More advance praise for
Not Too Late

"An adventure-filled journey of [Bounds's] transformation sure to appeal to others on similar paths . . . [and] an inspiring guide on how to unearth a "second wind," from someone who's been there."
—KIRKUS REVIEWS

"In a world plagued by isolation, alienation, and apathy, *Not Too Late* is an ode to the value of sport: a sense of belonging, intimacy, and mastery that's good for not just the body and mind but also the soul. Gwendolyn Bounds inspires and shows how you can reap these rewards at any age."
—BRAD STULBERG, bestselling author of *Master of Change* and *The Practice of Groundedness*

"*Not Too Late* proves that reinvention is possible at any age—and gives you the tools you need. Bounds not only changed her own life; her irresistible story will change yours."
—JOANNE LIPMAN, bestselling author of *Next!: The Power of Reinvention in Life and Work*

"Bounds's journey to that self-discovery, to embracing the inner badass that rests within so many of us, even if we don't think it does, is something that anyone who has ever felt the pull of the couch and midlife malaise will want to dive into."
—MATTHEW FUTTERMAN, author of *Running to the Edge*

"Honest, humble, and very funny, *Not Too Late* will inspire any mortal to push personal limits, whether it's on the playground monkey bars or in one of the planet's craziest endurance competitions."
—JASON GAY, *New York Times* bestselling author of *I Wouldn't Do That If I Were Me* and *Little Victories*

"A soul-nourishing smoothie of science, philosophy, and personal memoir, *Not Too Late* will resonate with anyone who has hit midlife only to wonder: Is this it? (Spoiler: It's very much not, with a growth mindset.) The joy of self-discovery through athletic challenge comes through on every page."

—JEFF BERCOVICI, author of *Play On: The New Science of Elite Performance at Any Age*

"A breathtaking work of jelly-legged genius . . . Writer slash (unexpected) action hero Gwendolyn Bounds dove deep into the pain cave for this one, and emerged with a captivating memoir about the transformative power of mud, sweat, and suffering. . . . For anyone who has ever wondered if there's more juice to squeeze out of life. So—basically everyone. This book is for everyone."

—SCOTT KENEALLY, writer/director of *Rise of the Sufferfests: A Film About Mud, Masochism and Modern Life*

"An intimate first-person story of pivoting in midlife to embrace challenge, persevere, and triumph."

—R. DOUGLAS FIELDS, PhD, author of *Electric Brain* and *Why We Snap*

"A gripping sports narrative: Screen-bound, middle-aged workaholic transforms her mind and body—hauling sandbags, throwing spears, crawling under barbed wire, leaping across fire—in a quest to win gold. But even more important, it's a serious, scientific exploration of how we age and what we can do to face down the inevitable march of time. Bounds has written a book full of both drama and sound advice for challenging preconceptions and living our very best lives."

—STEFAN FATSIS, *New York Times* bestselling author of *Word Freak* and *A Few Seconds of Panic*

NOT TOO LATE

By Gwendolyn Bounds

Little Chapel on the River

Not Too Late

NOT TOO LATE

The Power of Pushing Limits at Any Age

GWENDOLYN BOUNDS

Illustrations by Peter Sucheski

Ballantine Books

New York

This is a work of nonfiction.
Some names and identifying details have been changed.

Published in the United States by Ballantine Books, an imprint of
Random House, a division of Penguin Random House LLC, New York.

BALLANTINE BOOKS & colophon are registered trademarks of
Penguin Random House LLC.

LIBRARY OF CONGRESS CATALOGING-IN-PUBLICATION DATA
Names: Bounds, Wendy, author.
Title: Not too late: the power of pushing limits at any age /
Gwendolyn Bounds; illustrations by Peter Sucheski.
Description: First edition. | New York: Ballantine Books, 2024. |
Includes bibliographical references.
Identifiers: LCCN 2023056263 (print) | LCCN 2023056264 (ebook) |
ISBN 9780593599709 (hardcover) | ISBN 9780593599716 (ebook)
Subjects: LCSH: Bounds, Wendy. | Physical fitness—Psychological aspects. |
Exercise for middle-aged persons. | Obstacle racing. | Midlife crisis. | Self-
actualization (Psychology) | Women journalists—United States—Biography.
Classification: LCC GV481.2 .B68 2024 (print) | LCC GV481.2 (ebook) |
DDC 613.701/9—dc23/eng/20240124
LC record available at https://lccn.loc.gov/2023056263
LC ebook record available at https://lccn.loc.gov/2023056264

Printed in the United States of America on acid-free paper

randomhousebooks.com

2 4 6 8 9 7 5 3 1

First Edition

Book design by Virginia Norey

For Lisa

Contents

INTRODUCTION: I SHOULD NOT BE HERE   3

PART ONE

1: WHEN YOU GROW UP   17

2: SITTING AND SCREENS   23

The Obstacle: Walls *(commitment)*   31

3: STUCK IN THE CHORUS   33

4: PATH TO A BRIDGE (AND SUPERPOWER)   47

The Obstacle: Burpees *(personal accountability)*   55

5: FRAGILE FIRST NOTES   57

6: BE CONTENT TO APPEAR FOOLISH   68

The Obstacle: Heavy Carries *(willpower)*   80

7: THE POWER OF FIRSTS   83

PART TWO

8: COMING FROM BEHIND   103

9: DON'T LET YOUR CROP DIE   110

The Obstacle: Rolling Mud and the Slip Wall *(fear)*   124

10: WHAT'S ON THE OTHER SIDE OF FEAR?   126

The Obstacle: Monkey Bars *(adaptability)*   142

11: LEARN, UNLEARN, RELEARN   144

12: DIPS AND TURNING POINTS   *154*

13: EDGES AND EQUALIZERS   *165*

The Obstacle: Spear Throw *(take nothing for granted)*   *179*

14: DON'T FORGET THE PREVIOUS VERSE   *181*

15: DO WHAT YOU CAN, WHEN YOU CAN, WHILE YOU CAN   *196*

The Obstacle: Cargo Nets *(perspective)*   *206*

16: AGE IS A SECRET WEAPON   *208*

PART THREE

17: WHEN THERE'S NO BELL TO RING   *227*

The Obstacle: Tyrolean Traverse *(faith)*   *239*

18: FINDING FLOW AT FIFTY   *241*

19: THE FINAL STRETCH   *250*

The Obstacle: Fire Jump *(endings & beginnings)*   *264*

20: YOU'LL KNOW AT THE FINISH LINE   *266*

EPILOGUE: A NEW VERSE   *284*

ACKNOWLEDGMENTS   *289*

SOURCES AND NOTES   *291*

NOT TOO LATE

Introduction

I SHOULD NOT BE HERE

Empty Quarter Desert, Abu Dhabi, United Arab Emirates
Spartan Race—Age Group World Championship

December 4, 2021

Where does it end?
The wall of red-and-gold sand stretches up into a cloudless sapphire sky, a monstrous dune so steep I crane my neck trying to glimpse the top. Sweat drips into my eyes. I blink, stare, but standing here at the dune's base in the sun's glare, I can't make out the top. The same thought keeps looping: Where exactly does it end?

What I *can* make out are the black ropes dangling from its crest above, small squiggles of lifelines the race organizers have set out for competitors. Reach the ropes, and the summit is close. Just pull yourself, hand over hand, to the top. But first, you must reach the ropes, some four hundred feet up, and the cliff in front of us looms at a daunting fifty-degree incline.

I pause and tighten my hydration vest for the climb, savoring a short beat of rest while I'm still standing on solid earth here in the Middle East, nearly seven thousand miles from my home in New York. From down here, the racers who have reached the ropes look like big ants summiting a mound. And most of those just starting the climb are crawling up using both hands and feet, because the dune's pitch is too steep to walk upright easily without falling backward. Groans float down to me. Racers are sinking deep with every step, and those without gloves feel the deep heat of the desert sand on their flesh. I pull a thin pair with UPF 50 fabric onto my own hands, grateful for the last-minute purchase I made back in the United States.

We are roughly nine and a half miles into this half-marathon world championship obstacle course race, which combines running with military and hunter-gatherer-style obstacles and is designed to test strength, endurance, mobility, and speed. So far, we've knocked out twenty obstacles, among them slithering under barbed wire, throwing spears, hauling heavy bags and buckets of sand up, down, and around the dunes, ascending and descending a seventeen-foot rope, scaling walls, and carrying our body weight across monkey bars of staggered height.

Our race terrain is amid the largest continuous expanse of sand in the world, covering roughly 250,000 square miles, with dunes that rise to meringue-like crests and descend into salt flats. Called Rub' al Khali, or Empty Quarter, it is a part of the Arabian Peninsula that stretches into Saudi Arabia, Yemen, Oman, and the United Arab Emirates—the country in which we are competing. It is the land of epic movie backdrops—the planets Jakku in *Star Wars: The Force Awakens* and Arrakis in *Dune*. We've all made it here to race in the middle of the Covid-19 pandemic, crossing borders just as a new variant called Omicron surfaced in the news, adding frequent rapid testing to the list of obstacles we faced even before crossing the starting line. Roughly six weeks from now, when most of us are back home, Abu Dhabi—the capital city of the UAE, where we are racing—will be the target of a missile attack by Iran-aligned rebels threatening the country's reputation as a secure hub for international business in the Middle East. But right now, all we know is the endless, monotonous blur of bright sun, heat, and rolling dunes.

As racers, we represent sixty-two countries. For the last two miles,

I've raced alongside a man from Barcelona, Spain, and a chatty pack from Sweden. We communicate our mutual discomfort in spurts of English ("*This is bullshit*" seems to be universally understood) but mostly through the common, unspoken language of heavy breathing and persistent forward motion in this molasses of sand that fills our shoes and tugs at our hamstrings and Achilles tendons.

According to my life's major plot points to date, I should not be here. Not so long ago, my most significant physical competition was a 5K fun run for charity. I couldn't manage a single pull-up, and "athlete" was nowhere on the list of descriptors friends and family used to categorize me. I sat at a desk all day, uncalloused hands pecking at a keyboard, as an executive of one of the country's most well-known media brands, my legs stretching their limits only to race from one conference room to another in a gauntlet of meetings.

At fifty years old, I am a true latecomer to the world of competitive sports.

And now here I stand at the start of obstacle number twenty-one, the Cliff Climb. After this, we are just four miles and eleven more obstacles from the finish line. But I've seen enough racers being loaded into makeshift SUV ambulances, their bodies dehydrated and battered by the shadeless desert situated near the Tropic of Cancer, to know that finishing isn't a given. There's a constant ache in my toes, now blistered and bloodied from the sand that keeps slipping under my gaiters and into my shoes. I'm also pretty sure I may have refractured my tailbone in a fall I took off a slippery obstacle called Olympus, a few miles back. (The first fracture came twenty-five years ago on New Year's Eve when I slipped on a beer-soaked dance-floor staircase, an obstacle of a very different sort.) The injury throbs more with each step, and I am banking on endorphins and the two gooey-with-sweat Tylenols I jammed in my shorts pocket at the race's start to get me through. In Spartan races, there are no special allowances or handicapping for age. If you are forty-five or fifty-five or sixty-five, you still carry the same weight, clock the same mileage, as a twenty-five-year-old of your gender, and are scored the same way—by how fast you finish. And even though our finish times today as Age Group category competitors eventually will be measured against our peers, all of us out here now are racing the same course as the Elite category racers did yesterday—the ones competing for cash prizes, some of whom are professional athletes with sponsorships.

There are two options now: climb this cliff or find one of the SUVs and quit. I sip water and electrolytes from one of two hydration bottles strapped to my chest and stride onto the dune. Immediately, my foot sinks as if the earth has no bottom. A few more paces and I join the marching human ants, falling to my hands. The ground feels warm even through my gloves. The woman beside me has ditched her sand-filled shoes altogether and is attempting to summit in her socks. More groans float by, now joined by my own. Step after step, head down, I inch upward, each time losing some of the ground gained as my feet slide backward in this desert soup. We are all locked in our individual worlds of willpower. And there is no way out other than to keep climbing or slide back down to the bottom.

Midway up the dune, I lift my head briefly, feeling my blond ponytail lodged against my neck in a wet, gritty nest. The moment registers as both brutal and beautiful, looking up at this Arabian backdrop so far from the world I know and the people I love. And there is a strange comfort in this discomfort. Because it still seems impossible that I am here, and that my story has changed so late in the game.

And that this . . . this is now part of who I am.

In my late twenties, I was eating brunch with friends in a New York City restaurant where the lousy acoustics meant privacy wasn't on the menu. As we rapid-fired stories across mimosas and eggs about our latest career moves, love interests, and new apartments, the occasional sound bite from the next table floated over to ours. The group, not young but not *old,* were swapping their own flurry of tales about doctors' appointments and what seemed an endless list of declining medical conditions related to their eyesight, knees, hearts. As I sipped my drink, nested safely among the future-forward pronouncements of my cohort, it seemed impossible I'd ever reach a stage where the main topic of conversation would be decline.

And then, in what now feels like the amount of time it takes to snap your fingers *(Snap)* I'm seated at a dinner table in the Hudson Valley, and it's seventeen years later. There are six of us, ranging from our early forties to our early sixties. A man in our party has recently undergone multiple-bypass heart surgery, another member received a cancer diagnosis, and one woman iced her knee for an hour after our afternoon hike. All of us are rattling off tales of managing job boredom and the affairs of our aging parents and bemoaning the lack of time to pursue things we care about. And suddenly I'm transported back to that New York City brunch with my mimosa and big, open-ended plans.

Wait, I think with a flicker of bewilderment, when did they move me to the other table?

Search online for "midlife synonyms"—which I did while writing this book—and contemplate some of the results, which are hardly inspiring. Words and phrases such as "crisis," "breakdown," "the wrong side of 40," "stressful," and my personal favorite, "tube sock," popped up for me like hazard-ahead warnings. Another search for "health and middle age" yielded a particularly cheery list of conditions to look forward to, among them: arthritis, coronary heart disease, diabetes, hypertension, mental disorders, strokes, and genitourinary disorders. I don't know what the last one is, and I really don't want to find out.

Read enough of these entries and it begins to feel as if there's a stealth assassin waiting . . . patiently . . . in the rafters of the concert hall where our life's composition plays out. This assassin bides its time through childhood, with all its bright notes of infinite possibility, and through early adulthood, filled with crescendoing high points: pick a profession, get good at it, make money, find a mate, build a family, create a home, take vacations, save for the future. We don't all strive for or reach the same notes, but we generally feel our composition is building toward *something*. We understand our "why" when we wake up in the morning. And we move toward it.

It's when that momentum slows, when all the learning and box checking begins to feel no longer progressive but increasingly repetitious (rise, work, eat, family, bills, chores, bed; rinse and repeat) that we become most vulnerable. We sense it when we wake up and when we try to fall asleep. We're unsettled, slightly bored but too busy to know it, and something is now off-key. Like a drop from E major to E minor. Yet it's hard to hear, or to fix, amid the white noise of narratives that tell us that after a certain age, there's no point in pushing the envelope. That the time for ambition is over. That certain pastimes are only for the young. That we shouldn't try something new, particularly something hard, because the days of testing our limits have passed and there's simply not enough time left to get good at it. "What's the point?" the assassin whispers.

Meantime, our bodies are also in the crosshairs. Perhaps an unexpected injury leads us to stop running, playing soccer, cycling, or [*insert favorite activity here*] for a few weeks, and absent a powerful goal for our rehabilitation (I'm not on a team, I'm not competing, I'm getting too old for this anyway), we just never go back. And then the physical changes follow: an extra pound or two a year, loss of muscle mass and respiratory fitness, now compounded by doctors pointing to rising cholesterol and elevated glucose levels, until our bodies no longer look like our own in the mirror.

It's now, as the bright crescendo of our future and all its potential dampens into a subdued hum of maintenance and managing decline, that we are in the most danger. In danger of no longer seeking new passions. Of giving up on old ones. Of tipping into a belief state that we are fully baked as humans. Of believing our bodies are too far gone for any real redemption. Fully mired in the malaise of "this is just how it is at this age," we surrender. And so, the midlife assassin declares victory, another victim claimed.

But in the pages to come, you'll discover—as I did—that with some luck and, more important, some will, there's a way to fight back. A way to upend the dynamics of this battle for our middle-aged bodies and souls. This does not mean ignoring the reality of what's happening to us, including the very certain fact that we are all going to die. And let me say that again, because for me, it has proven no small matter to reconcile.

We are all going to leave this earth. And we cannot fully control how and when that time will come.

Rather, what it does mean is making different choices about how we spend the time that is left for us. It means rethinking who we believe we are and still *can be*. It is about tapping unexplored reserves inside all of us and learning to be good, and even occasionally great, at something completely new and even hard. Most critically, it's about realizing age can be a secret weapon in such a journey.

Let's start with the fact that the term "midlife crisis" is a relatively new construct, born of the modern age. The ancient Greek philosopher Aristotle theorized about middle age as being the prime of life, a time associated with having reached full competence and mastery, with the body being fully developed sometime between thirty and thirty-five and the mind at forty-nine. It wasn't until the mid-1960s that middle age—which today is thought to encompass roughly our forties to our early sixties, depending on whom you ask—really became firmly pegged as a period of "crisis." And while the "crisis" buzzword has stuck around, more research now identifies key strategies to awaken our physical and mental potential in midlife. To start, tackling something new and challenging can help ward off the many health problems associated with boredom, among them anxiety, depression, and the risk of making mistakes. If that new challenge includes physical movement, all the better, because the assumption that you're too old to reap real payoff from exercise has now been repeatedly debunked, even for the truly elderly. In fact, starting a new program in midlife can profoundly alter some of the negative changes coming for us, physical and emotional, and turn them into positives. Even your perception of aging matters. Casting growing older in a positive light has been shown in study after study to increase longevity.

Although I was a gangly, bullied kid who sat on the bench for many early-life sports endeavors and grew into adulthood never fully comfortable in her own physical skin, my strategy to fight the assassin came through an endurance adventure sport called obstacle course racing, or OCR for short. It was the catalyst that shook me out of an increasingly comfortable pattern of competency and, at times, complacency. By my midforties, I believed I knew what I was good at and what I wasn't, so that's how I rolled in life: leaning into what came easily and sidestepping what didn't. I liked words, stringing them together, and had managed to make a decent living out of it. So I focused on that. On the flip side, I'd pretty much given up on expecting anything noteworthy from my body—my physical disappointments chalked up to DNA and destiny. That is, until I discovered OCR, and specifically a global brand of competition called Spartan Race. And through it my openness to embracing incompetency became a catalyst to strengthen not just my aging body but also my mind and soul.

For perspective, obstacle course racing is a sport known for its unforgiving demands on every facet of the human body, requiring running endurance and speed, mobility, stability, and significant grip, core, upper- and lower-body strength. Ignore any one of these and you cannot conquer the litany of obstacles and challenges on a course. You've seen *American Ninja Warrior*? OCR has parts of that but usually with miles of running through mud, rocks, sand, water, woods, and sometimes mountains. Professional football players, seasoned triathletes, marathon champions, even Olympic sprinters might excel at one facet yet struggle at others. Over the past decade, OCR has been called one of the fastest-growing sports in the world, with serious talk of an obstacle race being included in the 2028 Los Angeles Olympics as part of the modern pentathlon. On a single weekend, anywhere from six thousand to twelve thousand racers might compete at a given Spartan race venue.

For most of my life, such an activity would have felt unthinkable— as off the table in my life plans as piloting a spaceship to Mars or singing at the Grammys. (To put things in perspective, I chose bowling to fulfill my physical-education requirement in college.) Yet, at the moment when the midlife assassin came to claim me, I embarked on this unlikely voyage to become a competitive athlete in a sometimes-grueling pastime. And in doing something so new, so seemingly out of reach, I dodged a lot of damage from midlife's stealth attack. I also got a chance to quiet some of my loudest childhood demons. In fact, the simple motions of swinging from bars and pulling my body weight up a rope patched holes as well as any therapist ever could.

Put most simply, at an age when so much seemed to be turning a corner toward endings, I found in racing a new beginning—one that let me see parts of my country still a mystery to me after half a century on earth: the rolling plains of Ohio and dense woods of West Virginia, the wild mountains of Northern California and lush rainforests of Hawaii. It eventually also led me far from home, across the globe to the vast desert of the Middle East, where I raced through heat and endless dunes of sand in a six-hour test of spirit. Equally important, by becoming a student again as I approached fifty, I learned to rethink my habits—from how I answered emails to my relationship with social media—and to question the way I approached problems and conflicts with others. I saw the old in a new way. I wanted more from my day job. I was less anxious. Ideas came faster. I woke up earlier. Drank less alcohol. I was more patient with other people, and with myself.

But perhaps the most revelatory change was the way becoming a student again made me realize the document labeled "me" wasn't a locked file but one that still could be added to or revised. That even in middle age and beyond, we can redefine who we think we are and recast the limiting constructs of who we believe we're not: "I'm not an artist," "I'm not strong," "I'm not competitive," "I'm not creative." And one way we can start to do that is by tacking on the word "yet," as we'll come to learn. In other words, "I'm not an athlete *yet*."

While each of our tactics to fight the assassin may differ, the strategy in these chapters can be a template for anyone. I wrote *Not Too Late* because there is a crisis of identity awaiting most of us if we are lucky enough to reach middle age and beyond—a moment when core things that define our sense of self start to irrevocably change, be it work, marriage, our roles as parents or as children, or something else. This upending certainly can start before middle age, but it becomes more acute as time reshapes our bodies, minds, and the circumstances around us. It is an existential challenge that exists across income levels and is heightened by the fast pace of change in our modernized, digital-first world where machines increasingly redefine what makes a productive and valuable human. Being able to address the question "Who am I?" with new, unexpected answers is like future-proofing yourself on a bunch of levels.

I too hit that crisis-of-identity moment, but in a stroke of dumb luck—or, more precisely, with a lucky stroke of my computer keyboard, as you'll soon see—I stumbled upon my weapon of choice. It took five years for me to fully understand all that I might have lost, and all that I might not have gained, had this not happened. That realization led me to try to distill what I'd learned into this book as a guide and tool kit for others. As a journalist, I followed my instinct to tap knowledge from a variety of experts, and woven through these pages is wisdom from scientists, longevity specialists, military leaders, a philosopher, doctors, and authors of bestselling books on motivation, fear, transformation, and performance. As you follow my journey, you'll find guidance on unearthing a "second wind," restructuring your days to focus on what's essential, learning to unlearn and to relearn, and pinpointing age "equalizers" in pursuit of mastery.

Ultimately, this book is a proof of concept for how you pull it all together and *do something*. It is a story, first and foremost, yes. But it is also a road map for action and change.

There is a potential upside of the midlife assassin's stealth attack for any of us. And that is the clarity of purpose it can bring when you realize that in all likelihood, you're closer to the end than you are to the beginning. With time not on my side, I learned to harness and adapt something known as my "crystallized intelligence": the vast accumulation of experiences, facts, and skills I'd acquired through-out my life, as well as the core attributes I'd been born with. All of us can use the edge age gives us, regardless of our pursuits—and regard-less of how far we go on the journey of mastery. You don't have to summit all the world's highest mountain peaks, win an Oscar or a world championship, or become an expert—though my deep respect if you do—to push limits in a way that is profound and life altering. What I discovered was there was still time to at least become good—and, by some measures, among some of the top contenders for my age for a time—at something totally foreign and hard. More impor-tant, by pushing the boundaries of my body and mind, I was able to metaphorically push back my seat and get up from the table that was focused only on decline. And while I couldn't move back to the vantage point of my idealistic mimosa-sipping youth, I ultimately landed in a spot with an even better view.

It wasn't because I had natural gifts for sports. That much will become clear. Rather, it was precisely because of the very thing that spurred me to race in the first place: waking up one morning and realizing I was moving toward death with something still untapped in my tank.

PART ONE

1

WHEN YOU GROW UP

Summer 2016

Saturday morning. The quiet click of the wall-mounted air-conditioning unit's fan turning on and the first pink daylight creeping over the hills through our windows bring me awake. I stretch my legs in the cool sheets and focus my sleepy eyes on the trees. They are fat and flush this time of year, dark-green leaves hiding a ridgeline of the Hudson Highlands. In the winter, when the landscape is stripped of its plumage, the hills are visible as a gently curved line, like a woman lying on her side.

Usually, I spend a few minutes studying the tree line and getting my bearings for the day, but this morning, something feels off immediately. I went to sleep unsettled, and the source of my unrest is fighting to surface from a night underwater in now fuzzy dreams.

I sift quickly through events from the past week. After nearly two decades working as a reporter and editor at *The Wall Street Journal*, I've taken a new job overseeing the magazine and website at Consumer Reports, a historic nonprofit that rates and reviews products and that fights for improvements in laws protecting what we eat, drive, and buy. My days are spent amid a sprawling network of laboratories where our engineers and scientists dig into the performance of everything from washing machines and smartwatches to cars and snowblowers. We're dealing with all sorts of new competitive threats to our business, but work isn't what's bothering me now.

My mind keeps sifting. There's a lot to do, as always, weekend catch-up kind of stuff—house chores, errands, email, calling my parents back home in North Carolina. I should probably try to get in some form of exercise, maybe a short jog. Same as most weekends.

I yawn. And then I remember. That little girl at the dinner party.

We'd been at our friends' house the night prior for a small gathering. The hosts' two almost-teenage children, a boy and girl, flitted in and out of the dining and living rooms, engaging briefly with the adults before retreating to their lairs and gadgets. At one point, a man in his late sixties, enjoying his gin, attempted to make meaningful contact and pulled the young girl's sleeve with a persistent tug.

"Young lady," he said with a formality that made her eyes narrow with suspicion as she instinctively pulled back to reclaim her sleeve. He held on firmly. "Young lady, so, what do you want to be when you grow up?"

I listened in, sipping my drink. The young girl's face relaxed and her eyes visibly brightened. This was a safe question. *A fun question!* She bounced lightly on her patterned-sock-clad toes, buoyed by the possibilities—so many they came spilling out in an excited, unorganized tumble.

"Well, I'm thinking I should be a veterinarian because whenever I see the dead birds on our road, I want to help them, but my dad says you need to go to school for a long time for that, and so I was thinking maybe I'd be a painter because I get good grades in art. I can show you something I drew of a unicorn marrying a caterpillar. *Oh!* And I'm better at the computer than my brother, so I could go work at Apple, that would be fun. . . ."

And it went on and on from there. I watched the old man's watery eyes fill with regret, sorry he'd ever asked, topped off my drink, and then stood up to look around the room for my wife, Lisa. After catching her eye and seeing her give me the Look (translation: Rescue me),

I joined her and two guests who had broken the unspoken "no politics" social rule and were debating the upcoming 2016 election.

As I began looking for an opening to change the subject, the old man's voice reverberated inside my head.

So, what do you want to be when you grow up?

I stood mute for a few moments, losing sight of my purpose until Lisa nudged me gently; she'd been at this conversation for a while and wanted out. Refocusing, I resumed searching for a cue to extricate us elegantly, but then it happened again.

So, what do you want to be when you grow up?

The phrase was still there, a hanging chad.

What do you want to be when you grow up?

And that's when it hit me.

Nobody was ever going to ask me that again.

Like, *ever.*

It was two months before my forty-fifth birthday, which, based on the average life span, brings with it a definitive declaration of being fully grown up and—*hard swallow*—having at least one foot firmly planted in the camp of the middle-aged. I've never been one to dwell much on the number. Ever since I survived fleeing my lower Manhattan apartment on the morning of the September 11, 2001, World Trade Center attacks, as the twin towers collapsed around us, I've known there are far worse alternatives to another birthday.

But still, all those things that little girl named, they sounded like fun things to do, to be. She might choose them. She might be them. She had time. Enough time. They were still possible.

I am a lot of things already, but there are more things I am not. I've always felt young enough to become those things in the future if I chose to. But what if I'm too old to be anything more than what I already am?

I drank too deeply from my champagne glass, a defensive measure to quell my mental ramble. Come on, I thought, pull yourself together. That's what people ask little girls and boys. It's fine. Get us out of this conversation.

And so I did, with some thin excuse about us helping the host in the kitchen. (She was in the bathroom.) But I carried the panicky feeling with me for the rest of the night and then took it home with us.

Remembering now, here in the clarity of morning, I shift my legs restlessly, which makes Lisa's rhythmic breathing next to me pause for a moment. I force myself to stop, be still, and recount all the good things I know to be true. I love and am still in love with the person I met eleven years ago and have since married. My job is hard, but overall, it has purpose and meaning. My parents are alive and healthy. I am alive. I've come to terms with not having children—maybe not completely, but without letting it burn up all else that's good—and filled my life with the kids of my friends. A lot of boxes are checked. And I'm busy—*so very busy!*—tending to the carefully constructed infrastructure of my adult life—commuting, house maintenance, dog walking, vacation planning, volunteering. There's no room or time to be or do something more, even if I wanted to.

Yet the unsettled feeling from last night . . . it won't go away. My laptop is lying next to me on the floor where I dropped it after answering some emails late the night before. I pick it up, give our fourteen-year-old golden retriever, Dolly, a kiss on her soft forehead as I do every morning, and walk into the living room. Scan the news for a bit. Make a pot of coffee and realize I'm a little hungover from the champagne and the conversation. Return to the computer.

Then I click open an empty Google browser.

I'm not sure what I think Google can do for me. And I'm not even sure what I'm looking for when I start tapping out the words "What are the hardest things you can do . . ." It's just a half-formed thought, but Google's algorithm is ready to help with suggestions of common search queries made by some of the other 7.4 billion people currently on this earth who've clearly wondered the same thing. I see a drop-down search option suggestion for "What are the hardest physical things you can do?" and mindlessly click that, since I don't have a real end destination in mind.

Among the search results is this post on Livestrong.com: "The 10

Toughest Endurance Challenges (You Can Actually Do)." I recognize things like the Boston Marathon and Ironman. That's serious athlete stuff—way out of my league. There's also something called "Spartan Race," which I've never heard of.

Mostly out of curiosity, I click the link and start reading. And then I keep clicking and reading more. Spartan racing apparently is some sort of extreme endurance sport—a "sufferfest" is what some people dub it online. Running up and down mountains, climbing ropes, hauling buckets of gravel and heavy sandbags, lugging blocks of cement, crawling under barbed wire—crazy stuff they call "obstacle course racing." It's apparently a booming business and nothing my angular, 122-pound, five-foot-ten frame can comprehend. I struggle curling a ten-pound arm weight for more than ten reps at the gym and still can summon the humiliation of childhood team-picking for sports and being among the last names called.

Still, it's a good distraction from the memory of last night.

I pour more coffee and descend further and further down this bizarre Spartan rabbit hole. Queued in the long list of search results, a 2014 *Outside* magazine story with the headline "DNF: The True Tale of Failure at a Spartan Race" pops up. I don't know what "DNF" means, but as a bona fide type A overachiever, I'm intrigued by someone who would write about failing. The author, Scott Keneally, is a writer and director who, while making a documentary about obstacle course racing called *Rise of the Sufferfests,* attempted a Spartan race in Malibu. Ultimately, he was so beaten down by some form of physical punishment called "burpees," which were dished out as penalties for failing obstacles, that he quit not far from the finish line after a disastrous attempt at a rope climb sent him plunging into a muddy trench below. That apparently was what "DNF" meant: Did Not Finish.

Keneally seems like a lunatic to me. Still, I read his last paragraph twice, something about it holding the promise of a future I don't yet know I might want.

"I want to be more than the filmmaker who champions OCR and

spotlights people who've found salvation through it. *I want to be one of those people. . . . I want to be strong, fit, ready.*"

People who've found salvation . . . I want to be one of those people . . . strong, fit, ready. His words maneuver around my brain like children in a bouncy castle, colliding with those from the old man's question. *So, what do you want to be when you grow up?*

I drain the last of my coffee, grimacing at the taste of a few stray grounds. Then I return to the main Spartan.com website and zoom in on something called "Workout of the Day." It's free—costing only the privacy of your email address.

I pause . . . type mine in. And hit Enter.

You know, just to see.

2

SITTING AND SCREENS

One of my strongest memories of childhood is the sheer hell of dodgeball.

Even now, I can transport myself back in time to 1979. I'm eight years old, with my back against the concrete wall of our school's cavernous gymnasium, wishing time would pass faster. It's the worst part of the school day, PE, which is bad enough on a regular afternoon with the billowing gym shorts swallowing my stick-figure legs. But today is worse. Today is dodgeball, with the cool, bigger kids hurling that hard red ball a million miles an hour at my birdlike frame. I hate running, because I have a left ankle that's so weak it makes my foot flop weirdly inward when I move fast. My parents tell me not to worry. I'm just what they call a "late developer." But I've heard them talking in low voices on the phone with Coach Cherie Fowler, the nice head of physical education at school, asking her if they should be worried.

Right now, all I want to do is go back to the school library, where I can read so many Trixie Belden mystery books, so fast, that the teachers give me lots of green M&M's (green is my favorite color) as a special prize. No one is giving me a prize here in the gym.

The first humiliation is the ritual of team-picking. My face grows hotter and hotter as we are winnowed down by the two team captains until there are just two of us left untaken, unwanted. It's me and a short boy with black Coke-bottle eyeglasses and asthma who my grade has cruelly nicknamed Darth Vader because of the way he breathes. My fear of complete loserdom overrides any sense of camaraderie or decency I might have, and all I can think is: Please don't let them pick Darth Vader before me.

A lengthy pause, and then I am rescued by Team A's leader, Chris, who is tan and blond and already has muscles that make the other guys eat more at lunch. "OK," he says. "We'll take Wendy." I'm only a little ashamed of my flood of joy and how fast I scurry over to his side, leaving Darth Vader to shuffle toward Team B as a leftover default pick, his name never even uttered. I don't have time to think about him for long anyway, because his captain is picking up that horrible red ball, and my next move is to hide behind Chris's sister, Louise. A competitive swimmer who is always picked first, she is the strongest girl I know. She's also my friend and never lets the ball hit me if she can help it.

Twenty minutes of hiding behind Louise, and then I can get more green M&M's.

Once, I heard that if you can take something you were made fun of for as a kid, and get good at it, then it will become your superpower.

There's a reason Keneally's words "strong, fit, ready" resonated so deeply when I read his *Outside* magazine story. The truth was, my body had never delivered what I'd been taught as a young girl to believe it should give me—beginning with those early days of dodgeball agony. I was born the year before Title IX was signed into law by President Richard Nixon, setting in motion a movement for women to gain equal footing in sports. By the time I was a teenager, the most popular girls in my school generally played competitive sports and were cheered on by the boys and girls alike. They were muscular, physically deft, and idolized for it.

By comparison, I progressed from being a bony kid picked last for dodgeball into a jumbled mess of angles who couldn't quite connect the dots on a basketball court or a soccer field. Moreover, I was a slow developer and thus the target of locker-room torment. Once other girls started wearing bras, I did too—desperate to fit in, even though it probably wasn't technically necessary. Unfortunately, my assigned locker was next to that of the Beast, my secret nickname for a strong, well-developed blond girl who was a gifted athlete with an older boyfriend at another school. The Beast wielded physicality as a social weapon, once holding me by my throat against the lockers to try to force me to help her steal a teacher's grade book so she could change her scores. (She wasn't so gifted on the academic front.) In the locker room, I kept turning my back to her when I removed my shirt, but it was no use. One day, as I was scrambling to pull on my green-and-gold gym shirt as fast as possible, the Beast declared loudly, with her big laugh, "Why do you even *bother* with that bra?" After that, I changed clothes in a bathroom stall.

On the competitive playing fields, I often made teams only as a last pick, or because our school was small and we needed bodies to fill the roster. Cheerleading found me struggling to keep my limbs moving in a coordinated fashion. (Add in pom-poms, and I was completely lost.) In soccer and basketball, I excelled at keeping the bench warm and helping put soft drinks into the coolers of ice. I performed better in softball, but only because there was nobody bigger trying to run me down.

Although things sorted themselves out once the late blooming eventually began, this sense of physical insecurity still followed me into adulthood. It was there as I bared my limbs on beaches and by swimming pools through my twenties and thirties. It was even there the day I donned my beautiful handmade wedding dress, fearful people might think I didn't fill it out well enough. People who knew me during childhood and early adulthood may be surprised to hear how I felt. Indeed, we learn to mask our insecurities starting from a young age. But the happiness and strength I felt in other parts of my life were always offset by this feeling of weakness in my body as

I moved about the world. Men can know this sensation too, but for a woman, the feeling can be particularly acute—especially when walking down a street alone at night or stepping into a cab in an unfamiliar city.

That was the outside me—the part you could see. On the inside, my body hadn't cooperated either. I still remember with clarity the day I *knew* I'd have a child. It was summer, and Lisa and I were driving. I was thirty-five and in the first full year of a relationship with this person who made the promise of "till death do us part" feel truly possible. We'd found each other after years of trial and error, broken engagements, and broken hearts. That those other relationships and loves had been with men and women for both of us—that it had taken much of early adulthood to find each other—didn't matter now. Everything felt fresh and new. Words and phrases such as *statin, sarcopenia, osteoporosis, stroke, assisted living,* and all the others describing complexities that soon would find us with middle age were not yet in our lexicon. All we saw was the possibility of the future and the good things it would bring: trips, house renovations, new jobs, and—I was sure of this to my core—*a child*. Even the song blaring from the radio, "Summertime" by Kenny Chesney, was new and full of promise, with its lyrics about two bare feet on the dashboard and young love somehow capturing everything we felt. The windows were down, Lisa's own feet on the dashboard, her long auburn hair whipping around her face, and we were humming along to the chorus, which was all about wine, smiling, and summertime.

Suddenly the song shifted into a more questioning key. The pace slowed. Kenny's voice even seemed a little wiser.

The more things change
The more they stay the same

"Great bridge," Lisa shouted over the music.

"What do you mean?" I shouted back, neither of us bothering to turn the volume down.

"That section that sounds different is called the bridge of a song," she yelled. "It's always the best part."

As a longtime entertainment reporter, first for *TV Guide* and then for Fox News, she knew far more than I did about music (and most pop culture matters), so I took her word for it and didn't ask questions. Later I learned the bridge is a transitional section of a song that adds variety, a new tempo, or a shift of key. A well-written bridge draws upon the best of what's come before to create harmony with what will come after.

As it turned out, she'd just pointed me toward a powerful weapon I'd eventually wield to combat the midlife assassin. But neither of us realized it back then. Because at that point, we were still writing our chorus.

Three years after that carefree car ride, we reached the part about children—checked all the right boxes in our research, our medical planning, and the preparation of my body. We'd found a sweet-faced anonymous donor through a sperm bank and paid for multiple vials of hope to be shipped to New York. Now thirty-eight, I knew I was late to the party. But I figured sheer force of will could make this happen, because after all, plenty of other people my age did it. My metrics of success were so tightly bound to my profession that I blindly assumed hard work and desire were enough to achieve this bodily KPI (key performance indicator, for those of you lucky enough not to be chained to this acronym).

And so, though I knew the challenges, failure never entered my mind as I lay on the table in my doctor's office, looking up at the paper mobile dangling from the ceiling while she worked her medical magic and added the DNA of that sweet-faced donor to mix with mine. When we'd left her office that morning, the first vial empty, I truly believed I could feel a new life starting inside me—like a glow that lit my body up and made the cabdriver see us and stop in the rain on Seventy-seventh Street and Madison Avenue. So certain was I that when the call came from the nurse telling me the subsequent blood test for pregnancy was negative, I remember thinking she misspoke.

Lisa and I were sitting on a bench in New York's Central Park, the rush of humanity before us filled with well-lit Hollywood-esque scenes of family: kids in strollers, children chasing a soccer ball, a little girl dragging a stuffed animal behind her on the dirty sidewalk and rubbing her eyes. When the words "I'm sorry" came through my cellphone, I turned my back to Lisa, instinctively shielding her from the news.

"Are you sure?" I asked softly, the glorious light of the scenes before us fading to dark.

After the nurse's first "I'm sorry" and then the second and third calls, I'd had surgery to correct the endometriosis that my doctor thought might be complicating things. Then, after the fourth, fifth, sixth, and seventh calls with the same news, we finally decided to take a break, give my body a rest from the fertility treatments. Consider adoption. Feeling powerless, I quickly doubled down at the table where I knew how to win, which of course was work. Months passed. We made inquiries on the adoption front. A year passed. Then another year. Inertia. Until one day, without ever saying "We're done" out loud, we must have packed this verse of song into our internal boxes labeled Regrets. Occasionally, we'd peek inside, talk about pulling out the contents. Trying again. But the more time passed and the more we aged, the more I knew we never would, even as we continued to pay storage fees for the vials of hope nearly a decade after I stopped trying to get pregnant. Instead, we made rough peace with what was not to be in our lives and pledged to focus on what we had. Most days, we kept that promise and worked hard to forgive each other when we didn't. But my own moments of longing, acute at unpredictable times—seeing a child fiddling with his mittens on the subway—were another reminder that my body's performance was seemingly out of my control.

And so it was that I regressed deeper into my core comfort zone of creating stories. I allowed inertia to take over. And that involved a lot of sitting. And a lot of screens.

* * *

That my own journey into the world of obstacle course racing began while sitting in front of a computer is no coincidence.

When I look back to the years of my thirties and early forties, I see myself sitting and looking at or through screens. The screen of my computer in the Manhattan offices of *The Wall Street Journal*. The screen of my cellphone, where Facebook was becoming the first online service of its kind to reach a billion users. The screens of TVs, where I chatted in three-minute strings of sound bites about my reporting on real estate and home improvement with *Good Morning America* anchors Robin Roberts and Diane Sawyer and on networks such as CNBC and DIY Network.

I also see myself sitting. Sitting at my tiny cubicle desk. Sitting on a subway. Sitting to get a manicure. Sitting in a movie theater. Sitting in a restaurant. Sitting in a car or train commuting almost four hours a day from my Hudson Valley home, where I'd moved after the 2001 World Trade Center terrorist attacks damaged my downtown New York City apartment—a morning of chaos, smoke, and death that imprinted on me the true impermanence of everything.

While sitting with these screens and heading toward middle age, I had managed to future-proof my career by moving away from my roots in print and into the digital world. *The Wall Street Journal* launched a series of live-streamed news and lifestyle video shows and tapped me as a host. So I sat some more, in a chair where a confident stylist named Maria fixed my hair and makeup each morning. And then I sat on a tall stool learning to read a teleprompter, yet another screen, and trying to find my "anchor voice." Lisa, a seasoned on-air TV personality, tried to help, but anchor voice never quite came naturally to me. Still, I faked it well enough until Consumer Reports came calling. There, I gave up the on-camera work to lead their large editorial team and quickly found that leadership involves a lot of conference rooms and meetings. And more meetings mean more sitting. And more staring at screens.

Through all of this, exercise took a back seat to my career. I belonged to gyms on and off, jogged a little, and mostly managed enough physical activity to feel like I was checking another box. And as modern technology evolved and our phones morphed into screens by our sides 24/7, everything I did became tied to them: email, weather, news, entertainment, even exercise itself with a virtual folder full of rarely used health apps. Occasionally I'd try to push back, always hoping I might find some untapped athletic gene that had eluded me since childhood. There was a brief stint where I took up boxing lessons and another where I attempted to learn to fence. A couple of times I even got fit enough to ride a bicycle several hundred miles to raise money for a charity. I clearly craved something I instinctively believed sports could give me, but I wasn't self-aware enough yet to figure out what that was. Nor did anything athletic come naturally. And so always I moved on, throwing myself back into work, where competence and victories were more readily at hand. More sitting. More screens.

Once I stopped trying to get pregnant, this cycle of professional and personal inertia only deepened. More waking up and going to sleep, and in between, doing the things I was good at, steering clear of the ones I wasn't, and doing little to push myself out of my comfort zone.

As a result, I was now—quite literally—a sitting target for that midlife assassin.

The Obstacle: Walls
(commitment)

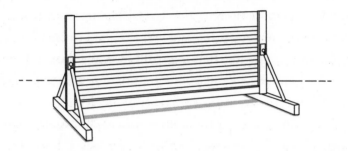

Walls are a common fixture in most obstacle course races. In fact, the first obstacle Spartan typically sets before its racers is a vertical wall. It's not a particularly high wall—roughly four feet. But surmounting it is the price of participation. You must climb over that wall just to reach the starting line. It's a literal and metaphorical gut check—am I ready? Am I prepared to commit and do what it takes?

Because that small wall won't be the last one. Depending on the race's length there will be multiple walls, generally between four and eight feet tall, to conquer on a Spartan course. And they all require a measure of strength, agility, and confidence. On the smaller walls, the best athletes often push their entire bodies straight up into the air with powerful arm strength and roll or vault themselves over, or they plant one foot atop the wall and swing the other leg across. It's fast and beautiful. On the taller walls, success is more a matter of strength and coordination—using a pull-up motion to hoist yourself up before getting your chest on the wall and then bringing your legs over. Some super confident racers run directly at the wall and plant a foot against it while still in motion, which catapults them up to the ledge.

Fortunately, there are tricks to make conquering the taller walls easier if your upper body isn't that strong. Like any obstacle—wall or otherwise—the key is figuring out what advantage to leverage, as I eventually would come to learn in my first race. In my case, this advantage was the long arms and legs that had carried me through my awkward, gangly youth into a still physically unsure adulthood. With a big jump, I generally could grab the top of a wall. And then, while pulling with my arms, I would walk my legs up the wall's face until I could hook a foot on the edge as an anchor to pull myself the rest of the way up. Coming down the other side, I'd use those long arms again to slowly drop myself down and avoid rolling an ankle or buckling a knee. The first time I summited an eight-foot wall was also the first time I truly appreciated the body I'd been born in, no caveats.

Walls aren't necessarily the hardest of obstacles, but they are an inevitable part of every race, and they're designed to wear you down and break your stride. Not giving up when you hit a wall, that's half the battle when you're starting something new.

3

STUCK IN THE CHORUS

If life were like the movies, I'd have closed the computer that lazy summer morning in 2016 when I first discovered Spartan, thrown on some workout clothes, and set off on my obstacle course racing journey with unstoppable Rocky-style grit and commitment, some Lady Gaga or Beyoncé version of "Eye of the Tiger" overlaying the scene.

Instead, I offer you reality—and my first "wall." After that dinner party and my caffeine-laden morning of frantic googling, six months passed before I ever thought of obstacle course racing again. I got swept back up in the inertia and repetition of my own chorus. Like most of us, my life was overflowing at this point with adult obligations I'd accumulated over four and a half decades. We didn't have children, it's true, but there were other seemingly all-consuming obligations to my job, where I now managed a team of nearly 150 people (which sometimes felt like having 150 grown children); my spouse; my parents, who were in their seventies; my increasingly narrowing network of friends (*narrowing because I'm so busy!*); the community organizations where I volunteered. And then there was the cooking, cleaning, taking cars for service appointments, booking those doctor checkups that were adding up with age, calling plumbers, taking out trash, shoveling snow, buying groceries, pumping gas, chasing down the plumber who didn't call me back, walking the dog, cleaning up after the dog ate sticks and vomited on the carpet, and a long list of other grown-up activities that seemed to guzzle the hours.

Yet despite being so consumed by such a vast array of activities, there was that sameness to the days that was emerging, blurring them into one another like in the movie *Groundhog Day*. Same work routine, same (fewer) friends, same dinners out with the same conversations, same restaurants, same Saturday chores, same Sunday prep for the week to come. The chorus didn't feel new anymore. More frequently now, as I had that morning after the dinner party, I felt the passage of time pressing like a dull knife into my chest, which spurred an undirected sense of panic. Monday quickly became Friday, and the sameness felt unstoppable even as I sensed there was something left sitting in my proverbial tank. Some kind of fuel. But I had nowhere to go with it.

How to fix this feeling was slippery to get my arms around, though, because I'd chosen all of these things—the person I loved, the place we called home, the way I earned money. There were a lot of boxes checked, and I wasn't interested in unchecking them. I recognize this isn't true for everyone. For some, middle age may legitimately touch down like a tornado, wiping out what was there before and leaving no choice but to rebuild. This may be needed and even welcomed in some cases, or a terrible shock in others. But because I didn't hate my existing life or want to blow it up in any obvious way, I wasn't sure *what* to do. It was more like a long stretch of overcast days that sneak up and leave you with the dull ache of being inside for too long. You don't hate your house, but you don't want to stay in there all the time either.

Describing what I felt back then as a crisis seems like a reckless overstatement, given the state of the world. Still, the *Oxford English Dictionary* defines "crisis" as "a state of affairs in which a decisive change for the better or worse is imminent." And indeed, a turning point is what was coming.

When I set out to write about my turning point, I felt a need to go back and better understand the enemy, this midlife assassin, and its powerful siege on our minds and bodies. That was so I could make sense of what had happened to me and how it had led me to obstacle course racing, and better explain what might be happening, or *have* already happened, to you. Which is how I found myself talking to a philosopher, a former physicist who now is a fitness and endurance expert, and one of this country's foremost authorities on aging.

Let's start with the fact that when that dinner-party exchange took place, I was more than halfway through my four thousand weeks on this planet. That's the rough calculation, anyway, if you live to be almost eighty years old. Maybe you'll get more, maybe less, but it's a back-of-napkin baseline used by a guy named Oliver Burkeman, who wrote a sobering book called *Four Thousand Weeks: Time Management for Mortals*. In his book, Burkeman ran the numbers on life span and thus cemented for himself—and his readers, including me—the astoundingly brief amount of time we may get to live and why the things we choose to fill that time with should be so carefully selected.

Once your four-thousand-week hourglass is half empty, it's natural to start taking stock of accomplishments, regrets, dreams, and possible plot points not yet hit. And then, pretty quickly, you're trying to figure out how you'll get it all done (though you obviously never will) before the sand runs out. I was surely doing this while listening to that little girl at the dinner party, the math running in a processor deep in my brain, and concluding I was very likely a good way through my own allotment of sand. The universality of this feeling has sent many academics, economists, and writers on a journey to probe and understand why this happens and what we can do about it.

One of them is Kieran Setiya, a philosophy professor at the Massachusetts Institute of Technology. After reading his book *Midlife: A Philosophical Guide,* I sought out Setiya because I hoped a philosopher would be, well, wiser than I am on this topic. In 2014, Setiya had penned an academic paper about the so-called midlife crisis in which he probed the puzzle of why a person would feel like something was deeply wrong at this stage of life when they were in fact busily engaging in the chorus of the things they'd actively spent their life *trying to do*—build a career and a family while also amassing a bucket of interesting activities and obligations.

Bingo, I thought. This is my guy.

Turns out, his paper wasn't purely an academic exercise. When we ultimately spoke, Setiya told me he too had reached a point in adulthood where, somewhere between securing tenure and writing a second book, he felt a yawning void and was deeply confused about why. "I still liked philosophy. I liked teaching. I loved my students, and it all seemed worthwhile. And yet at the same time, it seemed futile and repetitive to just keep doing it over and over again, writing another paper and teaching another class. And I thought, There is a puzzle about why you would feel like something is deeply wrong with your life when you are doing things worth doing and very fortunate to be able to do them and basically things are going well."

Setiya explained how he channeled his confusion into exhaustive research over the next several years. He discovered that while philosophers as far back as Aristotle had struggled with the perceived "rut" of middle age, they also had looked at this period as being the prime of our minds, the point where our accumulated wisdom and experience climaxed in an optimized way. Curiously, humans' sense of intense dissatisfaction with this period (to the extent of labeling it a "crisis") is really a more modern phenomenon, with the birth of the buzzword phrase "midlife crisis," often credited to a Canadian psychoanalyst named Elliott Jaques. In 1965 Jaques wrote a paper musing about this age when we supposedly face our limitations, mortality, and dwindling possibilities, thus planting the seed for the term "crisis." The word took firm root in the cultural lexicon roughly a decade later when journalist Gail Sheehy published her seminal book *Passages: Predictable Crises of Adult Life*. And since then, the label has continued to flourish, with more sunlight and water from various cultural and research corners.

Take, for example, the U theory. In the early 2000s, two economists, David Blanchflower and Andrew Oswald, published a paper titled "Is Well-Being U-Shaped over the Life Cycle?" As a former *Wall Street Journal* reporter, I was naturally curious about what two economists might have to add to the "midlife crisis" conversation. Their work shows midlife sitting at the bottom of a trend line of lifetime psychological well-being, as illustrated by a gently curving letter U. According to this theory, happiness starts high in youth, bottoms out in your mid- to late forties, and then ends higher in older age. This holds true, apparently, for men and women. While the data and some of their conclusions have been debated in certain academic circles, the general sense of a midlife slump awaiting us at the bottom of a U has proven sticky in our modern cultural zeitgeist.

So I put this question to my philosopher guide, Setiya. What is it about the modern, convenience-filled world we live in today that makes us feel, justified or not, so particularly prone to misery and a sense of drowning at this midway point? And selfishly, I wondered: Had he perhaps found a path others could follow out of the despair pit in the U curve?

What came next was like a one-two-three punch of "Aha, yes!" moments.

The first one, and this may hit home with you, because it certainly did for me when I heard him describe it, is the rise of FOMO. That is, the fear of missing out. Essentially, this means the more we have a sense of all the options available in life, the more we think they ought to be available to us. And when they're not, we feel anxious. Social media, of course, has accelerated this sensation in no small way. But even before we began scrolling through the carefully orchestrated feeds of our friends, noting all the ways that they seem to be living happily and that we aren't, the proliferation of cable channels and a 24/7 news cycle sharpened our perception of all the possible things to do, see, and be. At midlife, not only are we bombarded by these options but we also now feel like we're running out of time to pursue them.

"There is empirical research on the ways in which having more options available actually makes people more unhappy," Setiya explained.

And while our social media "families" are perhaps making us anxious, we've been losing the support traditionally offered when multiple generations lived close by and sometimes together. With relatives now so geographically dispersed, there's often inadequate means of familial support for all of life's pressures, including caring for parents or dealing with a medical emergency if you don't have adequate health insurance. Hence the drowning sensation we may feel at this stage in life. Setiya tied it together like this: "You've got your kids and all of their problems and your parents and all of *their* problems to deal with. And now we are no longer living in extended families where this work is distributed. Your parents are far away, and you have to travel to help them. And you may not have brothers and sisters and cousins around to help. There is just an immense amount of time and energy devoted to solving problems."

The third punch I really should have seen coming.

It's the idea that productive work defines our identities. In other words, there's been a large cultural shift with industrial capitalism that promotes the idea that your value as a person has to do with how much you produce. And while this may have originated as an economic metric, it's insidiously infected other parts of our lives. Even our social lives and relationships have come to be measured by how many likes and followers we have on Instagram, X (formerly Twitter), TikTok, Facebook, or whatever your platform of preference. This, Setiya concluded, seems precisely designed to generate the kind of crisis where you realize around midlife that you are a productivity machine, and your existence is defined by numbers that signal your value. Not only is this stressful, it's also inherently unsustainable.

Setiya's explanations felt like someone showing me the corner pieces of a jigsaw puzzle. From the age of twenty-one, when I started work as a young reporter covering manufacturing in *The Wall Street Journal*'s Pittsburgh bureau, I'd been measured by my productivity in the number of articles I'd published. That eventually morphed into how many videos I produced, or how many TV appearances I made, and then the quantity of likes, views, or shares those stories or appearances received. Meantime, my blood relatives, including my parents, all lived a ten-to-twelve-hour drive away in North Carolina. We saw each other twice a year if we were lucky. The idea of a familial safety net was a distant concept; we'd be there for each other if something really bad happened, but for most of our everyday trials and tribulations we were too far away from each other to offer much help beyond a text or quick phone call. As for FOMO, I certainly wasn't immune either, particularly when I saw pictures of my high school and college friends surrounded by their children fly through my Facebook feed.

Tie all Setiya's theories together and suddenly you've got a perfect storm that starts to illuminate why, starting around age forty-five, we might feel like we're dropping into the low point of that U curve of life satisfaction. We've got too much going on, not enough support, and impossible models of who we should be by now that stream into our smartphones 24/7.

So, what is the solution? Weirdly, the answer seems to be something of a paradox: acceptance and action.

"What becomes more evident to people as they age is that the issue is not about how to live your best life," Setiya told me. "It's about how to make the most of the complicated situation you find yourself in." Being the best and achieving everything are impossible tasks when most of us are struggling to deal with the fact that life isn't always ideal, or that there are simply problems that won't go away. "I've come to think that being willing to sit with discomfort and accept difficulty is essential to be able to think about how to live life properly," the philosopher suggested.

Still, I wondered, isn't there a risk of letting this kind of acceptance slip into passivity? Shouldn't we also consider taking action? Yes, perhaps, he conceded. In his own case, for example, Setiya said he was focused just on being OK with all his paths taken—and those he might have missed out on. "I didn't spend as much time thinking about 'How can I make a change and will it add agency and richness to my life that I don't have?' I think it takes a lot of courage to do that."

Before I was willing to let my philosopher go, I pressed him for examples. He talked about making a change to add agency and richness to our lives, but how do we figure out what precisely that change should be? After all, I'd stumbled into obstacle course racing through dumb luck during a hungover Google search. Certainly there was a better way?

Enter the telic versus atelic framework.

It's not about action for action's sake, Setiya believes, or cramming more to-dos into our already full lives. Rather, it's about making room for activities or pastimes that bring lasting existential value to us versus focusing on only those whose value may wane once completed. This is the difference between an atelic and a telic activity—the words being derived from the Greek word "telos," which means "end." A telic activity, Setiya explained, is designed for immediate or finite gratification and has a definitive ending, like eating a good meal, writing a report, or taking a vacation. By comparison, an atelic activity is in service to something greater that delivers ongoing internal fulfillment, like listening to music or practicing your fly-fishing cast. You'll never be totally finished, and that's the beauty of it. In middle age, when you're turning toward endings, such atelic activities can be far more fulfilling because they aren't finite.

Looking back now, I see how right Setiya was. My life before obstacle course racing revolved around mainly telic activities: write this story, go on TV for this appearance, meet these friends for dinner, take this trip. All of them mattered, but all of them were finite and telic. It wasn't until I stepped into my journey to master obstacle course racing that I firmly entered the atelic realm of "never finished"—and realized how electrifying that could be. There would always be something new to learn, some way to improve, something different to try on a Saturday morning in June. And that sure felt like a far cry from being stuck at the bottom of a U curve or going stir crazy in the house while it rained.

If engaging in an atelic activity is a strong defense against the mind's middle-aged malaise, then counteracting all the sitting and screen time would become an equally important defense for my body.

What exactly *was* happening to my body in middle age, however, was murky to me. All of us in the developed world have evolved a very long way from our ancestral origins, when we were constantly moving—be it running, jumping, crawling, or swimming—to seek nourishment and safety. Now we have ready access to food that we can order using those screens in our hands while sitting. Collectively as a population, our bodies have been changing fast. Obesity in the United States has been rising for decades and now plagues almost 42 percent of American adults. We've also got a new twenty-first-century medical condition to battle called "text neck syndrome." It might sound amusing, but what's happening is cervical spinal degeneration resulting from the repeated stress of forward head flexion while we text for long periods of time. In this sense, the gifts of modern life are also our physical kryptonite. Much of this has led to what author Michael Easter dubbed "The Comfort Crisis," which is the title of his powerful, aptly named book.

By age forty-five, when I first googled "What are the hardest things you can do?" there's no denying my own body and health were changing from this crisis of comfort, even if it seemed subtle at the time. A bit of stiffness now each morning when I rolled out of bed, my first few steps a kind of strained Frankenstein lurch until my calves and feet loosened up. The noise accompanying this move is so common that the well-known writer Jancee Dunn branded it "the middle-aged groan" in an essay for *The New York Times*. Then there was the sense of being out of breath after climbing stairs to my friends' walk-up apartments in the city. Picking up a bag of heavy groceries, once a mindless act in my twenties and thirties, now elicited an occasional warning cry in the vague nether regions of my lower back and hamstrings. One Saturday afternoon, I raced across a grassy field with my college best friend's young sons, Johnny and Julian, and not only didn't beat them but felt an ache in my Achilles tendon for two weeks, along with the ache of having been bested by people with legs much shorter than mine. (In my defense, Johnny and Julian are *really* fast.)

Those were just the changes I could feel. Other, less obvious ones were happening too, at least according to my doctors. My glucose scores apparently now hovered around prediabetes levels. (Fewer carbs and sugar, I promised during each annual physical, and actually kept that promise for a week or two.) My total cholesterol levels, while still normal, were ticking upward. A few benign polyps in a colonoscopy—*I was old enough to get a colonoscopy!* And some skin spots removed by my dermatologist who advised I wear a floppy hat and lather on SPF 70 sunscreen.

Yet despite these alarm bells, I lived my life pretty much as I always had. That meant eating what I wanted when I wanted, lying out in the sun (sunscreen, fine, but I couldn't bear the floppy hat), exercising just enough to almost justify my gym membership, and drinking alcohol multiple nights a week, like most journalists I knew. I didn't feel terrible and figured I must be doing better than the general population because I consumed salads and vegetables most days. If something *really* bad was going on, I certainly wasn't aware of it. And in my blurred days of busy inertia, I didn't take time to find out.

To understand what really was happening to my body during the entry into middle-aged airspace, I sought somebody as sharp as my philosopher, Setiya, to explain things in a way that a non-medically-inclined person could understand.

I found who I was looking for in Steven Austad. If anyone understands aging and what's going on behind the scenes with our bodies, it's Austad. He has been studying the causes behind humans' physical decline for decades, and what types of interventions might be successfully deployed. When we spoke, he was working, among other capacities, as senior scientific director for the American Federation for Aging Research. When I asked him what about our physical health we needed to be most concerned with in middle age, he met my request for clarity with this unequivocal response:

"Everything."

While I digested that mic-drop answer, Austad continued. "Anything you want to imagine. Muscle strength, endurance, immune system decline, nerve conduction velocity. Even a slowing of mental activity." All of those things decline, he said, and the decline picks up steam over time.

Our hormones can complicate things, Austad noted—a point later echoed by my own doctors. If you hit menopause in this time frame, a drop in estrogen may coincide with a cascade of problems, ranging from cognitive changes and an increase in weight and body fat to a decrease in bone density. If you experience decreasing levels of testosterone, that may be accompanied by lower energy, reduced muscle bulk, more body fat, and loss of libido—symptoms that also can be associated with aging in general.

Against this bleak backdrop, I asked Austad what he'd recommend as the best defense against the steady decline. He was unambiguous in his prescription.

Move.

We all must move more.

Not just move from one chair to another, or from the car to the golf cart or the elliptical at our gym once or twice a week—but move in a way that measurably builds muscle and upgrades our respiratory fitness. And we need to treat that movement like it's a job, because we only get paid if we show up, and show up with the same regularity with which we make coffee, brush our teeth, or pay our taxes.

Sure, muscle-and-respiratory fitness matters if you aspire to be a fifty-year-old running up and down mountains and hauling buckets of gravel in an obstacle course race. But it matters just as much if you want to keep up with your kids (and grandkids) on a family hike without your knees blowing out, walk down the icy driveway to get the mail and maintain your balance, or carry a heavy bag of birdseed to the car at Home Depot without a store clerk's help. How about squeezing yourself into a restaurant booth or a narrow airline seat without the embarrassing middle-aged groan? Or swinging that tennis racket, casting a fishing line, holding a heavy cast-iron pan in one hand, or spreading garden mulch without thinking, Uh-oh, is my lower back about to give out?

Obviously, not everyone will have the same options for working on strength and movement, given their personal health situations. The question becomes finding what you *can* do. And in case your mind was starting to go there, here is one excuse we're about to bury right now.

It's not too late to start, no matter what your age. And even small steps can make a difference.

Even as recently as twenty years ago, researchers in the aging field believed the later you waited to start healthy activities such as exercise and movement, the less benefit you'd get. Austad said that theory has been turned upside down. "We've now got plenty of evidence that you can get these dramatic impacts," Austad explained. "Starting a new program in midlife can really interrupt the pace of those not-good changes, those negative changes, and turn them into positive changes. . . . We know this now from a lot of work with animals and a lot of work with people."

To really paint the picture, I'll share this graphic story involving a big plate of raw beef.

It was told to me by a guy named Alex Hutchinson, whose writing I'd discovered somewhere along my obstacle course racing journey. Like me, he was a journalist, but unlike me, he'd started out as a physicist and had spent many years as a competitive runner, ultimately writing a book called *Endure: Mind, Body, and the Curiously Elastic Limits of Human Performance.* I'd started reading it in the bathtub after a particularly long run that left my legs feeling like jelly, and when the water finally turned cold, I got out and stayed up past midnight scouring the pages to figure out how I could better manage pain, fatigue, thirst, and all sorts of other discomforts I was starting to face with my training.

After speaking with Austad, I was curious what the *Endure* author would think about the impact of movement on aging, and so we set up a time to talk. Immediately, he told me about a story he'd written. It involved a professor of exercise physiology and nutrition named Luc van Loon. The Dutch professor had engaged in a well-funded experiment in which a large group of frail, elderly people were put through a six-month strength training program. The results were inspiring: those who had also taken a daily protein supplement put on an impressive 2.9 pounds of new muscle.

OK. So far, so good. If frail, elderly people can put on nearly three pounds of muscle, that seems like not such a stretch for many of us in middle age.

But then van Loon gave another account about how subjects of a bed-rest study lost 3.1 pounds of muscle in a *single week,* a loss starkly visualized in a photo taken by one of his students, showing a large plate piled high with cubes of beef. In other words, the muscle it took half a year to gain could be lost potentially in just seven days through being utterly sedentary.

"It shook me up," recalled Hutchinson, who wrote about van Loon's findings in his Sweat Science column for *Outside* magazine. "If I had to pick a number-one enemy of aging, it would be something called sarcopenia—loss of muscle."

The reality is, everything we could possibly measure in the labs starts getting worse before we realize it. By the time you are in your thirties, you are losing muscle on a continuing basis unless you are highly unusual, Hutchinson said. For most people, it's the thing that will affect them most in middle age. Press Fast-Forward and once you are in your seventies, that loss of muscle will be one of the most important things that limits your ability to live independently.

Pass me a kettlebell, please.

Bottom line is, if it's not too late to start, it's also not too early. And once you do, keep at it, because the point is to stay as strong as possible to:

(A) function independently when conducting even normal tasks, and

(B) store up muscle reserves for a day when you are injured, have a surgery, or get laid up in bed for a week or two from something like, say, a global pandemic.

In fact, today more hospitals are putting people who are not particularly fit on exercise programs before they have surgery as a kind of prehabilitation. "Even for people with some sort of catastrophic event, if you have a heart attack or break a leg, the better shape you are in, the faster you will recover," Austad says.

Perhaps what struck me most after talking with Austad was learning how science shows that physical activity, including resistance training to improve strength, can also be a powerful tool to slow cognitive decline. Austad calls such developments one of the biggest surprises to come out of research into the regular practice of physical movement in the past few years. "It's actually very good for your brain, and physical activity is one of the best ways to avoid later-life dementia," he explains. "We know now that there are these chemicals, these hormones that your muscles release when exercising, and they cross into the brain. Those have something to do with the protective effect of physical activity on mental function."

Now, thanks to Setiya, Austad, and Hutchinson, I could see very clearly why I'd been a sitting duck for the midlife assassin: FOMO, for starters. An incessant focus on finite telic activities and unsustainable—and ultimately unsatisfying—benchmarks for productivity. Disconnection and distance from family. Inertia. Sitting. Screens. Too much comfort. Too little discomfort. It all made what came next make a whole lot more sense.

4

PATH TO A BRIDGE
(AND SUPERPOWER)

The summer of 2016 quickly slipped into fall and then dropped into winter without my doing anything further to investigate this strange world of obstacle course racing. Christmas, which we'd decided to spend with my parents in Québec City, arrived. The four of us drove in two fully loaded SUVs up to Canada, each toting an aging golden retriever. Ours, Dolly, still generally acted like she was three even at age fourteen, charging up and down the mountains of our Hudson Valley town. She'd first come home with me at eight weeks old in the spring after the terrorist attacks of September 11, 2001—nicknamed by the breeder as the "bonus puppy" because she'd been born nearly twelve hours after the rest of the litter and was not expected to live. Her full name became Dolly Levi Garrison— an homage to the main character played by Barbra Streisand in the 1969 film version of *Hello, Dolly!*, parts of which were shot in the town of Garrison, near where we lived.

The first year of her life unfolded in a rental home nestled in the woods, a place where wild turkeys roamed across the front yard and coyotes sometimes howled at night. It was a fork-in-the-road time when I needed my dog more than she did me. The 2001 assault on the Twin Towers had unfolded just outside the downtown Manhattan apartment where I lived at the time of the attacks, and in those moments standing at the tip of Manhattan in a rainstorm of smoke, debris, and thousands of human souls from just-collapsed build-ings, I'd looked to the darkened skies believing my own life was over at age thirty. It was then that I'd made my vague Hail Mary promises to God about changing and being better, being different, if I some-how made it out alive. Bringing Dolly home, learning to put another being's needs before mine, was a first tiny step. And yet I had asked much of her in those first years, burying my face in her neck's downy fur each time a jet flew over our house and the roar sent me reaching with shaking hands under the small wooden desk where she would be lying at my feet. Sometimes I'd awake from a vivid dream of being strapped to the nose of an airplane while flying over the rubble of the Twin Towers, panicked we'd hit those souls now floating in the air around me. Then, again, it was Dolly who allowed me to put my head on her ribs and still my heart to the steady beat of hers. Many years later, once it seemed likely a human child was not in our future, Dolly's place in the household took on greater prominence, a canine salve for what wasn't to be.

Old Québec is the epitome of Christmastime, in a Charles Dick-ens kind of way. Lights, carolers crooning in English and French, and carefully decorated trees festoon the often snowy streets that wind between quaint shops and churches. On Christmas Eve, our hotel staged an elaborate arrival by sleigh of Santa bearing a large sack of gifts for the guests' children while adults drinking spiked eggnog snapped pictures. In another town, it would feel overly commercial and forced. Here, it worked.

Christmas Day, while everyone else napped, I walked Dolly up a narrow road called Côte de la Montagne. We paused midway for her to chase snowballs in a park before continuing up to the massive Château Frontenac hotel, a famous tourist landmark in the city. Dolly seemed slower than usual, which I chalked up to the steep climb and icy conditions. The roads had even tested my mother's knees when we'd all walked it a day earlier, although she'd pushed through gamely, never a quitter or a complainer. Still, it had unnerved me to see her struggle at all because, even though she was seventy-two, aging was not a word I'd yet come to attach to her or Dad. They remained fixed in my mind as scuba divers, skiers, sailors . . . always in constant motion: doing, fixing, and prepping for hurricanes bearing down on their coastal North Carolina home.

Dolly and I paused our walk in the shadow of the storied hotel to watch tourists haul red wooden sleds up a steep, icy toboggan slide and then plunge down on them, screams of delight filling the cold air. As always, she studied every movement and sound with laser-like intensity. It was this insatiable curiosity, as well as her fierce independent streak, that led my parents to joke that she was almost like any real child I might have had. Plus, she was blond! We always laughed at the last line, me with gratitude that they'd kept private whatever remorse they bore for what I, their only child, hadn't given them by way of human grandchildren.

Now I stroked her back absently while she watched the joyful mayhem, long feathered tail swishing a canine snow angel into the ground behind her.

A gift of writing is that sometimes you can get a better perspective of life's full musical score, note beginnings and endings for what they are and give them appropriate measure. This day was to be both. My last Christmas with Dolly and the true start of my obstacle course racing journey. There also are those rare times when writing cannot craft a better reality, and this cold afternoon on a frozen hill in a foreign city, my dog's warm body leaning against my legs, was one of them.

Our walk back down the hill was slower still. Dolly went straight to sleep in the hotel room, not even bothering to drink water or eat dinner, so I checked my email. In my inbox was a marketing message from Spartan Race. They'd kept coming ever since I'd originally given them my email address. Occasionally, I'd open one and feel the original tug but forget about it again once something else distracted me. This one touted an upcoming June race in New York, not too far from where we lived. Lisa had gone out for her own walk, so I stretched out on the floor beside Dolly, her labored breathing louder than the hum of the hotel's overworked heating unit.

The lure of that June race rose to a slow boil as I lay on the floor. After a few minutes, I rolled over on my stomach. And on that hotel carpet, face planted where thousands of other middle-aged feet had trod before mine, beside my sleeping dog who was dying from a cancer we hadn't yet discovered, I did five push-ups. My form was terrible, my arms shook, and I had to break after attempting the first two to rest and then perform the last three on my knees. But I did five, somehow imagining this effort would infuse Dolly with the strength to wake up and eat. And then I did ten sit-ups.

Like I said: with some perspective, you can see a beginning for what it is.

In many ways, obstacle course racing checks a lot of important mental and physical boxes as a weapon of choice against the midlife assassin. First, it's the type of atelic activity you can engage in but never be "done" with—in other words, the journey of training, learning, and mastery lasts well beyond any single race. Second, it requires strength, periods of lower-intensity movement as well as high-intensity movement for respiratory fitness, and certain maneuvers requiring complex coordination, which are all considered important fundamentals of a well-balanced exercise routine.

The growing popularity of the sport in past decades may stem from our instinctive need to move in certain ways as a species. *Climb, hang, swing, squat, lift, grip, run.* When we were hunter-gathers seeking our own food, such motions were pivotal to survival. And even without that motive, we knew how to do these things as children. Then, over time, with modern conveniences at our fingertips and busy adult lives under way, we just stopped. And soon, our bodies forgot how. These movements are necessary for obstacle course racing, yes, but they also can help us meet those daily life challenges of picking up heavy groceries, climbing stairs, and hoisting grandchildren in the air.

In other words, are you "strong to be useful"?

Indeed, the movements and challenges of obstacle course racing are rooted in military training designed to build the best warriors, from ancient Greece into more modern times. Historically, soldiers would find themselves crawling through ditches and pulling themselves over walls in battle, and thus needing a regimen of functional exercises. These included so-called "natural movements," such as rope climbing, running, and jumping. Credit for the natural-movement method, or "méthode naturelle," is often given to a French naval officer named Georges Hébert, who championed this form of exercise in the early 1900s as a means to "be strong to be useful."

In the twentieth century, obstacle courses became a regular part of military training in both Europe and the United States. Among other challenges, these courses included traversing horizontal ladders (aka monkey bars), crossing streams by balancing on a log, and scaling an unstable cargo net. By the early 1940s, colleges, high schools, and the Boy Scouts were adopting obstacle courses as part of their fitness requirements, with a major goal of preparing young people to be battle ready both physically and mentally.

But after World War II, interest in this kind of all-around fitness waned in the general population. Universities began allowing students to fulfill their physical education requirements with lower-key activities such as badminton, canoeing, and bowling (my personal pick). In the coming decades, as a more sedentary lifestyle of sitting and eventually screens began to take root in developed nations, a British man named Billy Wilson—aka Mr. Mouse—sensed an opportunity. A former soldier in the British Army with a white handlebar mustache and a penchant for eccentricity (he reportedly once dressed up as a horse for the London Marathon to raise money for his equine sanctuary), Wilson began staging "Tough Guy" races on a large parcel of land in an English village in 1987. His races were built around a cross-country run with obstacles including firepits, log jumps, rope bridges, and water immersions.

Entrepreneurs in the United States soon followed suit, including Spartan Race founder Joe De Sena. De Sena had moved his family to a seven-hundred-acre farm in Pittsfield, Vermont, in search of a life-style that could counterbalance the advent of always-on digital tech-nology, modern convenience, and an increasingly sedentary and overweight population. There he started something called the Death Race. Still going as of this writing, the Death Race is a multiday endurance event designed to test the limits of human potential. Challenges are generally kept secret before the race, though over the years many have become public after the fact: Baling hay for hours. Loading heavy manure into wheelbarrows with pitchforks and push-ing them around a field in timed laps. Searching for ping-pong balls frozen under a foot of snow. Chopping nine pounds of onions and then eating a pound of them. Twenty-two thousand feet of elevation gain and loss. And then, when your body is thoroughly taxed, come the riddles to test your mind: naming American presidents and assembling Lego structures by memory. A fraction of those who start the race finish.

Realizing there was likely a limited market for an event whose website vanity URL is YouMayDie.com, De Sena and a business part-ner launched a new series of events in 2010 that would become Spar-tan Race. Tailored for the masses as well as elite athletes, these races would take place under more controlled circumstances, with more predictable lengths of roughly 5K, 10K, 21K. The challenges, branded as "obstacles," would still be hard, but generally more doable for newcomers. And they would be based on those natural movements used in military training: climbing a rope like in gym class, scaling tall walls, lugging buckets of gravel and bags of sand through rocky terrain, crawling through mud under barbed wire for short stints, and carrying one's body weight across monkey bars and rings.

There was appetite. As the sport took off, a host of branded out-door races, such as Tough Mudder, Warrior Dash, Rugged Maniac,

Bonefrog, and Savage Race, gained in popularity along with Spartan Race. Smaller locally organized races also began to flourish. The TV show *American Ninja Warrior*, which features a series of complex obstacles, became a hit among the masses. Obstacle course racing began producing its own celebrities. Front and center was a corporate attorney named Amelia Boone, who helped put obstacle course racing on the map and herself on the cover of magazines such as *Outside* and *Runner's World*. Big-name sponsors of the sport, including Reebok, came calling. Media and websites dedicated to the sport emerged over time—Mud Run Guide, The OCR Report. One of them, Obstacle Racing Media, was founded in 2012 by a then thirty-nine-year-old softball-playing dad named Matt B. Davis. Davis had completed his first Tough Mudder obstacle course race the year prior, on a cold day when racers had to plunge into an ice water pit as part of the race. That moment transformed his career trajectory: soon after, he launched a podcast and website that eventually became a key place of record for the sport. "I wasn't out of shape, but I was never fit," Davis says. "My DNA changed coming out of that ice water. I was like, 'When is the next race?' In three to four hours, I'd had a life-altering experience."

Spartan and OCR hit the equivalent of the mainstream-media jackpot when *60 Minutes* on CBS ran a piece called "Races from Hell" about the competitions. De Sena was featured describing the motivation to launch his races. His blunt words created a timeless thread from the Colosseum battles of ancient Roman gladiators to the modern-day narrative arc of Netflix's *Squid Game*.

"Wouldn't it be great if we had an event that just screwed with people?" De Sena said to the smiling *60 Minutes* reporter. "That just got 'em back down to their basics and brought out that animal in them? And then we got to watch, who survived and who quit."

It was a great sound bite, full of bravado and a challenge to cease our sedentary lifestyle. But underpinning the swagger was a fundamental truth, which was that in many ways, obstacle course racing just might be a perfect pursuit to rescue us in the modern age.

* * *

Most of this was a mystery to me when I did those five lousy push-ups in a Québec City hotel room. At the time, I was only cognizant of being slightly unsettled as the faint specter of my mortality, and that of my parents and even my dog, was appearing on the horizon. With the advantage of hindsight, I now think something in my inner nature was taking over. And that while pressing my face into that musty hotel carpet next to Dolly, I instinctively recognized a door to something that would make this time of life not just more bearable but maybe better than the days I'd known before. Something that would help me find the storyline of my metaphorical midlife "bridge"—as in the powerful section of a song that adds variety, a new tempo, or a shift of key. And this bridge, with its unexpected pivots from the inertia of middle age, would make the midlife assassin's job of claiming my body and soul a whole lot harder.

One of Spartan Race's most famous marketing lines is a six-word vow: "You'll know at the finish line." It's deliberately vague, a tease crafted to promise that a profound answer awaits a first-time racer who logically might wonder: Why would anyone choose—much less *pay*—to participate in one of the events once dubbed "Races from Hell" by *60 Minutes*? More to the point, why would anyone actively opt to engage in an activity where they sign waivers acknowledging risk of "serious injury and/or death . . . drowning . . . fractures . . . hypothermia . . . animal bites and/or stings . . . contact with poisonous plants . . . falling from heights . . . permanent paralysis," and—if all that wasn't scary enough—"diseases from exposure to fecal contaminated water or slurry."

"You'll know at the finish line."

OK, maybe. But first I had to get to the starting line.

The Obstacle: Burpees
(personal accountability)

For many years, failing obstacles in a Spartan race meant that you would face the grueling punishment of a penalty known as the burpee—thirty of them, in most races. Burpees are a mainstay fixture of many training regimens, including those in fitness classes, professional sports, and the military. The Spartan version of a burpee is in equal parts torture and the perfect exercise, because it involves a complex full-body movement that consists of squatting with your hands on the ground, thrusting your legs back into a plank position, completing a push-up where your chest must touch the ground, jumping legs back to meet hands, and then rising into a small jump with hands over your ears.

That all counts as one burpee. As my former *Wall Street Journal* colleague, the sports columnist Jason Gay, once succinctly wrote: The burpee is "an ideal way to A) get your heart rate up and B) truly hate life."

Try ten and see how you feel. After you try ten, consider how thirty would seem after your arms and legs are weary from miles of running on rocky, muddy terrain and lifting very heavy things over and over and over.

Burpees are designed to force accountability for failure. You get the pleasure of planting your face in the dirt over and over and then must continue racing, far more fatigued than if you'd completed the obstacle itself.

Over time, Spartan began phasing out burpees in favor of penalty loops, which theoretically are easier to monitor for compliance. But when I started racing, burpees were still the staple penalty for obstacle failure. What struck me most about performing them, other than the pain, was how completion was really built upon an honor system. There were generally three categories of racers. In the Open category heats—a more congenial environment where the bulk of racers participate and sometimes help each other with obstacles—no one counted your burpees. You could do the burpees or not. Nobody knew but you. Yet, on any given race day, plenty of people would slog it out in the burpee pit with no lure of a podium finish, no hope of any glory beyond just crossing the finish line. And even in the Elite and Age Group competitive heats, where burpees were required and racers contended for podium spots and sometimes prize money in the case of the Elites, trust was implicit because it was hard for race volunteers and cameras to monitor everyone all the time.

I came to loathe and love burpees in equal measure. Early on, as an Open category racer, they just meant suffering to me. As I got better and began seriously competing for the podium in Age Group heats, I could feel that temptation to skip a few as I'd drop to the ground and watch women pass me by. I hated that temptation more than the suffering. Eventually, I devised a system to beat the urge to cut corners, which was to count out loud—and to count so loudly my brain automatically would comply.

In this way, I learned to hold myself accountable even when no one was watching.

5

FRAGILE FIRST NOTES

After those five labored hotel room push-ups in Québec City, I got up off the floor, opened my email back up, and registered for the 5K June Tri-State Sprint in Tuxedo, New York. From that day forward, I also stopped deleting the Spartan Workout of the Day emails. There was a real goal in front of me—this impending June race at a now-shuttered ski resort. You'll hear motivation experts preach about the power of having a firm goal with a deadline if you want to embrace something new. Maybe it's cliché, but it worked for me. Sure, I could have signed up and attempted the race with no training, likely failed most of the obstacles, skipped burpees if I felt like it, and probably crossed the finish line. But as a type A overachiever, I wasn't programmed this way. Plus, the prospect of ending up in a crumpled heap after falling from a rope like that documentary filmmaker I'd read about in *Outside* magazine was not something that appealed to me.

The issue was, I was unclear exactly how to get started, or what training should look like, or how much training I should do, with what equipment and at what times and for how long, and after eating what food and wearing what tracking device. Question after question accumulated like little procrastination building blocks until finally, as the Spartan emails continued collecting in my inbox, I threw in the towel on planning and just started fumbling around.

Because my days were already full and it hadn't yet occurred to me that there might be things in my life I could *stop* doing, I began setting my alarm forty-five minutes earlier every weekday morning to attempt those Workouts of the Day. But because the exercises were foreign to me, after crawling out of bed at 5:30 A.M., I'd spend five to ten bleary-eyed minutes on YouTube decoding things such as "hollow hold" and "bear crawl." Then I'd go outside in my frost-covered yard and attempt to replicate what I'd watched, hoping the neighbors couldn't see me wallowing around in the cold dirt like a wounded animal as they drove past our house en route to work. After I was done, I'd shake the dead grass out of my pants and shoes, toss my sweaty hoodie in the laundry basket, take a fast shower, gulp down some oatmeal and coffee, and start the hour-long commute to the office, where I generally found I now needed a second breakfast from the cafeteria. On weekends, I made up stuff that seemed Spartan-esque for longer workouts—like the cold February day when I hiked in the woods for forty minutes, lugging small logs and boulders I found along the way.

With no firm instruction, I didn't have an obvious way to track my progress. Because digital calendars already ruled my adult working life, I figured I could also log my so-called training there. Each day, I'd click on a little Google Calendar square and record my Spartan Workouts of the Day and any problems I'd had or other notes. The entries from 2017 look something like this:

February 15—Spartan "Hardship"

Dynamic Warmup
(2x) Main Set
1-minute hollow hold
10 push-ups
10 leg raises
1-minute plank
10 mountain climbers

1-minute hollow hold
1-minute plank
10 burpees
Stretch

March 1—Spartan "Big Stonehenge"

Dynamic Warmup
10-minute run (1 mile)
(x3 rounds—supposed to be 5 but ran out of time)
50 stone deadlifts (need to work on my technique)
50-meter Atlas carry
50-meter sprint
50-meter bear crawl
Stretch

Clicking back now through those first few months of fumbling, I can see amid the details crammed into small digital boxes how holding myself accountable was such a critical first step to getting started and not dropping the ball. If I didn't do the workout, I couldn't write it in the calendar box. If I didn't write it in the calendar box, the box would be blank. A blank box felt bad, and a full box felt good. So I did the workout. My psyche apparently was that easy to manipulate. I even recorded our hikes with the increasingly slower Dolly. It's true that my workouts weren't strategic or optimized in any way. I certainly struggled with form and couldn't finish every workout yet. But what mattered at this point was that I was doing *something*. No more life-inertia delays. No more procrastinating while surfing the Web reading about Spartan and other people doing Spartan races. No searching for cool equipment to help mask my skinny-kid insecurities. Just doing. With whatever I had on hand. Even if it was all guesswork.

In his book *Beginners: The Joy and Transformative Power of Lifelong*

Learning, journalist and author Tom Vanderbilt traces his yearlong quest to become an adult learner again, from singing to surfing to chess. One of his chapters is titled "I Don't Know What I'm Doing but I'm Doing It Anyway." It's a powerful message to me for two reasons. First, it's freeing and takes away the pressure to be wise and perfect, which tends to grow with age. Second, and this might be even more important, it breaks down that barrier of procrastination. If you want to try something new, sometimes the best way is to just dive right in and fumble your way around for a while. Eventually, if it's meant to be, the fumbling will give way to process, and the process will become part of your identity.

In other words, when the barrier to entry seems too overwhelming, think about it this way: "If you run, you are a runner." That's an often-repeated quote from a couch potato turned marathon runner named John "the Penguin" Bingham. Bingham transformed his sedentary life by becoming a back-of-the-pack runner (hence the Penguin nickname) and chronicling his journey for the magazine *Runner's World* in a column called "The Penguin Chronicles" as well as in several books.

During these first months of self-directed early-morning lessons, I began to understand what both Vanderbilt and Bingham meant. It's true that I didn't know what I was doing, but I was doing it anyway. I was doing athletic things! I had a record in my digital calendar to prove it, as well as the bruises on my knees from crawling around in our yard at dawn. As the weeks passed, the emerging baby calluses on my hands felt like a secret, something I proudly touched under conference tables at work as the monotony of meetings and my old routines swelled up around me again. I was still the same me, just more like me-plus. And miraculously, given my lack of supervision, I hadn't hurt myself. Maybe, I began to think, I'd be able to pull off this June Spartan race and not totally humiliate myself.

And then came those bigger walls.

* * *

As I was getting stronger, Dolly was getting weaker. Six weeks after returning from Québec City, I'd discovered a knot under her left front armpit during a routine brushing session. It was small but not as squishy as the benign lumps removed over the years. Still, when our local veterinarian took a syringe full of fluid from the mass and looked at it under a microscope, he assured us everything was fine. He even gave me a high five in the doorway of the examination room, which I accepted while tamping down an uneasy feeling in my stomach.

By spring, I could tell the knot was growing. We eventually sought a second opinion from a specialist in Manhattan, and the minute the surgeon touched the lump, he gave me no high five. Instead, he said flatly: "I don't like the way this feels." More biopsies revealed the truth the first veterinarian had missed: a fast-growing cancer that was inoperable unless we amputated her leg—which, given her advanced age, Lisa and I decided was not a viable option. The other options were radiation and chemotherapy or doing nothing.

We learned of her grim diagnosis during a twelve-hour drive to visit my parents on the North Carolina coast, with Dolly curled up tightly in the backseat, almost too tired to relieve herself at the random Hardee's restaurants and interstate rest areas where we stopped. I'd warned my parents about Dolly's lethargy. But the moment we pulled up in their driveway and she saw my mother and father, she trotted down the ramp we laid against the back of our SUV for her, tail up, and went right to their sides, seeming like a different dog. This small coastal town had been her second home since she was a puppy, the smells emanating off the salty water behind my folks' home a never-ending source of interest. Lisa and I looked at each other, not voicing what we both were thinking: maybe there was still fight in her. That evening, before dinner, I ran two miles to a recreational area called Western Park Community Center to shake out my legs, stiff from driving. Jogging around the ball fields and tennis courts, I discovered a metal pull-up bar nestled in a back corner adjacent to a wall of scrubby pine trees. That bar soon would become a place of refuge.

As we settled in, it was clear my mother also wasn't feeling well. She and my father had just returned from a bucket-list trip to Cuba, and my mom was now coughing, experiencing vertigo, had a strange full-body rash, and had mysteriously lost her vision for a few hours one evening. My dad, a retired veterinarian who always applied medical logic to his human family, was baffled and seemed uncharacteristically worried when I spoke to him privately. My mother shook us both off, but she was never particularly interested in giving much heed to anything that would slow her down.

Midweek, Lisa and I sat down to talk. Lots of things can hold a marriage together, and part of our glue is staying on the same page and adjusting during periods of stress. Dolly needed to start treatment soon if we had any hope of extending her life. Lisa, meantime, needed to get back to New York for her job, now as a video producer and news anchor at the international news agency Reuters. I needed to get back to work too, but I didn't want to leave my mother. And here, at least, Dolly would have company during the day after treatment versus being alone in our house while we shuttled back and forth to our offices.

I called my boss at Consumer Reports, Leonora Wiener, and explained with a hard knot in my stomach what was happening. I was conflicted by my ambition at work and this unshakable sense that staying here on the coast of North Carolina was the right thing to do, a moment in time I'd never reclaim if I left. One that might get filed into that mental box labeled Regrets. It was a morning that would forever shift my perspective on leadership and trust. In these pre-pandemic days remote work was not the norm, and I led a large team. But Leonora never flinched, telling me to stay put and do my job from down South until things were resolved. Her generosity and my good fortune to have a job where remote work was even possible loosened the knot. "I know you'll find a way to make it work," she said.

Lisa flew back to New York, and we made doctors' appointments

for my mother. My father then helped me find a good canine oncol-
ogy treatment program at a hospital in Cary, North Carolina, a two-
and-a-half-hour drive from their house. The next week, Dolly began
radiation and later chemo, a course of treatment that would take a
couple of months. She and I would awake before dawn once a week,
drive to Cary with two large cups of coffee for me and an empty
stomach for her. While she lay sedated, high-energy beams coloring
her skin purple as they blasted into the tumor, I attended meetings
by phone or Google Meet from the hospital's waiting room, hitting
Mute when the collective barking and meowing grew too loud. After
Dolly awakened, she'd eat a small meal in the parking lot, and we'd
drive back to my parents' home while I took more meetings by
phone. If it was this hard watching a four-legged creature I loved
undergo such aggressive treatment, I couldn't imagine how the parents of sick human children coped.

Weeks passed. The root of my mother's issues eventually was
pegged to a virus she'd picked up aboard the small cruise ship on
their trip to Cuba; the virus apparently had kicked her immune system into hyperdrive. Various medications were prescribed, and relief
set in among the three of us. As she improved, we fell into a routine.
My father and I exercised the dogs at Western Park early in the morning; on evenings when my mother felt up to it, she and I would walk
a loop around a local campground's nature preserve. When my work
meetings ended for the day, if I wasn't in transit with Dolly, I sometimes helped my father spread mulch or stack firewood on their
property. ("What did you do with our daughter?" he joked when I
lifted a particularly heavy piece of wood.) It was the most time we'd
all spent together since I'd left home at age twenty-one to drive north
for my first job at *The Wall Street Journal*'s Pittsburgh bureau. When I
needed to fly to Washington, D.C., for a work board meeting, my
parents took care of Dolly. Lisa flew back and forth, tended to our
house in New York, and we made the best of it. We were pulling away
now from those carefree days of Kenny Chesney's "Summertime"

lyrics, with two bare feet on a dashboard, and heading into a new verse of our life together, the realities of middle age planting our feet firmly on the ground.

As for the June Spartan race, it came and went without me. And this might have been the end of my obstacle course racing journey before it ever truly began.

Except . . . *except* I'd started to feel like training—even my improvised, faking-it training—wasn't really optional anymore. The calendar box checking, the small, incremental improvements in my body that I'd started to see (a little calf muscle!), the secret calluses and bruises, it all had lit a small flicker inside me. And I wasn't ready for it to go out. Through the summer, I ran alone before work, sweating in the dense coastal heat. On weekends, I would bike around the wetlands at the local campground, lift my parents' hand weights, and carry a cinder block from my father's workshop around their yard. I performed burpees in the coarse centipede grass, once discovering when I took off my shirt to shower that I'd forgotten a key childhood lesson to check for fire ants and had racked up a trail of angry red welts across my stomach. All the while, Dolly watched me vigilantly from the cool comfort of the screened-in porch. And each of those workouts still got recorded into those little Google Calendar boxes in between other notations: "Dolly's 5th chemo"; "Lisa arrive OAJ 11:07 pm."

On her good days, Dolly and I would sometimes drive those two miles to Western Park, where I'd practice hanging from that metal pull-up bar for as long as I could to improve my grip strength. My dog would wait patiently in the shade while I'd count seconds, telling myself every moment I held on was another day she would live. Soon fifteen seconds became thirty, and then sixty. Whenever I finally dropped, she'd come lie beside me for a few moments, panting a silent thank-you for the effort before returning to the shade. We'd listen as the thunder of training explosions coming from the nearby Camp Lejeune Marine base mixed with the crack of baseball bats in the park from the youth teams.

And so it was, amid so much uncertainty, that the fragile first notes of my bridge fell firmly into place. My unguided training evolved to become as core to my day as bathing or doing my job: something to be worked around, not put aside, even when other pressing obligations arose. I taught my mother how to perform a Spartan dynamic warm-up with gentle arm and neck circles, ankle rotations, and squats (which she still does to this day). My father often joined us. And with Dolly and their dog, Bos'n, lying at our feet, we stretched, rotated, squatted, and pushed back against time and the final toll it would eventually levy on us all.

By August, just before my forty-sixth birthday, my mother was feeling much better and Dolly's treatment was finished, so Lisa and I made plans to return permanently to New York. We said goodbye to my parents in their driveway beneath the protective arms of the live oak trees, all of us trying unsuccessfully to hold back our tears as we optimistically spoke of returning at Christmas.

Dolly lived three more months. During that time, she swam again in the Hudson River, slowly walked some of her favorite flat trails, and slept in her own home. But the cancer eventually spread to spots on a hind leg. We tried another round of radiation in New York, but this time, the treatment just seemed to make her feel worse. On November 26, we drove into Manhattan and checked into a hotel so we could attend the opening night of a friend's play. That night, we awoke to the strange sound of Dolly thrashing on the floor against the hotel bed in a seizure. At 1 A.M. we packed our bags, checked out quickly with a baffled desk clerk, and drove home. At daylight, Lisa helped Dolly outside to relieve herself. I woke up and looked out the kitchen window in time to see our dog collapse by a dogwood tree.

I ran outside, squatted, picked her forty-eight pounds up off the ground, and carried her to the back of our car. Only many years later, as I became aware of how obstacle course racing impacted basic life tasks, would I connect my early days of training to that moment when I was able to lift and carry our sweet dog one last time. I lay curled up with her in the back tailgate section of our car while Lisa drove the fifty miles back to Manhattan. As soon as we got to the hospital where she'd been receiving treatment, Dolly lapsed into another seizure. The doctors were kind but firm. They believed the cancer had spread to her brain and that the end was near. If we waited longer, she would suffer.

Lisa stroked Dolly's head while I signed the papers that would take her from us forever. I remember the unfairness of having to shake the pen to get the ink flowing. And as I watched my right hand scrawl my name, I flashed back in time to a moment a couple of years earlier when the three of us hiked a hill near our Hudson Valley home. Tiny purple flowers peeked up through the grass. A healthy Dolly was chasing her ball down the hill. Lisa and I walked behind, the spring sun warming our backs, and I felt profoundly complete. We did not have a human child, that much was true and likely now final. But we were a family. That same night I awoke in panic and started crying. "What, what is it?" Lisa asked as she came awake herself, frightened. I spit out my poisonous thought: "One of these days, I'm going to live long enough to see you, Dolly, or me die." The finality of it, the inevitability of that outcome, of the ultimate truth about aging, struck me as a maze with no way out.

I put down the pen and handed the signed papers to the veterinary technician.

What came next I preserve as a memory for the three of us. Anyone who has said goodbye in this way to an animal they love will know the dense heaviness that filled the room when it was over and the doctor exited, like a cold quiet pressing in from the deepest part of an ocean. Once again, and for the last time, it was the three of us alone—two of us breathing, the other one perfectly still as we whispered all the love we had inside of us into her ear.

The entry in my Google Calendar box for that day reads: "Dolly Levi Garrison (2002–2017)."

* * *

A month later, I sat in our living room watching the Christmas tree lights and feeling the emptiness of the house. We'd driven Dolly's body to North Carolina the day after she died and buried her on my parents' property, head facing the water so she could satisfy her eternal curiosity. My father dug the grave with his tractor. My mother outlined it with conch shells after Lisa and I filled in the dirt. I read an essay about the bonus puppy that I'd written one night that summer, listening to her breathe while she slept and twitched after her radiation.

And then we drove home to New York without her.

After so many months of squeezing my workouts in between these bigger concerns—worrying about my mother and treating Dolly—the obvious question loomed: What now? Another Spartan race was coming up in April at Citi Field, where the New York Mets play baseball. There was nothing to stop me from signing up now. Was I ready? The truth was, I had no idea. I'd never touched a real race obstacle. And I had no real benchmark for my progress beyond those calendar boxes.

So once again, I turned to Google for help (*Sitting! Screens!*) and searched for gyms that specialized in obstacle course race training. And that's how, almost a year to the day after that perfect quiet moment with Dolly on the snowy hill in Québec City, I landed in a nondescript strip mall gym under the instruction of a steely former army sergeant named Vince.

6

BE CONTENT
TO APPEAR FOOLISH

"Let's try a timed dead hang for thirty seconds," Vince says.

He points to a long, skinny black bar dangling off metal chains attached to the ceiling, one of a series of floating monkey bars. "Climb up on this box and hang from that bar with an overhand grip, palms facing away from you. It's a test of your grip strength."

We're nearing the end of our hour together, and things haven't gone as well as I'd hoped. It's a few days after Christmas. I'm alone in a small White Plains, New York, gym called Epic Hybrid Training, which is tucked next to a battery store in a strip mall off Interstate 287. There is no one here but me and Vince Liguori, an army sergeant turned personal trainer who makes body fat and aging seem intended for a different species, even though I'll later learn he's eleven years my senior. When I'd looked Vince up on Facebook the night before, there were photos of him holding himself *at a ninety-degree angle* to a vertical pole. Dressed in a tank top and gym shorts, with muscles you could bounce coins off, he makes me feel like Olive Oyl from *Popeye*.

When I first arrived, Vince was finishing up leading a small group class. Trying to play it cool, I took a seat on a long bench near the door in what I hoped was a casual, athletic position and watched the other students, drenched in sweat as they jumped onto boxes, crawled around cones, climbed ropes, and swung from bars and rings inside this small, steamy space. All the while, Vince barked at them military-style.

"You should have come hydrated already," Vince admonished one guy who stopped during a set of exercises to sip from his water bottle. "If you're drinking water now, it's TOO LATE! Everybody, give me twenty tuck jumps, because our friend here DIDN'T HYDRATE." The class members groaned but were clearly too tired to even shoot the offender a dirty look, so they just started jumping up and down, bringing their knees to their palms, while Vince counted: "FOUR-TEEN, FIFTEEN, SIXTEEN . . ."

But now everyone else has vacated the gym, and it's just me and Vince here sweating it out together. Well, to be more accurate, I'm sweating. He looks calm, cool, and dry. I've booked a private lesson with him to try to assess my fitness level, and throughout our morning together he's put me through a series of moves he says I'll need to complete obstacles in a Spartan race. Jumping with both feet onto a sixteen-inch-high box from a standing motionless position is doable, but I'm surprisingly winded. Not doable is swinging across hanging rings. With no clue yet how to shift the weight of my hips properly for momentum, I fall the minute I release one hand. Then there's the rope climb, something Vince can do easily using just his upper-body strength as he pulls himself up to the ceiling rafters and rings a bell. He instructs me how to use my feet, wrapping them around the rope in various positions so I can take the pressure off my arms. Again and again, I attempt what he shows me, but my feet keep slipping, and I keep falling.

It's increasingly obvious that, while my makeshift training has left me in decent shape for the average forty-six-year-old, I still am woefully underdeveloped when it comes to the upper-body strength and the techniques needed to conquer the basic tasks of obstacle course racing. It's all so much harder than I'd imagined while running laps around my parents' property and doing burpees in a pile of fire ants.

Panting and demoralized, I can barely imagine what Vince-who-looks-like-a-statue thinks about his wasted morning with me. At least he's getting paid, I remind myself. I've got this one last task, the timed dead hang, and then I can go home. Get into bed with a book. Nobody can make me do a Spartan race, I think, telling myself I don't care if I sound like a five-year-old.

I step up onto the black box, grab the bar, take a breath, and step off. My feet dangle about two feet above the floor as the bar swings a little on its chains above my head. I see Vince absently check his cellphone.

He thinks I'm going to just drop off.

The seconds tick by. Twelve . . . thirteen . . . fourteen. At twenty-five, Vince finally looks up, his raised eyebrow an indication he's surprised I'm still on the bar. He watches now. We get to our target of thirty seconds, and I don't let go. After a summer of hanging alone from a bar in a rural southern park, hot sun burning the back of my neck while I counted magical seconds to keep my dog alive, muscle memory is kicking in despite my fatigue and humiliation. I stubbornly cling to that bar as the clock on the wall moves to forty-five and then sixty seconds. My hands are throbbing, my forearms tight and burning. I keep hanging, thoughts jumbling amid my pain into a mix of fantasy . . . *A few more seconds will bring Dolly back* . . . and reality . . . *You are wrong about me, Vince. I want to race.*

At 105 seconds, I let go of the bar and rub my throbbing forearms. Then I press my white, clawed fingers against my leg to force them back into their normal position.

Vince walks to the front desk, leaving me behind—the bar I just released still swinging, its chains clanking over my head. With his back to me, he calls out flatly: "Well, you might not have much fun, but you'll probably get through a Spartan race."

The words sink in. He didn't say no. He didn't say I *couldn't* do it. I cross the floor to gather my phone and car keys, a tiny bubble of hope inflating in my chest, and take out my credit card to pay him.

He studies me for a moment. "Don't pay me," he says finally. "If you really want to do this—if you want to be here and commit and learn to get better—just come back."

The ancient Greek Stoic philosopher Epictetus mused about the will of humans and the importance of distinguishing what we can control from what we can't. One of his widely shared thoughts: "If you would improve, be content to be thought foolish and stupid with regard to externals."

Epictetus's words can be interpreted in several ways, and one of them is that humility is a good thing and it's OK to fumble around in front of other people who may judge you. (As opposed to crawling around in the dirt alone in your backyard, like I'd been doing.) For those of us not blessed with natural talent or gifts in a particular area, adopting this mindset is crucial if we're to have any chance of success in a new endeavor—be it a new job, sport, or skill, such as computer coding or painting. And it means relinquishing the illusion that we've got the Master Control hub at our fingertips, which can be deeply uncomfortable when you're older and accustomed to calling the shots in your life. But it's the only way to learn requisite new behaviors and habits and unlearn old ones, as we'll discover in subsequent chapters.

This is where the word "yet" becomes a really important tool. Ask yourself this question: Do you believe more strongly that your abilities are fixed and innate (i.e., you probably were born with them) or that they have been cultivated and developed through hard work? If you fall in the latter "hard work" camp, then you've likely got a "growth mindset," according to the well-known Stanford University psychologist, author, and professor Carol S. Dweck. And that mindset can help you flourish in something new and hard a lot more than if you land in the "fixed mindset" camp, believing your abilities are predetermined and set in stone. In speeches, Dweck sometimes tells the story about one Chicago school's unorthodox but effective grading protocol. It works like this: students needed to pass a certain number of units to graduate, and if they didn't pass a unit, instead of a failing grade, they got the grade "Not Yet." Embedded in the word "yet" is the promise that with hard work comes a future with potential improvement.

Taken a step further, I think "yet" also gives you carte blanche to look foolish for a while because you believe it won't last forever.

Indeed, the moment I'd stepped out of the privacy of my backyard and into the sanctum of Epic with Vince, I'd been forced to park any inhibitions I might have had about looking stupid at my age in front of strangers. In the months to come, my physical weaknesses and ineptitudes would be on full display publicly. I'd have to get comfortable picking my bruised ego up off the sticky gym floor again and again. Such indignities are the price you pay to learn any significant new skill. Want to master diving in a swimming pool? Be prepared to land a bunch of embarrassing belly flops first is how one mastery expert named George Leonard puts it. Thinking "I'm not an athlete *yet*" instead of just "I'm not an athlete" made all this humiliation more bearable for me.

There's also a powerful and beneficial physical component to cultivating this growth mindset. In fact, each time we learn something new, particularly something hard, our brain has the potential to form strong new connections by rewiring itself. This is often called "neural plasticity," and contrary to long-held beliefs that it only happens when you're young, newer research shows the adult brain can be capable of rewiring itself into middle age.

The Seattle Longitudinal Study, which started in 1956, bills itself as one of the most extensive psychological research studies of how we develop and change cognitively throughout adulthood, with more than six thousand participants ranging in age from twenty-two to over one hundred. One of the study's central findings is that as individuals, we generally tend to gain in our intellectual abilities into early midlife and then remain stable until our sixties before declining. (This trend obviously can differ by individual.) Some abilities, such as word skills, tend to increase into our sixties and beyond, particularly for women, while others, such as spatial abilities—think assembling furniture or reading a map—hold up into the eighties for men. That's certainly hopeful news for us middle-agers.

But there's more. Tackling something new and hard may also chip away at boredom, which itself is thought to be a health hazard correlated with anxiety, depression, and an increased risk of making mistakes. In other words, by learning new things and continually making choices, you are adhering to the adage "Use it or lose it." For example, as the study's founding director, K. Warner Schaie, bluntly put it: "There's nothing worse than being a couch potato and spending your time in front of the television. As you begin to stop making decisions, it won't be long before you have difficulty actually making decisions. The notion that you can no longer do anything becomes a self-fulfilling prophecy."

As I'm about to find out, it's very hard to be bored when you're out of breath, surrounded by people decades younger than you in a steamy gym, looking stupid over and over again while learning how to scale tall walls, throw a spear, and swing through the air like a monkey.

I meet Vince's challenge and show up at Epic two days later for one of the gym's regular "Blast" classes. It's the day before New Year's Eve, so there are only a few attendees, and the instructor happens to be the gym's owner, a guy named Pete Jones. At fifty-nine years old, Pete is small, lean, and strong, with a personality far bigger than his physical frame. As the class gets under way, he leads us through a grueling series of maneuvers where we go hard for forty-five seconds jumping, crawling, or sprinting between cones, rest for about fifteen seconds, and then repeat. It's a type of exercise I'll later learn is called High Intensity Interval Training, or HIIT for short. We do everything barefoot on the mats, and I'm blown away that Pete, who is older than any of us, performs the entire workout while he also coaches, cracks jokes, and races around the gym to tweak our forms. Not once does he seem winded.

Conversely, I am gulping for air and gulping water from my bottle every break we get. (And really glad Vince isn't there to witness my dehydration.) Within fifteen minutes I've soaked my shirt through with sweat. After twenty minutes, my legs are like Jell-O. Everyone here is faster than I am, and, evidently, more coordinated. But Pete's mood is infectious, and the intervals tick by quickly as rock music blasts throughout the small gym until suddenly we are done, and I realize I've finished the forty-five-minute class despite aforementioned Jell-O legs. I may not have any technical obstacle skills yet, but all my running around the Hudson Valley hills and the marshlands of North Carolina have at least made me fit enough to endure this first cardio outing with other people.

"Heyyyyy, not bad," Pete says to me after class while I'm lacing up my shoes. "This is one of the hardest classes we teach here." The other students nod their agreement as we wipe off our faces with little orange towels. "If you can do this, you'll have no problem with the other ones," he promises.

It's not true—I'll have a *lot* of problems with the other classes in the weeks to come. But this first nod of encouragement lands like a big cup of fertilizer on my budding dream to tackle an obstacle race. It dawns on me then that, despite the secret pride I've felt fumbling around on my own, it's been lonely. The surge of excitement coursing through my body from today will lead me to drive home and immediately start examining my digital calendar to see how many sessions with Pete I can squeeze in each week before and after work. As it turns out, Pete's ownership of Epic is the byproduct of his own midlife epiphany, and once I learn his story, I tell myself that if he could change his ways so late in life, so can I.

Because watching him zip around the gym, it's hard to believe that just a few years ago—well into middle age—Pete had been overweight, with serious back problems and zero interest in physical activity. He graduated from high school ("barely" is how he remembers it) and went on to community college. But math, which was his gift and passion, was way too easy for him at the school.

As a result, Pete says, he spent most of his time drinking beer at the local pub until realizing three months into college that he needed to "sober up and get serious." So he ditched the chance for a college degree in favor of enlisting in the U.S. Air Force for a four-year stint working on electronics, specifically for a short-range attack missile system. After the Air Force, he transferred that knowledge into a lucrative career working in technology and database management for a host of big-name clients ranging from Citibank and Reuters to Johnson & Johnson, multiple hedge funds, and eventually, the financial services and investment bank company Jefferies.

This next part will hit home for anyone who's ever gotten trapped in a desk job with long, grueling work hours. It does for me. For most of his adult life, Pete describes his physical activity this way: "None. But I didn't know I was out of shape because I never tried to do anything." Sensing a vulnerable target, the midlife assassin was relentless. At five feet, six inches, Pete's weight at one point crept up to 165 pounds. He also suffered from a condition called spondylolisthesis, a painful spinal issue stemming from problems with the connections between vertebrae. It would take him five minutes just to get out of bed in the morning. He couldn't lift his kids. In 2005 he attempted the J.P. Morgan Corporate Challenge, a large corporate running event—just out of curiosity, because so many of his colleagues were doing it. It was a disaster, Pete says. "Everyone beat me."

Still, inertia is powerful. Which meant it took almost another decade before the switch flipped that changed everything for him. It was 2013, and Pete was working for a midtown Manhattan hedge fund, commuting in and out of the city daily from his suburban home, the back pain excruciating and his overall health declining. He often ate lunch at a Thai place close to the office and would stare across the street at a new fitness studio, where he watched what he calls "this medieval crazy workout class going on." The studio was Epic Hybrid Training, and the equipment inside included floating monkey bars, kettlebells, heavy sandbags, and climbing ropes.

After a few months of watching the classes between bites of sauce-laden food, Pete got tired of his mindless voyeurism and signed up for a class. He lasted two-thirds of the way through and then got sent to the bench by the instructor. "It was brutal," he says. "But I was hooked." He was fifty-five years old. Soon Pete began forgoing lunch at the Thai place for classes at Epic. He was one of the oldest students, and it took him months before he could handle a full class five days a week. But then things started changing. He could see definition in his abs. His back stopped hurting, and for the first time in his adult life, getting out of bed didn't require a five-minute delay. He got lean, dropping his weight to 138 pounds. Looking back, Pete believes if he hadn't discovered Epic and started his training, "I'd be crippled by now."

At the end of his first year of Epic classes, Pete attempted a Spartan race at Citi Field in an Open heat and was stunned when he noticed his time was among the fastest of men his age. Soon he started racing competitively in the Age Group heats, and the first-, second-, and third-place medals began racking up from the Spartan and other obstacle races he entered. At his own gym, which he eventually opened in 2017 as a second career with his wife, Anne, students call him Podium Pete in honor of his rows of bling hanging over the front desk.

The fact that Pete is about to turn sixty quickly takes age off the table as an excuse when tackling anything taught at Epic. He flies across the swinging monkey bars and rings effortlessly due to his bicep strength and his now-slender frame, heaves fifty-pound sandbags around like they are small beanbags, and is quicker during sprints than a lot of students in their twenties and thirties. I'm particularly in awe of his ability to explode from a standing position up and onto a box that is forty-two inches high through the power and mobility of his hips. Out in the parking lot, Pete has erected a bale of hay on a stand and demonstrates how to properly land a spear in it, rarely missing.

Because I've got a full-time job with, generally, no break for lunch, I end up taking either very-early-morning or evening classes, sometimes with Vince or another instructor but often with Pete. The classes' focus ranges from cardio-intense sessions to more strength-training-based ones as well as workouts specifically designed to build the core, mobility, and endurance. From the get-go, it's humbling. There's a gifted squad of regulars—the cool kids, I dub them—who include a joke-cracking guy named Keith Grasmann, who's in his early forties and teaches French to junior high and high schoolers; a handsome cardiologist named Amit; and a quiet, muscular woman with tattoos, named Danielle. Danielle is so strong she can climb two ropes at the same time, holding one in each arm as she hoists herself upward toward the ceiling, reminding me of Scarlett Johansson in the movie *Black Widow*. The superstar of most classes is a dark-haired, always-smiling guy named Eric Florio, who races in the Elite category of the Spartan races and is second only to Pete in his seemingly boundless energy.

They are all so far beyond me in their abilities that I feel guilty no matter which cool kid I get paired with during class to race between cones or hurl a heavy ball back and forth. It's like a flashback to my dodgeball days. I imagine them thinking, *Why do I have to work out with the weak girl?* when I drop the ball or knock over the cones as we race. Epictetus would have been very proud, I think later, as I shower off my chagrin in the Consumer Reports company gym and dash, still flushed, down the hall, past the testing labs to my first meeting.

Fortunately, Pete seems to be of the Carol Dweck "Not Yet" school of training and sees something in me that I don't. He lets me spend extra time after class trying out the different techniques Vince had shown me for rope climbing, where the secret is more in the feet than the arms. They all look super simple when Pete demos them, but when I try pulling them together myself, my legs flail about like a panicked spider falling off its web.

Looking foolish transfers over to the floating rings, which, like the monkey bars, hang from chains anchored in the ceiling. The goal is to move from one ring to the other across the gym. But I can't even move from the first ring to the second one without slipping off. Many of the strongest guys, including Pete, can muscle their way across with bent arms. Most of the women who are skilled in this obstacle swing from arm to arm using momentum and grip strength. They are flowy and beautiful with their movements, and I watch from below on the floor mat with an unfamiliar envy lit hot in my chest. The feeling follows me into the parking lot, where I stand beside smelly dumpsters watching spear after spear leave my hands and sail straight past the target to land on the concrete or dirt beyond.

Here at this strip mall gym, everything else about me—any success I've had—doesn't help me in any way or hold any weight with my companions. My merit and worth are based solely on whatever performance I can muster during the forty-five minutes we work out together. There is no life hack or clever turn of phrase, no name in my virtual rolodex, that's going to get me across those rings or make my spear soar straighter. Politics play no role here. In fact, there is nothing I can do to help myself succeed except to keep coming back and looking as foolish as necessary until I figure it all out. As the days pass and this new reality sinks in, the anonymity and simplicity of terms between us all begins to feel remarkably freeing.

And, in baby steps, I do get better—at least sort of. After about four weeks, I'm able to make it clumsily about halfway up the rope, which earns a (very small) nod of approval from Black Widow. There are other modest advancements, like not needing to gulp water in between every HIIT interval or graduating from shouldering the lightest twenty-pound sandbags on my back to the twenty-five-pound ones when we practice weighted lunges around the gym. One weekend, Pete and Anne take us on a field trip to some nearby hiking trails, where we lug the sandbags up and down the mountain while their champion Welsh springer spaniel, Tucker, runs bored circles around us. Afterward, we practice our spear-tossing technique in the woods, and Darryl, one of the other students, tells me to hold the spear with my thumb facing backward so it flies straighter. I follow his instruction, and it's there in the woods, for the first time, that I hit my target and let out a yell so loud you'd think I'd just killed dinner after a three-day hunt rather than impaling a bale of hay strapped to an unlucky evergreen.

Do I appear foolish? Maybe. OK, sometimes definitely. But I'm also (hat tip to Epictetus) improving.

I'm toweling off after a class in mid-March when Pete points to a clipboard hanging from the front desk. "Did you sign up?" he asks. I pretend to not know what he's talking about, but I know exactly what's on that clipboard. It's a sheet of paper to sign up for the Citi Field Spartan 5K Sprint race in April, the one I've been secretly eyeing since Christmas as my goal. "We're all going to race as a team," Pete says. "You gotta do it."

Despite how much I think I want to do this, I just haven't been able to cross that Rubicon and commit. It's one thing to tell yourself you're going to race while rolling around in the privacy of your own lawn. It's another to publicly pledge to do it with all these people I now respect. What if I can't keep up? What if I hold them back? What if I fail every obstacle? What if, if, if . . .

"Hey," Pete says, interrupting my excuse loop. "Come *on*. You told me you wanted to do a Spartan race. There's only one way to make that happen." I nod, swallow hard, and pick up the clipboard—mostly because I don't think Pete will let me leave unless I do. Then I print my name slowly underneath my classmates' names.

The date of the race is Saturday, April 21, 2018. It's been almost two years since a little girl and an old man with his gin set this whole thing in motion, and I'm finally about to reach the starting line.

The Obstacle: Heavy Carries
(willpower)

Carrying heavy things is a challenge you'll find at many brands of obstacle course races. In Spartan races, some of these heavy carries have been designated as mandatory obstacles, according to the rule book. This means racers are not supposed to continue and theoretically can be disqualified from the event if they don't complete them—although this technicality really is enforced only with racers competing for a podium spot in Elite or Age Group heats and not with Open heat racers.

Sometimes the carries consist of a log to haul through water, for instance, or a ball of concrete attached to a handle to move a certain distance. Some of the most taxing Spartan heavy carries involve moving sandbags or buckets of rocks. The sandbags, for instance, weigh about sixty pounds for men and around forty pounds for women. These carries are a test of strength, yes, but also of determination and willpower. Depending on the venue, the carries can require already exhausted legs to lug the load up steep, uneven mountains or through shoe-sucking mud. The distances vary. It's sometimes hard to know where the end is. You just carry until it's over, however long it takes, however often you need to stop and rest.

Occasionally people give up and drop their bags or buckets and leave them in the woods. But most of the time they don't. Instead, if you look at the faces around you, you'll see grim determination setting in. Bodies of all shapes and sizes experiencing different levels of pain and discomfort, carrying their load however they can—slung across one shoulder, draped around their neck, in their arms. You'll hear encouragement among racers, even highly competitive ones, during heavy carries: "You've got this"; "Come on, just a little bit farther."

For me the secret was learning to find comfort in the discomfort. Sure, there were techniques that helped make things easier, like getting a sandbag or bucket up on your shoulders with the weight evenly distributed. But more than anything, heavy carries seemed to be about willpower—and as a skinny, unmuscular kid who'd wanted to do physical things, I had learned to rely on that a lot. After our high school graduation, my closest friends jetted off on a cruise; I instead chose to attend a fourteen-day Outward Bound wilderness camp in the Colorado mountains—a decision I began to regret the moment I first picked up the heavy pack I'd carry for two weeks and strapped it to my then 110-pound body. Nearly every loaded step I took in those mountains was an exercise in willpower, up until the final day when I got to dump that awful pack and they made us run/ walk another six miles just for kicks. Hungry, sore, scratched, and filthy from head to toe, I completed the distance, and then promptly fainted during the subsequent group photo.

So, to me, willpower was something that could be honed even without picking up weight. I eventually learned to get out of my warm bed even if it was raining outside and go running, and not mind being wet. When our dirt roads became covered in treacherous ice, I'd strap spikes on my hiking shoes and carry boulders up and down the hills. Heat, mosquitoes, lightning, a hangover? I hydrated, sprayed, rolled the dice, took some Advil. And then I went outside and threw a spear, practiced burpees, or climbed a rope.

Each time I chose discomfort over comfort, it helped me with heavy carries in races. Because to finish, you don't have to be fast. You don't have to have the strongest biceps. You just need to be able to gut it out, one step at a time, and not give up until you're done.

7

THE POWER OF FIRSTS

Citi Field, New York
April 21, 2018

On any other day, the vehicles snaking through the main gates of Citi Field in Flushing, Queens, would seem to have made a wrong turn. Instead of being plastered with blue-and-orange bumper stickers announcing LET'S GO METS!—an homage to this stadium's hometown professional baseball team—they are stamped with red, blue, and green circles featuring a menacing warrior helmet. It's the official Spartan Race logo, which borrows from an ancient Greek helmet that covered a warrior's head and neck, with menacing slits for the eyes and mouth. Right now, as I sit in the passenger seat staring at the stickers lining the SUV in front of me, the sight makes a very nervous me feel as if we're entering some ancient battlefield instead of the familiar ball field where Lisa and I come to cheer on her favorite childhood team. Around us, racers are walking from their vehicles to the registration tent, many of them clad in Spartan Finisher shirts earned in previous races. I have an overwhelming sense of being an outsider, sneaking into a club where everyone knows the private handshake except me.

Spartan races that take place in baseball stadiums, like today's, are dubbed "Stadions." Stadions are generally held in major sports venues around the United States, such as Fenway Park in Boston, Nationals Park in Washington, D.C., and Oracle Park in San Francisco. Stadions are the cleaner, faster version of Spartan races, which are more typically staged in the mountains, on farms, or in other rugged terrain. While non-Stadion race lengths may vary—a 5K Sprint, 10K Super, 21K Beast, or 50K Ultra—these stadium races are fixed at the shorter 5K distance, making them perfect for newbies. Even the obstacle failure penalty is more lenient, at fifteen burpees instead of thirty. This will turn out to be a good thing for me today.

Temperatures are hovering in the low forties with a stiff breeze coming off Flushing Bay. I'm wearing only a long-sleeved white shirt over my sports bra and thin workout pants, and I realize, not for the last time in my racing career, that I didn't plan my apparel very well. My guts are churning from nerves and last night's meal. Worried about traffic, I'd booked a cheap room in a nearby hotel the night before and ordered what I figured was race-friendly grub from their limited menu: mac and cheese (carbs!), greasy chicken wings (protein!), salad (greens!). Now it's all congealed into a gluey mess in my intestines while the yogurt, granola, and fruit I scarfed down in the room this morning sits in my anxious stomach. Lisa is driving, and I sip her coffee tentatively, worried I'll have to pee during the race. I feel completely out of my league when I think about what will happen today, so I've attempted to control what I can—which pretty much boils down to setting the alarm for 4:30 A.M. so I'm not late. As a result, we've arrived at Citi Field way too early, and we're both tired.

"I don't feel very good," I tell Lisa as she hands the cashier our parking fee. I watch a procession of very muscular humans walking in front of us. "Look at these people. They're all so hardcore."

She moves our SUV forward, smart enough not to indulge my whining. "Whatever," she says in the flat, deadpan tone I depend on when feeling insecure. "They have a bunch of stickers and some T-shirts. So what?"

After parking, we pick up my race registration packet (waiting twenty minutes in the cold because the computer systems are down) and enter through the dramatic Jackie Robinson Rotunda that leads into the bowels of the stadium. The nineteen-thousand-square-foot space is teeming with racers and staff organizers milling around a large sculpture commemorating the iconic 42 that Robinson wore on his jersey. We find a space clear of foot traffic on the chilly terrazzo floor, and I squat to open my packet. Inside is a black headband with the number 14965, a red timing chip, a yellow plastic wristband, a paper wristband with my start time, and another one that says 1 FREE DRINK—good for a beer at a local bar after the race.

"I guess I wear all of these?" I say to Lisa, who is also shivering, not really expecting an answer. She's probably wondering why I couldn't have chosen beach volleyball for this midlife athletic adventure. I fumble around with the timing chip and the yellow plastic band I'm supposed to use to attach the chip to my wrist. After about five minutes of unsuccessful attempts with cold fingers, I pull on the yellow band too hard and its latch pops off.

"I broke it!" The panic in my voice is not commensurate with the situation, but at that very moment, I'm sure this means I'm doomed to die on the course. The waiver I signed did say that is a possibility. "I BROKE IT," I exclaim more loudly to Lisa, panic now moving to despair. "What do I do?"

Again, calm reason comes my way. "Let's just get you a new one." She points to a table of race volunteers. We walk over and explain my ineptitude. They are sympathetic but don't have extra wristbands. Maybe back at registration? they suggest. We look outside at the lines still stacked up from the computer glitch, and it's clear I'll miss my start time if we queue up again. We stare at the red chip together. I have no pockets in my shirt or pants, so that's not an option.

Finally, Lisa points downward. "Can you tie it to your shoe?" My laces are thick, but I can just squeeze one through the openings on the chip and secure it to the top of my foot. Years later, deep in the woods of another race while slogging through mud and watching racers lose their shoes, my own race chip expertly secured to my wrist,

I'll remember this moment with something that approaches fondness. But right now, in my beginner's mind, I've just barely avoided catastrophe.

I swallow hard. "OK, I need to find Pete."

By the time we hit our midforties, we start running short on "firsts" and, equally true, we often stop trying for them. Throwing a baseball. Standing up on a surfboard. Threading a needle. Watching our fingers climb an octave on a keyboard. Hoisting a sail. Speaking a full sentence of a new language. Standing onstage before an audience. Talking into a camera. Making an incision. Casting a line. Dipping a brush into paint. Hearing a clear note emerge from our vocal cords.

There is nothing that registers quite like the first time we try something that sticks and later becomes a fundamental part of our story of self: "Ah, yes, this is who I am." It's the moment when all our strengths and potential, and all our weaknesses and limitations, are still unknown. Only possibility lies ahead.

There are powerful mechanics at work in the brain that determine which firsts imprint and become meaningful to us and which ones we throw out. Much like an email inbox where we decide what is important enough to save, our brain sifts through experiences to determine which ones might have value for the future and should be stored in our long-term memory, and which ones are less important and can be discarded. For instance, I can't recall the first time I ironed a shirt or took out the trash. But I will remember the tiniest details from my first Spartan race—spilled water on the floor, the texture of locker-room carpet where I do push-ups—in crisp resolution for years after the event.

Why would today register so profoundly? When I went looking for answers, I found R. Douglas Fields, a famous neuroscientist then working at the National Institutes of Health who'd spent decades decoding the mysteries of our brain and the rest of our nervous system. He told me that emotion clearly played a large part, as did the fact that I was seeking something deeper out of obstacle course racing, even if not fully cognizant of that desire in the moment. "The amazing thing is that the brain has evolved to have ways to evaluate which experiences might have value in the future. Are they novel? Are they highly emotional and highly unusual? That's the kind of thing you are talking about being imprinted. The flashbulb memories."

You can probably pinpoint some of these emotional "flashbulb" memories in your life. Moments where you recall the circumstances surrounding the event like a vivid snapshot. It might be around a major event, like a natural disaster or the assassination of a public figure. But it can also be around personal moments: the birth of a child, the sudden death of someone you love, or the first time you experienced a sensation that was so unique and powerful, you wanted to feel it again. (Or avoid it at all costs.)

For instance, I still recall the first time I played in an official game on our junior varsity basketball team. From what I recall, they pretty much let anyone join the girls' team, because the adults were too nervous about demoralizing you at this fragile, hormone-fueled age. However, suiting up didn't mean you got to compete, and I spent most of the season warming the bench during games or tossing free throws alone in a corner of the gym during practice while my teammates ran plays. The only sign I'd even registered on the coach's radar was the nickname she'd bestowed on me: Bones.

But finally, there was one game when we were so far behind that even Coach D. had given up, and she sent me in to play with ninety seconds to go. I was so nervous I ran to the wrong spot on the court and then had to course-correct like a panicked chicken. Our point guard tossed me the ball, and immediately I got tangled up in the arms of some monstrous girl on the opposing team while Coach D. yelled from the sidelines:

"Go, Bones! Shoot the ball! Shoot the ball!"

I staggered back and forth looking for the basket, but my short, permed 1980s Kristy McNichol haircut kept bouncing in my eyes, and the monster was relentless, so I finally just gave up and hurled the orange globe in the general direction of the basket. The ball didn't go far because the monster slammed her massive forearm onto my thin wrist.

Foul.

I stepped to the free-throw line, rubbing my wrist. This was familiar territory at least. "All right, Bones. You've got this!" Coach D. screamed. I took a deep breath, aimed, bent my knees, and shot, watching as the ball arced toward the basket . . . and then bounced off the rim with a loud thud.

"It's OK, it's OK. One more, Bones. One more."

I imagined it was just me practicing alone again, aimed, bent my knees, and launched my last shot, watching as the ball circled the basket, teetered, and then dropped through the net. My first point! In my first game! The buzzer sounded. Game over. I heard a lot of people stomping their feet in the bleachers and looked up eagerly, thinking they were showing their support of my triumph, but realized they were just hurrying to leave and to beat the traffic.

Still, thirty-five years later, I recall this day with something resembling a low-emission sense of pride. The level of my emotional response during that event clearly made it imprint in my memory. It was the first time my body physically did what I asked it to in a moment that seemed to matter. I didn't forget it because clearly, I wanted someday to feel it again.

Which, unbeknownst to me, is about to happen inside this massive, cold professional baseball stadium.

Lisa and I wind our way through Citi Field's chilly halls, where the wind is whipping through the vendor kiosks and rock music is blaring. The sun is starting to shine on the field and the spectator stands, but its rays aren't making their way to us yet. All racers are released in groups—otherwise known as "waves" or "heats"—at various start times spread throughout the day. Elite category racers go first; they are supposed to be the fastest and include professional athletes. The Elites compete for a single gold, silver, or bronze medal among themselves (one for men, one for women), regardless of their age. Then come the Age Group category racers, who vie for first, second, or third among their peers and gender in a five-year age range—25–29, 30–34, 35–39, and so on, up to the last group, which is 60+. They are just now starting to release the Open category of racers, who race under the more relaxed rules I mentioned earlier (they sometimes help each other at obstacles, and burpee penalties aren't strictly enforced). Open racers don't compete for a podium spot but do still get a finisher medal, as does everyone who crosses the finish line. I'm in one of the early-morning Open heats with the rest of our Epic team, but when Lisa and I find the starting line, there is no Pete or anyone from our gym in sight. So I retreat to the bathroom to warm my hands under a metal dryer, watching women expertly adjusting their racer headbands and ponytails in the mirror. Self-assurance appears to fill every corner of the echoey bathroom except the little sliver where I stand huddled against my dryer.

Fifteen minutes before our start time, I reluctantly abandon the warm air and return to Lisa. They are starting to queue up racers for our heat. Finally, I spot one of the Epic cool kids—Keith, the French teacher—who is wearing a backpack and hiking boots along with a blue fleece cap and his glasses.

"Hello!" He smiles brightly. "Are you ready?"

"I hope so," I say, attempting an equally bright tone. "Where are Pete and everybody else?"

"He'll be here," Keith says, adjusting his backpack. "He just gets to the starting line late, because first he races competitively in his age group."

I don't quite process that Pete is running the race twice, because I'm so fixated on Keith's wardrobe. "Why are you wearing your backpack and those boots?" I ask, confused. "Aren't you going to change for the race?"

"Nah. The boots are just for fun." He shrugs confidently. "The backpack is so I can fill it up with the freebie samples the sponsors give out at the end. Easier to race with my bag than wait in line at bag check. Hey, look." He points while I stare at him in disbelief. "There's Pete."

"FRIEEEENNNDS!" Pete draws out the word when he sees us, beaming as always. "Are we ready to race?" Immediately, I relax a little in his presence. A few other members of the gym, including the other cool kids, are arriving now. Like the weaker animal on the savanna, I feel protected in the pack.

The voice of an announcer somewhere commands us to move to the starting line. But all I see through the crowd is a wooden wall with the Spartan helmet emblazoned upon it.

"Where's the actual start?" I whisper to Keith, not sure why I'm whispering.

"On the other side of the wall. You have to climb the wall to get there."

I look at Lisa, who reads my mind: *What if I can't even get to the actual starting line?* "You'll be fine," she says quickly before I can come up with excuses, though she later confesses she was worried too. "Have fun!" And just like that, the lifeline to my old world recedes, and I'm tethered to the new pack.

As we make our way forward, I carefully watch how everyone hoists themselves over the wall, which is only four feet high but stands as the gatekeeper between me and becoming a Spartan racer. We've climbed onto soft square boxes stacked up at Pete's gym, but never over actual walls. "Go, Wendy," I hear Lisa say somewhere deep in the crowd. There are people lined up behind me, so it's now or never. I use the full advantage of my height and push up off my toes with both hands on the top of the wall. My arms shake precariously for a moment, but I manage to swing a leg over, and then a second leg, and drop to my feet.

I'm in.

I stick close to Keith, fidgeting nervously with my black headband and blowing on my hands to stay warm. Earlier that morning, I tucked Dolly's dog tag over my heart into my sports bra, a talisman to keep me safe. It's the beginning of a tradition that will become a religious part of my race routine. Today, I simply touch my heart quickly to make sure the hard disc is in place.

"Who's ready to RACCCCEEE?" the announcer standing at the front of the pack calls to the crowd. He rattles off a few important details that I try desperately to remember, about the number of water stations and how we should make sure to follow the arrows as we run.

Then his voice drops what seems like an octave.

"Today you will embark on a quest like those of legends old," he intones.

I look around to see if people are laughing. They aren't.

"Where you will face unimaginable obstacles and push yourself through them. In order to prepare yourself for that, I will ask you one simple question: 'Who am I?' To which you shall reply, 'I am a Spartan.'

"WHO AM I?" he demands.

"I AM A SPARTAN," the crowd screams back. Not one for participatory chants (I can't even bring myself to om in a yoga class), I half-heartedly mumble something that comes out like "I ram artan."

Unfortunately, the announcer is just warming up.

"The day may come when the courage of Sparta fails, when you forsake all friends and break all bonds of fellowship, but *today* is not that day. For this day we *fight*. We are honored by your courage and commitment to excellence, but know this: free your mind, body, and spirit, as they will be put to the ultimate test.

"Look at the Spartans on your right and your left." I look at Pete. I look at Keith, who high-fives me.

"You will draw strength from them as they will draw strength from you. You will *not* let them fail. In the name of all you hold dear on this good earth, I bid you stand, sons and daughters of Sparta, stand and fight. For today is the day you rise to glory, not tomorrow, not next week. Right here, right now, in *your* house, Neww Yooorrrrrk!

"Who am I?"

"I AM A SPARTAN" comes the return roar. I hear myself clearly this time. That's weird.

"WHO AM I?"

"I AM A SPARTAN." Louder again, and now I'm screaming too. My heart is pounding, and I've suddenly got so much adrenaline coursing through me that it feels like someone stabbed me with an EpiPen.

"SPARTANS, WHAT IS YOUR PROFESSION?"

"Aroo! Aroo! Aroo!" comes the chant, pronounced ah-ROO. I don't know what "aroo" means or how that's actually a profession, but none of that matters right now as I *Aroo* away with everyone else.

"LET'S RACE!"

Of the firsts I recall about this day, one of them is the feeling of immediately falling behind and willing myself to keep up and not quit. Keith is quickly ahead of me, loping in his hiking boots up several flights of stairs on the outskirts of the stadium. I am trailing most of the Epic crew and, within the span of about sixty seconds, breathing very hard. While we've done all sorts of high-intensity training in class, there's something different about running in a competitive pack. I want to fall back and let everyone pass me so I can relax a bit. But at the same time, I am annoyed each time someone does pass me, which makes me speed up. I am seriously out of my comfort zone, and the conflicting emotions seem to suck unnecessary energy from my already tired body.

On the plus side, I am warm for the first time in two hours. And from the moment we take off, I stop worrying about anything except whatever, or whoever, is right in front of me. This freedom from fretting and all other thoughts—work, money, obligations, the rest of life—is obstacle course racing's very first gift. In fact, years of meditation will never bring me as close to living in the now as a race with my heart beating close to its max, legs burning and mind gripped around the immediacy of doing whatever it takes to keep moving forward.

After a long climb up multiple flights into the upper decks of the stadium, we crawl under some thick rubber bands designed to mimic the barbed wire used on outdoor courses. The bands are, as I'll later painfully learn, a ridiculously gentle substitute, since they don't literally tear your clothes or skin. So far, so good.

Next up, we come upon bins of long, malleable sandbags, of different weights for the women and the men. They are a bit different from the bags at Pete's studio, so I study how the other racers are carrying them before slinging one over my shoulder like it's a small sleeping child. We enter the sunlight on the stadium stairs and start to haul our bags up and down several flights. Suddenly the pace slows, which suits me. I find that some of the speedier girls struggle to keep their bags balanced, and I'm able to pass them. My legs burn, but that's overshadowed by the memory of lugging that awful backpack on the Outward Bound mountaineering trip so long ago. All I need to do is keep moving, even if it hurts.

And so, as I pass a few more people, another first happens: the realization that I might actually be OK at lifting and carrying heavy things.

Now that I've lost most of the Epic people from view, the world before me changes. Without the pack for protection or instruction, my senses heighten as I start noticing small details. Water on the ground that could make me slip. How faster racers are skipping stairs or gripping a handrail to turn corners more swiftly. Verbal protocols as people pass me—"On your left." All these little bits of information register and will get reinforced later, in future races.

I head back into the bowels of the stadium and into a locker room where we must knock out fifteen push-ups, putting chest to floor. We do lots of push-ups at Epic, so this one's easy, though I wonder—

pressing my face into the rough rug over and over—if you can pick up athlete's foot in your nose.

Push-ups completed, I'm feeling pretty good as we head outside the stadium for the Spear Throw obstacle. There, a line of rectangular black foam boxes about the size of hay bales are mounted onto a row of frames. Spartan spears are attached to long lines that are tied to metal barricades about twenty-five feet from the targets. (Racers stand behind the barricades to throw, and the lines are to keep the spears from flying all over the place.) Choosing my weapon, I carefully toss the line over the metal barricade like Pete has instructed, so it won't catch on the barricade while the spear is in flight. Then I aim, pull my arm back, and throw. The spear sails straight—so straight I hold my breath with hope—and soars over the top of the target. And with that I have another first, an obstacle failure, and am down on my belly doing my inaugural set of Spartan penalty burpees on the asphalt. (I'm immediately grateful the penalty is only fifteen for Stadion races compared to the typical thirty.)

Soon comes an eight-foot wall. There's a small red block attached to the bottom of the wall that women are allowed to use as a step, but even though it helps me reach up and grab the top of the wall, I still am not nearly strong enough to pull myself up and over. After multiple attempts, I'm about to give up when I instinctively start walking up the wall sideways, manage to hook an ankle over the top, and drag myself up. My calf cramps, but I finally haul myself over the wall. Well, I think, at least these long, awkward legs are good for something.

I'm still rubbing my calf when I reach a giant contraption called a multi-rig. I know from Pete that this grip challenge is standard at many brands of obstacle course races, though it comes in different formats. Depending on the race length, he's told me, the Spartan Multi-Rig typically has some combination of swinging rings, bars, or ropes that you must grab to move yourself across the rig and hit a bell without touching the ground. Today, there are only rings. I've never actually made it across the rings at Pete's gym but am hoping there might be one more swig still left in my Beginner's Luck cup. I step up onto a starting bench, grab the first ring with both hands (it's red, soft, and slippery), take a deep breath, and lunge. Instantly, I realize there's no way I'm coming close to grabbing the next ring, so I dangle like a frantic fish on a line for a few moments before my grip gives out and I collapse underneath the rings. Grateful no one from Epic is there to have witnessed this sad attempt, I slink over to the burpee pit and perform my penance.

After this, we jump rope with a resistance band around our ankles (the rope is heavy; it's an exercise in strength and not tripping), and then there's a long stretch of running around the stadium. I regain my composure and take a moment to look out across the baseball diamond, where sunlight bounces off the neatly mowed grass. The once deafening music has receded a bit. And that's when I'm overcome by a sense of absolute clarity that there is nowhere I'd rather be at this moment. Endorphins are overriding my senses, and I feel vaguely euphoric.

It's now, jacked up on this new chemical cocktail that is masking how fatigued I am, that I come upon the Rope Climb obstacle. From where I stand below, it sure looks a lot longer than the rope at Pete's gym (which I've still only climbed halfway up) and is skinnier and slicker. I take a couple of deep breaths, wrap my right calf around the rope so the top of the rope lies flat across my foot—something called an S-hook, which Vince and Pete have taught me—and reach up with my arms and pull, stepping onto my right foot with my left to pinch the rope. Shockingly, it holds. I do this a few more times, pulling my knees up, rewrapping my feet, and then using the foothold as leverage to walk my hands upward.

I'm nearly two-thirds up to the bell when the rope gets loose from my feet, and I'm dangling by just my arms. Common sense warns me I need to use what's left of my strength to ease down the rope safely. And yet the bell is taunting me, just another pull or two away, and this endorphin cocktail is surging through me and hijacking my brain.

It's at this moment, you'd think, that I'd somehow remember my first encounter with Spartan. That I am here in part because I was googling and read about that filmmaker Scott Keneally who fell from a rope during a Spartan race and didn't finish. You'd think I'd remember his sense of humiliation and how he'd wished for aliens to swoop down and abduct him.

Nope.

Instead, I make a hopeful rookie error and try one last time to get a foothold—a big mistake, since I don't have this move committed to muscle memory. The rope flails away from my dangling legs, an angry black serpent, and those few seconds are all it takes for my hands to give out. I drop like a sack of flour, landing with a loud thud in a crumpled heap on the mats, ten to twelve feet below. For a moment I lie there, immobile, looking up at what seems like a cruelly cheery sign announcing WELCOME TO THE COCA-COLA CORNER. Two other racers hurry over to help me up, asking worriedly, "Are you OK?"

I don't know if I'm OK. Fear and panic have swiftly replaced the glorious, hedonistic endorphin cocktail in my body, and I feel like I might cry. Doubt smells its opportunity and pounces. Why am I doing this? Who am I to think I even had a shot at completing this race? I'm a skinny kid who sits on the bench, never gets playing time, and gets a nickname like Bones. Still, when I finally stand up nothing seems to be broken except my pride. So I thank my two helpers and stand there, hands on my knees, deciding what to do next.

To my right is the burpee pit. To my left, a ramp that leads out to the parking lot and the safety of our car. With that ramp, this could all be over now. I can go home, take a hot bath, and return to what I excel at. I don't have to go back to Epic or see Pete or Keith or any of the cool kids again. Nobody will ever remember, or care, what happened here today.

Except, blinking back my stupid tears, I know someone who will. And I have to wake up in her body tomorrow.

Fine.

Another fifteen burpees later, I'm up and running again.

The rest of the race is not so awful. I conquer something called the Z-Wall, where you move your body across a series of walls connected at acute angles in a Z form, using wooden blocks for foot- and handholds. And then I accidentally pick up two enormous forty-pound water-filled jerry cans (women only have to carry one) and haul them up and down a flight of stairs before the obstacle volunteer tells me my error but applauds me at the same time for being a "beast."

I laugh and tell them I was just dumb and didn't know the rules, but the thought gets reinforced again:

I might be OK at lifting and carrying heavy things!

The final minutes are a blur. I climb up and over an enormous netted structure called the A-Frame Cargo, where the biggest challenge seems to be not getting kicked in the face by the racer in front of you. After that, I scale a few more short walls on the warning track, hoist a heavy ball overhead and slam it down onto the ground a bunch of times, and jump on and off a big box for fifteen reps. Then I turn toward the finish line.

And that's when it hits me.

I am going to finish.

Spartan shrewdly spends a good deal of effort capturing photos of racers that they can download and post on their social media accounts. When I look back at these first race photos, I see one that captures me making this turn toward the finish line. I am midstride and seem for the moment to have Citi Field all to myself. Sunlight glints off my chest as I pass underneath a colorful tapestry of MLB and Spartan signage projected on the screens. I am clearly tired, probably as physically tired as I've been in my recent adult life, and my eyes squint with emotional disbelief—but my head is held high and my shoulders are back, Dolly's dog tag tucked out of sight, lying flat against my heart.

Just after this photo gets snapped, there is a collection of swinging kickboxing bags standing between me and the end. It's not a real obstacle in the sense that people fail it. At worst, you might get your sunglasses or hat knocked off. Mostly, it's just another great photo op. I hold my arms in front of my face like a boxer and charge through, the black bags bouncing off my body and messing up my hair. As I run alone amid the bags, my chest tightens and Spartan's marketing line floats through my mind.

You'll know at the finish line.

And sure enough, it is there amid the claustrophobic pummeling of those bags—a nobody forty-six-year-old wannabe athlete who fell off a rope, missed her spear throw, and dangled like a hooked fish from floating rings—that I understand. Because despite all my blunders and failures today, there is once again the most inexplicable feeling of physical completeness and control, one akin to the moment in junior high when the ball left my hands and dropped through the hoop before an uninterested crowd. Today I have scaled walls, carried heavy things, fallen, gotten back up, and not quit. Vince was right, I think. Maybe I *can* do this. Suddenly, my brain's synaptic connections are exploding, as if a secret door has revealed itself—one opening onto a part of my world I thought was walled off for good.

After they hang my first finisher medal around my neck, I spy Keith with his backpack and jog over to him. He clearly crossed the finish line not that long ago, though he is barely winded and talking fast. "Oh my God," he says. "Where did you come from? Good job. Let's have them take our photo together and then go get all the free samples out in the parking lot."

After the photographer snaps our picture, Keith quickly removes his medal and crams it into his backpack while stuffing a banana into his mouth. I stare at him in disbelief. He looks at me, misreading my expression. "Oh, I'm sorry, do you want me to hold your medal too?"

I reach up and clutch the heavy metal chunk dangling against my chest, its weight in equal measures a promise of the future and a talisman against the past. I shake my head at Keith.

"I'm never taking it off."

PART TWO

8

COMING FROM BEHIND

How is it possible to become good at something when you are already so far behind and time is running short?

That was the question pressing against my brain in the days after I crossed the finish line at Citi Field. I finally did remove the finisher medal from my neck. (I'd kept it on at the pub with Pete and the Epic crew celebrating after the race *and* for the drive home.) But I slept with it on my bedside table in a gesture of gratitude for the day, giving birth to a tradition that would last my entire racing career. The clarity I'd felt during my first race, the sureness that there was no place I'd rather be, and the freedom to abandon all my other concerns, at least for an hour: I wanted—no, I needed—to feel that again.

I also wanted to get better. To figure out all those obstacles I'd failed. Even with the humiliating rope delay, my performance hadn't been too terrible, suggesting the early training had paid off. I was 33rd out of 244 women my age and 418th out of 2,852 women in total. And 1,705th out of 6,590 overall (men and women). To be sure, these stats needed to be taken with a grain of salt, since I'd run in an Open category with its looser rule enforcement. Plus, the best racers generally ran Elite or Age Group heats. But since I'd completed all my burpees and received no aid from anyone (mainly because all the other Epic racers had left me in the dust), there was a glimmer of hope.

I knew later-in-life success was possible. After all, our culture is filled with celebrity proof points. The culinary rocket ship that was chef Julia Child took off as she turned fifty; previously, she'd worked in advertising and government intelligence. Author Laura Ingalls Wilder of *Little House on the Prairie* fame was penning columns for a farm magazine before she published the first book in that seminal series at age sixty-five. U.S. president Ronald Reagan, as most of us likely know, was an actor before moving deeply into politics in midlife and eventually becoming the oldest sitting American president up to that time.

In the area of entrepreneurship, where the lore of the twentysomething start-up founder turned billionaire looms large, research from MIT's Sloan School of Management found that for the highest-growth new ventures, the mean founder age was forty-five. "Our primary finding," the MIT research team notes, "is that successful entrepreneurs are middle-aged, not young." Martha Stewart was closing in on fifty before she signed a deal to launch her eponymous magazine, *Martha Stewart Living*. The founders of Geico and Home Depot were roughly the same age as Stewart when they launched those businesses. At sixty-two, Harland David Sanders franchised Kentucky Fried Chicken for the first time.

Regardless of whether they'd been working at their craft for a long time or dug in for the first time in middle age, the collective forces needed to propel them to success united well past their youth. Clearly, the desire to keep evolving flickers inside many of us. At the time I was writing this book, *The New York Times* published a column chronicling the feats of people in middle age and beyond attempting to become comics, cellists, water polo players, theologians, mountain climbers, and more. My longtime mentor and friend from *The Wall Street Journal*, journalist and author Joanne Lipman, explores tales of profound career pivots in her book *Next! The Power of Reinvention in Life and Work*. Her subjects range from bestselling novelist James Patterson to a burly telephone repairman from Massachusetts who finally embraced his dream to design women's shoes after being diagnosed with prostate cancer at age fifty. He eventually landed on the show *Project Runway* and, at age sixty-one, was dubbed the "newest fashion superstar" by *Boston* magazine.

Lipman interviewed more than one hundred people about their life changes for the book. There was one key trait all of them possessed: an openness to listen to their gut feeling, even when it seemed to fly in the face of rational thought. "Whether it was switching careers or getting out of a toxic relationship, personal or professional, they were open to listening to that gut feeling," she tells me.

Even in my own life, and probably in yours, I have known people pushing to become more than what already defines them. One of my parents' closest friends is an attorney and forensic scientist named Beth Whitney, who is my age. After Beth spent nineteen years working in the criminal justice system solving cases involving homicides and sex crimes against children, she and her husband, Clarence, sold or put most of their possessions in storage to live and travel on a small sailboat. During their visits to different warm islands, Beth began volunteering at local animal shelters. At one shelter, she grew increasingly frustrated that she couldn't enter the "Medical Staff Only" part of the building, where the sickest and most needy animals were treated. So she decided to become an official veterinary assistant. This meant studying coursework online aboard their boat while continuing her volunteer work injecting donkeys with dewormer and assisting neutering surgeries at the Antigua & Barbuda Humane Society. "I know it's weird, but it's my life," she says.

In my birth state, North Carolina, a math teacher named Bettie Parker created her own second act as a politician at age sixty-nine when she became the first female mayor of Elizabeth City. It was an accomplishment even more notable for a Black woman born into segregation who, as a child, couldn't use her city's public swimming pools. She later was recognized for her extraordinary transition in *Forbes*'s "50 over 50" list, which is produced in partnership with MSNBC host Mika Brzezinski.

My mother-in-law, Stella, started college at almost forty—more than twice the age of most of her classmates. It took her six years to graduate with a degree in fine arts because she insisted on being present when Lisa and her sister, Jennifer, arrived home after school. The coursework took her beyond her roles as a wife and mother, nurturing an innate talent for design that soon manifested in photographs, oil paintings, and drawings that hung at home. But Stella's gut told her she could do more. And after she graduated—just one year before Lisa received her own diploma—she parlayed her skills into a career as an antiques dealer, eventually selling to celebrity clients, including Martha Stewart, Mariah Carey, and Glenn Close.

And then there are the Mother Puckers, a group of New York hockey moms who grew antsy rooting for their kids or husbands on the ice and formed a competitive team themselves. Some of the Mother Puckers were nearing age sixty when they began. Lisa wrote about their team for *The New York Times*. As one Mother Pucker explains: "When I'm on the ice, I think about nothing else. Not the laundry, not the dishes, not the parent-teacher conferences."

What I wanted to know after my first race was, how?

How could I not only find the time to tackle something new and hard like racing but also really get better and become more successful at it? Despite the examples above, with age fifty just around the corner, I felt very late to the game. What were the tactics, tools, and time-management skills needed to move beyond novice and toward the admittedly far-fetched goal of mastery, while at the same time holding together an already full and, often, fulfilling life? And how not to get derailed by the inevitable interruptions and challenges that accompany aging?

One well-known framework for advancement of a skill is the Dreyfus model, and it's a framework that would track with my own experience. The model, developed by two brothers for the U.S. Air Force, presents five stages of adult skill acquisition: novice, advanced beginner, competent, proficient, and expert. In the coming months, as I carved a path forward from novice to advanced beginner, an important revelation began to emerge: instead of fighting age and viewing it as the enemy, I needed to make it my ally.

In his book *Mastery: The Keys to Success and Long-Term Fulfillment,* author George Leonard offers all of us aspiring midlife masters a big pour of hope. Mastery isn't reserved for "the supertalented or even those who are fortunate enough to have gotten an early start," he writes. "It's available to anyone who is willing to get on the path and stay on it—regardless of age, sex, or previous experience."

While each person's path to mastery will wind a bit differently, seven key guideposts eventually anchored my own journey, as we'll cover in coming chapters:

First was the realization and true belief that there could be something inside me still **untapped,** even in middle age. A founding father of modern psychology, William James, described the human capacity for a "second wind" as a captivating perplexity. He suggested that the ability to tap deep stored-up reserves of energy in pursuit of excellence is there in all of us—except that "most of us continue living unnecessarily near our surface." In other words, we don't push ourselves to dig deep and often quit when we hit hard patches. (Think walls.) This sentiment was echoed many decades later by the long-distance runner and trained physicist Alex Hutchinson (whom we met earlier fretting about muscle loss). In his book *Endure,* Hutchinson underscores the thought that endurance in any form is simply the struggle to continue against a mounting desire to stop—and that we're always capable of pushing a little further.

Second was figuring out how to manage my **time.** If I likely was at least halfway through my days on this earth and felt those remaining were already completely consumed, how did I find capacity where ostensibly there was none? One key was having the emotional discipline to say no to anything not critical to my family, health, earning a living, or advancing this new pursuit.

Third was learning to live in concert with **fear and the unknown** as well as discomfort. So much of early adulthood is spent pushing to have enough money, enough love, enough success, so we can be comfortable. Seeking to be uncomfortable, whether physically or mentally, is counterintuitive in middle age. But it's critical to pushing limits and, as our philosopher Kieran Setiya suggests, to facing the multitude of life obstacles that inevitably surface in midlife and beyond.

Fourth was developing a system of practice that I could sustain and that would advance me. You may have heard about **deliberate practice,** which entails spending sustained effort learning to do something in a manner that is purposeful, generally with feedback from teachers. This means breaking apart pieces of an activity we *can't* do well versus mindlessly repeating the parts that come easily. Separate but equally important is **unlearning** habits that hold us back from our goals, such as procrastination, insecurity, and a desire to please, and **relearning** skills we once possessed.

Fifth—and this one is *really* hard when you feel like you're running out of time—was finding **patience** to keep practicing when hitting a plateau or walls, and **conviction** to try again after backsliding. On any journey to get good at something, as Leonard notes in his book *Mastery,* we will spend most of our time on a plateau feeling like we're getting nowhere. And inevitably, he warns, we will experience "dips" of soul-crushing failure that threaten to derail us altogether. Not giving up (*Why am I doing this? The clock is ticking. I should try something else!*) is what will ultimately lead to a key turning point in my own progress. Understanding the difference between **intrinsic** and **extrinsic motivation,** which we'll learn about, can help ground us.

Sixth, if we are to harness age as a secret weapon, we must locate our **edges and equalizers**—those attributes or skills that give us an edge and do not necessarily tip the advantage to youth. That includes harnessing something known as our **crystallized intelligence,** which is essentially drawing upon learnings from our past experiences. The older you are, the more you've tried, failed, succeeded, and learned. Your situational awareness and bank of stored knowledge are vaster than they were when you were younger. Draw from that bank.

Seventh, unless we want to blow up everything we value in our life, we need to **not forget the previous verse** and be mindful of our new journey's impact on those we care about. Remember, the bridge is a link between what's come before and what will come after. It doesn't have to be an entirely new song.

And with this context, let's pick up where we left off—with a humbled first-time obstacle racer who had achieved no glory but wanted nothing more than her next competition.

9

DON'T LET YOUR CROP DIE

O*h my God, I'm so sore.*
This is one of three thoughts I cannot shake in the days following the first race at Citi Field. I lumber around the house like a sailor whose sea legs are adjusting to dry land and stifle moans while sliding into Consumer Reports conference-room chairs as my quads scream, "NO!" It seems inconceivable that three miles of baseball stadium stairs and some burpees and obstacles could wreak this kind of havoc on my body despite all my training with Pete.

Dulling the pain, though, is a lingering buzzy thrill unlike anything I've ever felt after a hard gym workout, which is driving thought number two:

When can I race again?

That question is answered soon enough when Pete posts a sign-up sheet at his gym for another three-mile Spartan race, this one taking place in roughly six weeks in the woods of Tuxedo, New York—the same race I'd missed last year when Dolly and my Mom were sick. Which in turn quickly triggers my third preoccupation:

How can I do better?

Right now, I am squeezing in a couple of classes at Epic each week. But those forty-five-minute sessions, even coupled with my unstructured running workouts or carrying rocks around my property, clearly aren't enough. To advance from novice mode in the Dreyfus model of skill acquisition and meaningfully improve, I need to find additional hours and mental bandwidth for learning and practice. This reality gnaws at me as I continue to gerbil-wheel it around the day.

I wake up with the best of intentions to fit in an extra thirty minutes of running or strength training or another session with Pete, but inevitably I get derailed. There's a recall notice for the car, which needs to go back to the dealer. Then, as I'm returning home from the dealer, the gas tank needs refilling. A health insurance claim is denied, resulting in a painful forty-five-minute call with customer service to resolve the issue. My watch battery dies and needs replacing. The dry cleaning needs to be picked up. Taxes need to be filed. We committed to dinner at a friend's house months ago. You get the picture. Until by day's end, plagued by the feeling I've been rushing around without ever getting to my best intentions, like much of America I crawl into bed and scroll through Facebook and Instagram to catch up on whatever important goings-on are happening without me. Finally, I boot up Netflix for thirty minutes, only to find that Roku needs me to reenter my password. And so the last few moments of the day slip by in a frustrated first-world-problem fit of punching in letters with a clicker before zoning out watching money-laundering schemes unfold on *Ozark* as I fall asleep.

Most of us know this frustration of juggling so many little things that we never get to the big things we want to do. There's a well-traveled quote often attributed to a pastor named John C. Maxwell, who is known for his bestselling books and speeches on leadership. It goes like this: "You cannot overestimate the unimportance of practically everything." The resonance resides in the phrase's simultaneous simplicity—*Yes, of course deep down we know this to be true*—and its complexity—*But how do we manage our lives accordingly?*

Because to me, everything in my life initially seems immovable. Or to put it another way, nothing seems unimportant enough to ditch. Endless meetings are part of being an executive, or so I tell myself. And I can't disappoint people by not accepting their invitations. The car must be fixed. Not paying my taxes is a bad idea. And of course, if I don't keep up with my social feeds, I might miss something important happening to someone I care about (since screens are now where this happens). I turn this conundrum over and over in my mind on a trip to visit my parents in North Carolina, not long after the Citi Field race.

Late one afternoon, I'm driving home on the back-country roads after running an errand inland for my mom. Before my parents retired to the coast permanently, I had spent most of my childhood weekends in this eastern part of the state, vacationing in a small trailer with a screened-in porch that was my family's getaway fishing camp. The sight of farmers on their tractors, working the land, raising corn, cotton, and tobacco, was such a constant that it's now the equivalent of visual white noise to me.

Today, I'm driving past that exact sight when I see a text from a colleague at work pop up on my phone. I pull the car over to answer it and, while awaiting her response, watch a farmer traversing his rows of crops on a John Deere tractor. He's staring straight ahead, moving methodically. At first, I only kind of see him, my mind still churning with the text exchange. And then my brain brings him into sharper focus. His worn baseball cap. Two hands on the wheel. The hum of the engine. The number of rows he's got left to finish. And it dawns on me that he's not looking at *his* cellphone. Not on text or Facebook or checking email. He's just doing the work in that field. That's his priority.

And then, with a clarity that reeks of the obvious, I think: If he doesn't get on that tractor, his crop dies.

For the rest of the drive home, and long after we've cleared our dinner plates and the sun has set over the inky White Oak River, I can't shake the image of the farmer. That night I open a spiral notebook I'd bought several weeks ago with the good intention to record more workout information than those small Google Calendar blocks can hold. It's still blank. And I write down these words on the first page:

"Don't let your crop die."

* * *

For those of us living in the developed world with so many of our basic needs already met, the luxury of deciding how to best spend our numbered hours is both a privilege and clearly also a mystery, judging by how many time-management books there are on the market. While the challenge of how to parcel out our precious and constantly dwindling minutes can vex humans at any age, it can be particularly acute in midlife. As our philosopher guide Kieran Setiya points out, this is the stage when so many facets of adult life suddenly collide and compete for the generally insufficient twenty-four hours allotted each day. Thus, the notion of slotting in something else, particularly something new that requires a significant investment of time for learning, can feel like the water that makes the bathtub finally overflow.

But what is truly indispensable? What is our crop?

I hold no illusions that finding time to train and improve at obstacle course racing carries the same universal karmic weight as growing food. But still, there is something about the prioritization and simplicity of the latter that gnaws at me. Which is probably why, a day or so after watching that farmer, I too start hunting online for information on time management (*Sitting! Screens!*). YouTube quickly tees up this passionate speech by a guy named Greg McKeown on something called "Essentialism: The Disciplined Pursuit of Less." It's a catchy title—and also the name of his book—so I click Play and start to listen.

McKeown is polished, wearing a well-fitted suit with no tie, and sports an enviable head of hair to frame his hip squared-off eyeglasses. He charms his crowd, explaining how success often leads to a proliferation of options and opportunities. While this may seem like a good thing, he counters that it's a problem if the options and opportunities lead to "the undisciplined pursuit of more." Those two words—"undisciplined" and "more"—hit me hard. I don't think of myself as undisciplined, but if I'm not, how is it that I'm struggling to find time to pursue something that clearly matters to me?

That night, I forgo Netflix and *Ozark* and try to figure out where all my "more" really comes from and, equally important, what I can begin saying no to. It's a small first step in what will become my option/opportunity detox program. I take notes in that spiral note-book below the words "Don't let your crop die." It's probably the first time I've written down lessons about anything since college, but the practice is oddly familiar and soothing. I had liked being a student once upon a time: the ingesting of knowledge from others and the anticipation of what I might do with it in my own world.

It's not until I examine the blocks of hours on my work calendar that I realize how much of it is filled with hour-long, one-on-one weekly meetings that serve as general catch-ups with my team and peers. At one point I add it all up and tally around twenty to twenty-five hours per week. Sometimes we get things accomplished in those sessions. But a lot of times we spend fifteen to twenty minutes chat-ting about life or discussing work items that don't truly require my input or guidance. And those hours of one-on-one meetings then push my other work into the evenings. So I try a change: I cut many of these touch-base meetings back to twenty-five minutes, switch some to biweekly, and tell everyone they can book extra time when-ever they want for anything urgent. At first, I'm nervous that impor-tant items will slip through the cracks. But this one decision turns out to be a powerful mechanism for both focusing conversations and empowering my highly capable team to make more decisions without me, and to grow their own leadership skills. It requires both trust and parking my proclivity to thinking I can always orchestrate perfection if I'm involved. Equally important, it means standing by my team when they make decisions that are different than mine would be. But 95 percent of the time, I come to find, things go fine. And it's easy to course-correct the remaining 5 percent. I get back roughly ten hours a week that way.

Meantime, how to say no more? This is tougher. I like a lot of the things I say yes to: volunteering for our local Audubon community group, helping my journalism school think about its future curriculum, those wine-filled dinners with people who are sort of friends but not core friends, which are fun in the moment even if they leave me sluggish the next day. But right now I need a filter. And so, if anything doesn't fuel my few vital, true priorities, which I define as family, health, work, and obstacle race training—my "crop"—I begin to write polite notes saying I need to decline, step away temporarily and revisit in the future. It feels selfish and terrible at first, like I am letting people down, but surprisingly, most don't push back and many say they understand. And with that, I get a few more hours back.

Saying no to other people is just one step. I also have to say no to myself. Being on a computer all day for work and having a smartphone constantly at my side makes it easy to dip in and out of nonessential pastimes, including random scrolling on social media, playing a quick word game online, clicking through to a sale on trail-running shoes, engaging in nonessential email and text threads with friends, checking the weather, and making playlists on my Spotify account. As most of these passive activities don't actively cultivate my crop, I set about eliminating or time-boxing as many as I can. To start, I unsubscribe from dozens of email lists (shoes, wine, airlines, news updates). That removes the temptation to click on what interests me and saves a few seconds of hitting Delete on what doesn't. I trim my Instagram "follows" to focus on obstacle course racing accounts and begin to use that platform primarily as a learning tool rather than a diversion. Facebook gets limited to a single biweekly check-in; Twitter (now X) I essentially pause altogether. My podcast list also gets temporarily thinned to shows that actively contribute to my obstacle course racing goals. Among them are Peter Attia's *The Drive* for health and longevity; a wellness podcast from an ultra-endurance athlete named Rich Roll; a popular show on performance and optimization by Tim Ferriss; and the irreverent yet instructive podcast from Matt B. Davis of Obstacle Racing Media.

Admittedly, there's a twinge of panic each time I hit Delete or say no. Is this something I'll miss? On the plus side, the difference between me in my late forties and me in my twenties is that I have some perspective now about what's dispensable to me and what's not. I've gone to enough parties, concerts, and movies and met enough new people that my FOMO level is slightly more manageable on this front. Frankly, I need fewer, not more, items crammed in my closet. All the extra podcasts were causing angst because I couldn't catch up. It's a matter of stopping the inertia.

Equally treacherous are the "time-suck slices," as I come to think of them. These are the five-, ten-, and fifteen-minute expenditures of energy on little tasks that randomly occur to me throughout the day. Ordering new water pitcher filters on Amazon, replacing a lightbulb on our lamppost, making a dentist appointment, remembering we also need AA batteries and going back on Amazon. All the little adulthood necessities that seem like quick to-dos, particularly because many are now just a click away on my phone or computer. But they prevent me from finding concentrated blocks of time for anything important. Instead, I begin making lists and bucketing these activities for defined hours of specific days. Saturday mornings are reserved for longer blocks of training; the afternoon is for small house chores (after a nap). I save all bills, paperwork, and Amazon ordering for Sundays so I'm not time-suck-slicing them throughout the week. Calls to insurance companies get made while I'm eating lunch at my desk. In the occasional small chunks of five and ten minutes between meetings, instead of socializing in the hallways, I climb our back stairwell at the office up to the roof to do push-ups, or perform squats in my office. This requires summoning my Epictetus teachings about not being afraid to look foolish, because there definitely are no other Consumer Reports vice presidents panting, at least intentionally, in the stairwell.

At home, Lisa and I also create more fixed routines and responsibilities: who cooks on each night of the week and who does the dishes; who buys groceries versus doing laundry; and years later, when we finally get another dog, who takes him out at night and who does so in the morning. By formulating clear divisions of labor in the household, we aggregate time blocks we both can count on and use for meaningful activities instead of wasting time negotiating in the moment, again and again, who will do what.

In fact, the more I study how my time gets spent, the more I realize how insidious and ubiquitous these time-suck slices are. One morning I'm leaning over the bed and drop my earring back as I attempt to screw it in while hurriedly dressing for work. The tiny piece of metal lands on the comforter and doesn't move. This is a magnificent revelation to me. Why? Because at least twice a week I drop an earring back while rushing across the bedroom and trying to multitask. Which means the back then bounces on the hardwood floor and rolls under the bed somewhere, requiring me to spend precious minutes hunting it down on my hands and knees, my stress rising because I'm already late for work. But not today. And that's because I was leaning over the bed and the back didn't bounce on the comforter. And in what might go down in history as one of the most banal yet satisfying of life hacks, I begin to pause and lean over the bed each morning to screw in my earrings. And with that, approximately 416 minutes annually of my remaining weeks on this planet get reclaimed. If you don't wear earrings, you've surely got another similar time-suck slice to be solved: losing your keys, misplacing your glasses (my mom now leaves a cheap set of readers in every room), taking off your favorite baseball cap and forgetting where you put it.

It will take years to fully develop and fine-tune my option/opportunity detox system. And sometimes it all blows up. Lisa and I wake up to discover our chest freezer has quit, leaving a pool of bloody meat juices that now needs cleaning up. (No morning run.) We can't wait on Amazon to deliver more toilet paper, so I need to run to the store. (No YouTube obstacle training videos.) My boss unexpectedly wants to see me at the end of the day. (No class with Pete.)

But many days the new system holds. And as my time gets freed and chunked, minute by minute, I'm slowly able to concentrate on moving up to become an advanced beginner in the Dreyfus model of skill acquisition. I get to Epic early to spend ten minutes alone trying to master swinging from the rings, watching my patient coach Pete demonstrate over and over the subtle hip-drop movement required. When class is finished, I stay fifteen extra minutes throwing spears at the hay bale set up outside near smelly dumpsters. The Spear Throw feels to me like that free-throw line in seventh grade. Nobody can outrun or outmuscle me here, so I might as well get good at it. (We'll get to other powerful equalizers like this in a subsequent chapter.) In the remaining extra bits of time I haven't bucketed—say, if someone is late for a meeting, or while I'm waiting for a doctor—I watch replays of the top Elite category Spartan racers on courses, freezing frames to study how they carry buckets of gravel on their shoulders, how they climb the rope, what gear they use. Little details get recorded in the notebook that's now always with me: flip the bucket so the lid is on the bottom to make it easier on the hands, flex the foot so the rope doesn't slip.

On the Monday before the June race in Tuxedo, New York, I take a class at Epic in which attempting the rope climb is part of the circuit. Classes are performed barefoot, which normally isn't an issue. Today, though, for the first time my S-hook footwork clicks, and suddenly I'm at the top, near the rafters and bell. Normally, at this stage, I get a belly full of fear remembering my fall at Citi Field and ease myself down. Today, though, it's like I'm on autopilot, and before I can think myself out of what I'm doing, I've swatted the bell. The class cheers, including Black Widow.

I'm so elated I climb to the top again and again over the next forty minutes—so many times that at the end of class, I suddenly notice the top of my right foot is oozing and raw where the rope has been pressing into my flesh. In my elation, I hadn't felt a thing. The next day at work, my boss Leonora's executive assistant—Maria T., as we call her—looks down at my sandaled feet and flatly suggests, "Um, don't you think you ought to do something about that?"

Maria's right. My entire foot is bright red and swollen now, and the gash looks gross. That night at urgent care, in addition to a tetanus shot and antibiotics, I receive a lecture from the attending physician about all the disgusting germs that can cling to ropes (a lecture later repeated to me by my exasperated father). No shoes, and keep it elevated and clean, the physician instructs.

In other words, no racing in the mud this weekend.

And so, just like last year, the New York Spartan race in June comes and goes without me as I sit on my couch, foot propped on a pillow, watching the Instagram feeds of my Epic friends after they cross the finish line in what becomes my first brush with obstacle course racing FOMO. Yet, it's tempered. Because I feel like that dim light of hope inside me that clicked on at Citi Field has brightened a few lumens. I can now climb a rope! Six months ago, on that most humbling of afternoons with Vince, this wasn't even a faint possibility. That knowledge makes me believe that I've been living near the surface of my physical potential all these years. That maybe there's something truly untapped.

With my ballooned foot elevated on the couch, I set my sights instead on a late-August race through the rugged woods surrounding the U.S. Military Academy at West Point, across the river from where I live. One morning, a few weeks before the race, I'm reviewing some new video concepts at work when my cellphone vibrates. It's Lisa calling at 11 A.M., which isn't normal.

"Are you OK?" I ask her, walking out of the room, my stomach knotting.

"*I'm* OK," she says, her voice indicating otherwise. "But my mom just called from San Francisco. She found my father unresponsive this morning. He's been rushed to the ER and she's on her way there."

We fly to San Francisco that night. My father-in-law, Alan, a former advertising executive with a razor-sharp wit and enviable verbal quickness, has suffered a serious stroke. The prognosis for him walking or fully communicating again is unclear. In the immediate hours, while focusing only on "will he live or die," what we can't foresee is how profoundly his situation will impact all our lives in the years to come—his most acutely, but also Lisa's, her mother's, her sister's, mine. Suddenly, with no warning, we've arrived at another tipping point of middle age, one dropping us into a ravine filled with new obstacles to navigate—challenges that soon will include Hoyer lifts and wheelchairs, cross-country medical flights, live-in care, power of attorney, the byzantine Medicare system, and ultimately the assisted-living circuit.

In these first days, as we digest the new reality descending upon us all, we take brief respites from the hospital to shower, eat, and rest. During one break, I pick up a paperback book that Lisa's sister, Jennifer, has left at her parents' house for me to read. She's a super-fit Pilates instructor and runner focused on health and wellness. "With your new Spartan thing going on, I think you'll like this," she tells me.

The book is called *Finding Ultra: Rejecting Middle Age, Becoming One of the World's Fittest Men, and Discovering Myself*. It's written by one of the podcasters who made my cut: Rich Roll, who was a competitive swimmer at Stanford before alcoholism and a sedentary life left him struggling to walk upstairs by his fortieth birthday. I've never read a book about an athlete before; it never would have occurred to me I'd be interested. And yet, as I wind my way through the pages of Roll's story, carrying the book with me to the hospital, Roll's athletic odyssey is like a bellows fanning the small flame that got lit inside me at Citi Field.

Maybe I won't become one of the world's fittest women, but what can I do—what can any of us do for that matter, in the time that is left to us? This is what I think reading Roll's book in the hospital hallway outside of my father-in-law's room.

Lisa and I fly home a few days before my forty-seventh birthday, with plans to return soon to San Francisco, and I prepare for the West Point race. In one way, it feels like a serious disconnect to attend an obstacle course race after having just been in a hospital with Lisa's father on the brink of death. But in another sense, racing feels all the more urgent now—as if at any moment, the privilege to move could just be seized and not returned.

By now, the rope burn has settled into a three-inch scar (a good reminder not to climb a rope in bare feet). My mom and dad have scheduled a visit to celebrate my birthday and we all slog out to the race venue early on a Saturday morning. My parents gamely brave the long hike from the parking area to the race festival area, where we're greeted by blaring rock music. Much like at the Citi Field race, a new batch of "firsts" begin imprinting on me—starting with the loud music, which jolts awake my still-sleepy soul. There's also the smell of smoke from the final obstacle, a fire jump, which I register, along with the hum of generators from food trucks and the constant slam of the porta potty bathroom doors. All of it so new and slightly overwhelming now, yet all of it destined to become as familiar as walking in my front door.

It's been raining a lot recently, and everything is muddy. As my mom picks her way through the fields in her no-longer-clean hiking shoes, she says to me, "Do you actually have to run in this stuff?"

"Pretty sure, yes," I tell her. She grimaces.

And sure enough, as soon as I cross the starting line, it's a whole different game than the clean urban confines of the Citi Field race. Immediately, we're immersed up to our ankles in mud, which is a lot deeper and wetter than it was in the parking area. A guy in front of me curses and starts fumbling around in the muck until he plunges into it face-first.

"My shoe!" he mutters when he surfaces. "I lost my shoe."

Mud splatters up into my nose, across my bare shoulders—there's no escaping it. When we slog through it later carrying heavy sandbags, a test of balance that inspires more than a few frustrated racers to abandon their bags, I realize I haven't been this muddy since I was a kid. Which makes me start to laugh in a way that feels like my soul is loosening. Because I'm an almost-forty-seven-year-old woman sprinting through the mud on a Saturday morning and carrying heavy sandbags near a training ground for young soldiers. Like, that's about as far from bemoaning aches and pains at brunch as you can get.

Once I give in to this new reality, I decide dashing around in hilly rugged terrain covered in grime is a whole lot more fun than racing in a clean baseball stadium. Being filthy is freeing, and I charge happily through rocky streams and up and down the hills, trying not to get knocked down by the other off-balance, inexperienced racers careening around me. We hit the monkey bars, and I fall immediately with my muddy grip. Thirty burpees later I'm dirtier than ever, sand and silica caking my belly.

My first true test of improvement comes at the Multi-Rig rings. After managing to grab the first two red rings today, I swing back and forth between them, gaining momentum, nervous to let go, and remembering my dangling-fish episode at Citi Field. Random spectators start cheering me on, and I realize I can't just swing back and forth here forever. Finally, I let go of the back ring and hold my breath as I drop my hip as Pete has taught me and float through the air on one hand, over to the next ring. I grab that, hold tight for dear life, and awkwardly repeat before I have time to think. In jerky movements, I move from ring to ring. It's not pretty, but my grip strength holds, and soon I'm at the end and hit the bell.

Progress.

The next big test comes at the Rope Climb near the finish line. My parents and Lisa are there watching. I'm worn down from thirty burpees after missing my spear throw (clearly more dumpster time is needed) and nervous because the three people I love most may witness me failing.

In video taken on Lisa's cellphone, you see me walk up to the rope, head low, seeming unsure. I stand with my hand on the rope for a minute, almost as if I'm deciding whether to try or just give up. But then you hear my father call loudly, "Go, Wendy!" And something about his voice causes me to pick up my head and look up at the rope. My arms reach out and grasp above me. My chest inflates with a huge inhale, and on the exhale, I pull up and start scrambling to wrap my feet. I don't get very far on the first pull; the rope is slippery with mud, and my arm strength is depleted. But after some flailing, I wrap again and move up a bit. And then I do it again, and again, until I'm near the top and swipe my long Olive Oyl arm for the bell . . .

And miss.

In the video's audio you hear the collective gasp of my family as I hang fourteen-plus feet in the air, a muddy mess of a wife and daughter who very much looks like she may fall. ("It's OK, she'll be fine," you hear a not very convincing Lisa assure my mom.) You can sense my indecision about what to do next. And then in the next moment, almost in slow motion, you see my feet wrap again instinctively as I rise up a bit more and stretch out my fingertips to lightly tap the bell.

I barely remember any of this. What I do remember is safely sliding back down the rope, crossing the finish line, and landing in the arms of my family. I remember rinsing off the mud, the cold water from the hose hitting my bare, now-kind-of-muscular shoulders and painting my running tights with a flood of orange. I remember seeing the founder of Spartan Race, Joe De Sena, milling about the race site and introducing myself. And I remember sitting on the ground in the hot August sun with Lisa and my mother and father, eating barbecue as the rays beat down on my bare, still-sweaty skin, believing that today's modest advancements are a tipping point. That from here on it will be nothing but an uninterrupted road to improvement and a glorious, if filthy, racing future ahead of me.

It was a little-girl type of dream, blissfully uncluttered and devoid of walls. And, of course, it was also fantastically unrealistic.

The Obstacle:
Rolling Mud and the Slip Wall
(fear)

Some obstacle course races are affectionately dubbed "Mud Runs." That's because, as I discovered in that West Point race, mud along the course is a challenge in and of itself, creating gooey hands and slippery feet, slowing down the pace, and snatching shoes from racers who haven't laced up tightly.

Spartan has taken mud to the extreme by creating a specific obstacle called "Rolling Mud," where racers encounter a series of deep pits filled with reddish-orange muck that sometimes transitions into a pool of dark, dirty water. Once in that water, participants face a "Dunk Wall" they must duck under while fully submerging themselves. This is a mandatory obstacle—no skipping, no burpees allowed. You *will* get wet, you *will* get gritty water in your eyes, you *will* get disoriented and possibly very cold, depending on the weather. And in some cases, as I one day learn the hard way, you *may* get an ear infection or nasty rash if you don't properly hose off all the grime as soon as the race is over.

Immediately after the Dunk Wall, there's typically another obstacle called the "Slip Wall." To complete it means emerging from the Dunk Wall to then—with eyes blurry, hands and shoes slick, hair dripping in your face—run up the inclined wall and grab for one of several ropes that dangle from the top. Once you get the rope, you use it to walk up the wall. To me, it is an exercise in overcoming fear, because frankly, it's counterintuitive to run up a steep metal wall while you are slippery and wet. Sometimes the ropes are long and it's easier. Other times, when the ropes are shorter, I've seen people miss their grab and slide back to the ground with a hard thud. In one North Carolina race I attended, they closed a crowded, muddy Slip Wall after a crush of people kept falling back on one another. (Here's where that waiver comes in.)

Mark Mathews is a professional big-wave surfer who once smashed into a reef while in Australia, tearing ligaments and severing a leg artery. He said this about fear on a podcast called *Finding Mastery*: "You've got to want the result on the other side, or you've got to want the experience that you're going to have when you overcome that fear, more than you fear doing what it takes to get there."

In a sense, that became my code to the Slip Wall. You must run hard and trust you'll reach the rope. And then once you do, you must trust your grip on the rope when you lean back and walk up the wall. But most of all, you must want what is on the other side of that wall more than you fear what it takes to get there.

10

WHAT'S ON THE OTHER SIDE OF FEAR?

About six weeks after the West Point race, I step out of the shower after a morning run and notice a voicemail banner alert on my cellphone. It's from my dermatologist. Initially, I think her office has misdialed, because I already had my annual checkup a week ago. *Why are they calling? Oh, right . . .* Now I vaguely remember her taking a scrape of a small, dark freckle on my leg as we chatted about our summers and the fact that she'd taken up golf at age sixty. Her young male assistant had complimented my calves—"You must be a runner"—after the doctor finished putting on the Band-Aid. I blushed; this new skin of athleticism still feels like wearing someone else's clothes.

Now, brushing my teeth, I hit the voicemail button to play the message, leaving a smidge of toothpaste on the touchscreen. "Hi, Ms. Bounds," they say and announce themselves as being from my doctor's office. "She would like to speak with you. Please call us back when you can." I spit, rinse, and wipe the toothpaste off my phone, feeling vaguely annoyed they didn't just leave my results on the voicemail. I've got a two-hour meeting this morning; I'll have to try calling her in the car driving to the office.

My SUV is humming along Route 9, just past the Croton-on-Hudson train station on the river, when I dial my doctor's number.

"Doctor's office," the bright voice chirps through my car's speakers. I steer into the left lane, preparing for the turnoff to Route 9A, simultaneously fingering my left palm. There's a callus tearing on my hand, which is starting to bother me.

"Hi. This is Wendy Bounds. Gwendolyn Bounds. You left a message for me to call her."

A pause. *Is there a pause?* "Yes, Ms. Bounds. Please hold."

Traffic. Steering. This callus is annoying. Do I have clippers in my bag? Why is she taking so long? Glance at the car clock. I'm definitely going to be late to my meeting.

"Hi, Ms. Bounds." It's my dermatologist's voice.

"Hi," I say. "Your office said to call."

"Yes," she answers. A pause. *Why all these pauses?* "Are you driving?"

"Yes," I tell her. "I'm on my way to work."

"Why don't you just call me when you get to the office."

My stomach knots. *Why can't she just tell me what's going on now?*

"I've got a lot of meetings when I get to the office, and a very busy day," I tell her, my confidence in the power of a full schedule and obligations to ward off bad things still very much intact.

Another pause. And then, suddenly, "I can't," the doctor says, her voice rising a notch. "I just can't. Please call me when you aren't driving."

And she hangs up.

My SiriusXM satellite radio blasts back on as the phone disconnects from the car's Bluetooth, sending a jolt through my body, which is itself disconnecting from my mind. I carefully turn down the volume and begin moving in very precise ways, registering sounds and sensations that will stay with me long after today—another flashbulb memory in the making. The loud motorcycle with a rusted tailpipe. My heartbeat pushing against my bra's underwire. The tight black leather stitching on the steering wheel irritating my callus.

I need a place to turn off. There is a shoulder on the road ahead where cars sometimes pull over. *That is the place where I will pull over. I will pull over and call her back. She will tell me the news.* Doctors don't hang up. Something is off in the narrative.

I pull over. Instinctively, I take out my spiral notebook and a pen. *Reporters' tools. Information gathering. That's all this is.* Dial the doctor's office and tell the receptionist politely that "we got disconnected." Disconnections happen all the time. That feels normal.

"Ms. Bounds?" Hearing the doctor's voice come on the line, I am equally happy and concerned.

I force precise calm into my voice. "I'm parked now," I tell her, hoping she can't hear the cars and trucks hurdling by me so close that my SUV shakes from the wake.

"Hi, yes, I'm sorry I hung up. I just couldn't talk to you while you were driving."

Got that part.

"So, what I'm telling you shouldn't take years off your life, but ..."

Years off my life ... I scrawl the words into my notebook.

"Your biopsy report came back, and you have a malignant melanoma."

Melanoma. Melanoma. That is obviously skin cancer. I've heard of it. It's not one I've had before, like basal cell or squamous. It's the really bad one. How bad? I don't know. Wait—what? This doesn't make sense.

"I'm sorry," I interrupt. "Are you sure you have the right report? You mean that small freckle on my right calf?"

"Yes. You'll remember that I thought it looked different from the picture we took last year." She seems relieved to have the diagnosis delivered and to be back to the data.

Did she think it looked that different? We were talking about our summers when she scraped it off. The male assistant complimented my calves after she made the scrape. Melanoma. That's the bad one. I need to get rid of it. What do I do to get rid of it?

"OK," I say, my natural bias toward action now kicking in. "What do I do? Have surgery? Do they dig it out? Radiation? What's the treatment?"

The rest of the call I remember as disjointed pieces of information that I log as best I can in my notebook. They've caught it early, it seems. But I'll still need some tests. Bloodwork. A chest X-ray. A surgeon.

When can I come to her office? she asks.

Now, I tell her, my very important meeting receding from view. I am coming to her office now.

Most skin cancer deaths are caused by melanoma. The earlier it is caught, the better chance you have of surviving five years after it is diagnosed. The kind of melanoma I have is a "superficial spreading type" situated in my epidermis (the outer layer of my skin) and the upper part of the next layer. It is considered stage T1a, because the cancer is invasive but is less than one millimeter in thickness and believed to be localized. Two hours later I'm sitting with Lisa in front of my doctor's big desk, learning all of this while she pulls up two pictures on her computer of the now missing mole on my leg. A young medical resident observes our conversation, learning the protocols of delivering cancer news.

"See the difference between the images," she says, enlarging the screen. "It's a little darker here, and the edges have changed." They both look equally brown and gross to me at this scale. In real life, the mole wasn't much bigger than the *i* typed on this page in the word "bigger." But I nod because it seems like the right thing to do.

I'll need bloodwork and a chest X-ray immediately, and then surgery. If there are clean margins from the surgery, then I shouldn't need more treatment. For the next year, I'll come to her for a detailed skin check every three months. After that, every six months. At the five-year mark, back to annually, assuming another melanoma hasn't been detected.

When we get home that night, I piece together how lucky I am. I've had good healthcare from my employers. Which means I've been going to a dermatologist annually for a skin checkup since I was in my twenties. The dermatologist I'm seeing now caught this early because she takes pictures of moles on my skin to compare between visits. There's a plan of action and a to-do list. I'm good with to-do lists. I put my list inside a blue file folder and staple a piece of paper inside the cover and carefully write out the names of all the doctors I'll need to see in the coming days. Organization, action. That's the way forward.

The next few days, we check items off the list. My chest X-ray is clear. So is my bloodwork. My dermatologist removes two more spots on my right leg as a precaution; both are benign. The results get filed in my blue folder. My general practitioner finds me a melanoma surgeon named Richard Shapiro at the NYU Langone Health medical center. He's confident, calm, and reassuring, explaining how he'll need to cut a long incision into my leg to remove the cancer, taking a much wider margin than the mole itself. Then he'll stitch it back together.

As is often true with the truly unexpected, the timing of my diagnosis is awful, arriving just as we're supposed to fly back to San Francisco and help with Lisa's father. In the days leading up to my surgery, we postpone the trip, Lisa now shouldering the weight of worry for her father *and* me. In between the surgery prep, I stick to my workouts, not knowing how long it will be before I can run again. Two races I'd planned to tackle that fall, in New Jersey and on Long Island, get shelved. At this point, I've canceled more race plans than I've run races. Still, the training sessions are both a distraction and a promise of the future. The day before I head to the hospital for surgery, my calendar records the following:

Dynamic Warmup
10-min rowing machine
Main Set (4x)
1 min pull-ups + single hand swing grips w/ black band
(4 total pull-ups)
Jog .40M
1 min rest

The surgery itself takes less than an hour. When I awake from the anesthesia, a nurse hands me orange juice and animal crackers, which I loopily spill down my chest while trying to cram them in my mouth. I've got a big bandage on my leg under a compression sock. Lisa has talked to Dr. Shapiro, and he tells her things went well and that the final biopsy results on the margins he cut will be back in a few days. The hospital attendants dispense a bottle of antibiotics, another of opioids, and bring me a wheelchair to exit the hospital. I look at it for a moment and then shake my head.

"I don't need it," I tell them. When the nurse starts to protest, I say firmly, "Really, I can walk." I'm not entirely sure that's true. But I don't want to say what I'm really thinking, which is: *I am a Spartan. A Spartan would walk out of the hospital.* I don't say it because it seems like a silly, drug-induced musing, especially from someone who's only run two races. Still, it's the first time I attach myself to this new identity, and the thought feels grounding—a promise of a moment that doesn't involve biopsies, surgery, and unexpected bad news on the side of a highway. A future where the choice about what's happening with my body belongs to me. So I reject the wheelchair and amble outside, into the noisy Manhattan twilight, stiff-legged yet unassisted, and climb into our SUV. Then Lisa drives us home.

The next morning, I peel off the bandage and gauze around my leg. There's a four-inch-long row of thick stitches with a surprisingly significant indentation on my inner calf where they removed tissue. All for something the size of a large sea salt fleck. I think about the decades of my flesh baking under a blazing sun on the beaches of North Carolina, by the pool as a teenager with friends as I worried about my underdeveloped frame, fishing on the open water with my parents. People didn't seem to worry about skin cancer in the seventies and eighties, or weren't as aware of the dangers as they are now. Being tan was equated with beauty and good health from being outdoors.

Still, once I digest the size of the incision and the future scar, my immediate physical recovery is smooth. The pain is manageable; I don't even take a Tylenol. On Saturday, my cellphone rings, showing an unknown New York City number. It's Dr. Shapiro. The margins he took from the biopsy were clean. In another timeline, another narrative, another life—if I were writing fiction—this chapter might end here with this call, our tears of relief, and my return to running and racing as soon as the incision heals.

But that is not my story.

In the coming weeks, with my "get into surgery as fast as possible" to-do list completed and nothing else to chronicle in my blue folder, I start to feel strangely off. Little things at first. I strip off a new pair of denim jeans and see the skin around my stitches covered in blue and think it's severe bruising. My body goes cold, my chest constricts, my heart rate jacks up, and it takes a few minutes before I consider, logically, that it's just dye from my new pants and wipe it off.

Then I fly to visit my parents in North Carolina for my father's birthday while Lisa heads out west to help her mother care for her father, who is still in acute care. Dr. Shapiro decides to leave the stitches in for the trip, a week longer than planned. "I know you," he says. "You'll take off running too hard and tear one of them." The skin is swollen around the stitches and slightly red—very normal after someone cuts your leg open and sews it back together. But as days pass on my trip, I begin to think the skin is growing over my stitches and the doctors won't be able to remove them and I'll get a deadly infection and lose my leg. Yep, this is what I think. My father, a veterinarian who also possesses stellar surgical skills, assures me this isn't the case and says he can remove them now if I want. But my brain is stuck in this odd gear and can't process this truth as real. Flying home, during a layover in the Charlotte, North Carolina, airport, I break out into this unfamiliar coldness again, my chest tightening, heart rate rising, and lock myself in a bathroom stall, crouching on the floor with my head pressed against the red metal door until I can breathe OK.

I hope things will go back to normal once my stitches come out. But not long after, while sitting in a conference room at work, I notice a mole on the hand of the colleague next to me and am so engrossed with examining its edges for irregularity that I don't hear my boss call my name. Then I start identifying new freckles on my own body and wonder if I should wait a full three months before seeing my dermatologist for a checkup. A small bump on the roof of my mouth sends me down a surreal rabbit hole of fear one evening after dinner, with my heart pounding, thinking for sure I must have melanoma in my jaw. I drink more alcohol to calm my nerves, and it helps me sleep. But by morning I awake shaking like I have a fever, scared to leave the bed and feeling like someone has tied a rope around my chest and is pulling it tighter and tighter.

My unraveling, as I come to think of it, is quick and acute, spanning the course of several weeks while my leg heals. I fake my way through meetings, smile reflexively in the hallways at colleagues who I don't really notice. What's happening is so foreign and so inexplicable that I have no context. Words like "panic attack" and "anxiety" are not in my lexicon. I'm confused and worried. Eventually, Lisa convinces me to call my general practitioner for help. He listens and delivers his opinion without hesitation.

"This is normal," he says. "Happens all the time after people get diagnoses like this." He gives me the name of a psychiatrist. "She'll fix you."

The psychiatrist's office is a big, cavernous room with dark wood in a quiet Upper West Side neighborhood of Manhattan. My experience with therapy is very limited. Nobody, *nobody* talked about mental health—or even fear, for that matter—in my family. Toughness, both physical and mental, was a prized attribute. As a small kid, I once stepped on a catfish spine at a lakefront beach, and the spine deeply punctured the webbing of my toes. The nearest hospital was two hours away, and I was in a good deal of pain. My dad doused the area with vodka, gave me a few small sips of the vodka with orange juice to take the edge off what came next, and then deployed his veterinary surgical skills to remove the bone with whatever tools he had on hand. I remember sitting very still and biting my lip while he worked, wanting him to be proud of me for being brave. My folks modeled this same DIY approach, a credo of "Buck up, put on a good face" when things got rough emotionally too. "Just get out into nature and you'll feel better" was the common prescription. (Which, to be sure, often worked.) No one I knew went to therapy, or if they did, they kept quiet about it. I don't know if it's a Southern trait or just the world I lived in. And you never know what goes on behind closed doors. But in my mind, therapy was associated with weakness and an inability to "just get on with it."

As a result, the scene here feels to me like a Hollywood movie version of "shrink's office." The doctor sits in a tall-backed chair with her feet outstretched on an ottoman. A white-noise machine is humming nearby, its job to absorb whatever secrets I spill so they don't travel out of this room. A long couch for patients—do people really use these? I opt for a chair. Also, a stupid box of tissues on the table next to my chair, taunting me. The doctor stares and stares, waiting for me to speak. Finally, she offers this: "How can I help you?"

I cross my legs. Uncross them. Sit up straighter. Try to remember what's real.

"So, I was diagnosed with melanoma on my right leg," I begin, my voice sounding confident, boardroom level, and then, seeing the empathy on her face, quickly add: "But they caught it early. I'm fine now."

And with the dishonesty of the "I'm fine now" burning my mouth, that tight rope around my chest uncoils. And the words come pouring out in a rush that's only slowed by the tears as I reach for the stupid tissue box over and over and over.

The call from my dermatologist. Parked on the side of the highway with my SUV shaking as traffic flies by. "Shouldn't take years off your life, but . . ." I wrote it down in my little notebook. What if this happens again? I mean, we're all going to die. Lisa's father nearly died a few weeks ago. My dog is dead. My parents are getting older. I could die soon. I'm at the age now when people die. One of my colleagues at *The Wall Street Journal* died of colon cancer at age forty-eight. What is the point of the human condition if we're just on a path to death? I know how lucky I am. I'm embarrassed to be sitting here with you. People think I'm strong. I used to think I was strong. But now my heart is caught in this bear trap, and I can't think straight.

She takes notes, nods a lot, and then prescribes some pills and suggests I come back once a week. I don't really want the pills, because I'm worried they will mess up my training once I resume running hard again. But, desperate for a path back to normal, I agree.

The next morning I awake, rope squeezing my chest so tightly I can barely breathe. Lisa already has left for work by the time I get out of bed. I swallow half of one of the pills from the psychiatrist and somehow shower, dress, and find my way out the door. I pass the spot on the highway where I took the call from the dermatologist and stare straight ahead, forcing myself not to look too hard lest, somehow, I'm still sitting there taking notes.

At the office, I'm so cold I leave on my heavy green coat for my first meeting, which, looking back at my Google Calendar, is something called "Paid Conversion Project Steering Team Meeting." I remember nothing about what's said other than the surrealness I feel as our vice president of testing speaks in his calm British accent. How can he be at this same faux wood table in room 2-59 with me, under these same awful fluorescent lights, during my unraveling? When the meeting ends, I find my way back to my office and curl up on the cheap red couch, still in my heavy green coat. I miss my next meeting. The glass of my office is lightly frosted, so I hope people walking by can't see me lying here in a ball. An executive curled up in a ball. It's not good. But at this point, I don't have the capacity to care.

It's my friend Erle Norton who ultimately finds me immobile. He also works at Consumer Reports and has an office nearby. I've known him since I was a cub reporter at *The Wall Street Journal,* working alongside him in my first job out of college. Erle calls Lisa and then tells me matter-of-factly, "I'm taking you home." Once there and safe again under my sheets in bed with my teeth chattering, I cancel an afternoon meeting with my boss, Leonora, telling her I have the flu.

Maybe I just have the flu, I tell myself. It's November and flu season.

And then I fall asleep.

Fear is an age-agnostic chameleon, a shape-shifter revealing itself to each of us in different forms at different periods: fear of public speaking, fear of closed-in spaces, fear of failure, fear of physical pain or harm, fear of rejection, of heights, of spiders, of being alone, of death itself. In certain circumstances fear is a friend, releasing the adrenaline needed to launch our fight-or-flight instinct to outrun a predator, jump out of the path of a moving bus, or lift something heavy in an emergency. But in other circumstances fear is insidious and sticky in a way that, at its best, isn't helpful and can be paralyzing at its worst.

When fear is associated with strong emotion, or flashbulb memories that feel traumatic or deeply uncomfortable, the emotion can encode in our brains in ways that are enduring and difficult to unlearn. This is how R. Douglas Fields—our neurologist memory expert, who helped me understand the power of memory and firsts during the Citi Field race—explains it. And then when a similar stimulus arises, the neural pathway to that memory gets strengthened through repetition. Eventually, without something to break the cycle, we can readily become trapped in a fear loop that's more harmful than helpful, particularly when there's no real predator around the next corner. Destructive thoughts can slide across our minds, picking up momentum like sleds on a luge course. In this form, fear to me is like the "mind-killer" author Frank Herbert describes in his seminal book, *Dune,* "the little-death that brings total obliteration."

It took a long time to understand the role fear played in my own unraveling—this "flu" that caught me in the autumn after my melanoma surgery—and how this unraveling was triggered by the sudden but complete realization that, in middle age, there's a lot of sand already at the bottom of our hourglass, and nobody's pouring in more at the top. It's a moment that will come for most of us somehow, some way. Until the call from my doctor came, I hadn't spent much—or any—time truly digesting this truth. Maybe none of us do until our hand is forced.

There's a lot of evidence in this book to undermine the clichés of middle age. But one I cannot dispute is the sharpening sense of leaving. People we care about start to leave the world with more frequency. And then there's the acute realization that we ourselves are going to disappear and no longer be part of the carefully constructed existence we've built with everyone and everything we love. And that if we get the privilege of more days, there will inevitably be that stripping away of abilities that make all of us *us*. We can do things that improve our chances of putting off this final leaving. But there are no guarantees, and as of right now, science has not yet discovered the elixir for immortality. And so our certain, ultimate exit remains a fact. In this sense, I find the story of humanity to be in equal measures the most beautiful and most cruel of narratives. We are born to experience the wonders of life, only to inevitably lose it all.

This inevitable loss became my fear loop—one set in motion by my dermatologist's words, "This shouldn't take years off your life, but . . ." and then compounded by the sense of endings already circling around me. Intellectually, of course, I understood the incredibly good fortune that we caught things when we did. Intellectually, I understood the common denominator of our collective mortality. But subconsciously, I was terrified by the lack of power we wield over our ultimate leaving. The more I turned it over in my mind, the more my fear loop strengthened. With the immediate to-do list of my surgery completed, there seemed nothing to do but wait. Wait for the next skin check. Wait for the next biopsy report. Wait for the next malignancy. Wait for the next diagnosis to be worse than the first one. Wait for the phone to ring and someone to tell me that information. Wait for my parents to die. Wait for Lisa to die. Wait to die myself. *And I could do nothing about this.* Or that's what it felt like. It wasn't so much that I feared the act of dying itself. It's that I feared not having the choice about when and how and from whom the verdict would come about any of these events.

We all have our addictions and weaknesses. Maybe it's food or alcohol or cigarettes or sex or approval from others. Maybe it's winning. My addiction, it turns out, is having control over my circumstances. If I could make choices and wield some control, I generally believed, things would turn out OK. As an only child, I'd been trusted by my parents as a third vote in our family and learned early the power of good decision-making. I knew how to write sentences that could convince people of my point of view. My comfort, salve, sense of well-being, was firmly rooted in the ability to [*insert your own addiction here: drink, smoke, win, eat, be thin, be liked*] control my outcome. (And for those who are curious: yes, I'm a Virgo.)

With that sense of control now dispelled, however false it was to begin with, the fear and subsequent anxiety set in. And I felt broken and ashamed. I was in my late forties but had almost no experience working on my emotional health. Now this part of my identity needed to change too if I wanted to get on with things and be happy again. At first, given my buck-up upbringing, I just wondered why this was happening and prayed it would go away. The people closest to me felt helpless. My mother couldn't hug my anxiety out of me or show me a beautiful enough sunset to make the badness disappear. Lisa couldn't cheer me up with a song we loved or a drink at our favorite bar. Erle, who'd known me since I was twenty-one years old, couldn't find an activity that would loosen the ropes around my chest and make me OK again.

It would take years before I finally found a framework that made sense for me about what had happened in the weeks after my surgery. It came, curiously enough, from a 2016 Olympic runner turned author and filmmaker named Alexi Pappas, who, while promoting her book, *Bravey: Chasing Dreams, Befriending Pain, and Other Big Ideas,* referenced a "scratch on my brain" to explain her depression. A doctor had told her it was "just like when you fall down rollerblading and you get a scratch on your knee." It would take time to heal, but it could heal just like any body part. This was language I understood and could borrow hope from. I fell down and scratched my brain, but a scratch can get better. In other words, a fear loop could be interrupted.

Unlike with a scratch, however, this kind of healing wouldn't take a week or two. And I couldn't do it on my own. My middle-aged misconceptions about emotional health meant I needed to unlearn everything I believed about being strong. I needed to seek help. Help through counseling. Help through medication and meditation apps. Help even through a very brief stint of psychedelic-assisted therapy. The latter entailed taking a microdose of ketamine under a doctor's supervision and working through my fear in an altered, calmer mind state while a counselor read me that passage from *Dune.* (Another notable first for someone who'd never even tried recreational drugs before.) The spiral notebook in which I took notes about time management now also contains notes about fear and anxiety, culled from the dozens of books and podcasts I've consumed on the topic. On one page, there's a scrawled thought I heard on one show from a man named Tony Blauer, who is a self-defense and performance coach. The essence is this: without fear, there is no bravery. I reread this page before nearly every doctor's appointment. There is comfort there. We can choose bravery.

Perhaps the biggest turning point came one afternoon more than three years after my original melanoma diagnosis. I was out running while listening to a trauma expert and physician named Paul Conti talk on one of my allotted podcasts. He spoke plainly and clearly about psychology and brain biology, defining trauma as anything that causes emotional or physical pain and leaves its mark on us. This can be trauma with a capital *T* or a lowercase *t.*

I didn't believe what happened to me qualified as trauma, but it was revelatory hearing a doctor talk in such a relatable, matter-of-fact tone about the mind as just another part of our body the way Conti did. When I finished running, before even showering, I located his medical practice in Oregon, and eventually I signed up to be counseled remotely by a therapist on his team who was licensed in New York. This man, Jonathan Horey, became the trainer for my mental and emotional health, someone I came to rely on for my overall fitness and well-being, the same way I did Pete or any of my future coaches. He helped me unlearn behaviors associated with my control and fear, the same way I eventually would unlearn the placement of my feet when I ran. He also blew up my misconceptions about what therapy is or should be. He was a talker, not just a listener, which I personally needed. He called me out when I dodged his questions and laughed at my jokes.

But perhaps the most critical lesson he helped me understand is this:

There is freedom in giving up control. Yet, just because we don't have ultimate control or choice over everything that happens to us doesn't mean that we have *no* control or choice.

After Erle drives me home from Consumer Reports on the day he finds me curled up in my green coat, I do not leave the bedroom for forty-eight hours except to use the bathroom. He sleeps in our guest bedroom during that time, helping Lisa make sure I eat, which feels like choking down sawdust. It's Thanksgiving week, so most meetings are canceled and the office is closed on Thursday and Friday. Lying on my side, watching the last rusty leaves blow off the trees outside, I drift in and out of an unstable sleep, thinking again about Lisa's father and the inevitability and suffering of human aging and decline. A show called *Longmire* hums low in the background on Netflix, something Erle left on, about a Wyoming sheriff piecing his life back together after a tragedy.

On day three in bed, I awake at some point and scroll habitually, glassy-eyed, through the calendar on my iPhone. (*Sitting. Screens. Even now.*) That's when I see the entry for Thanksgiving Day, which is tomorrow. It says, "Epic—Turkey Burn." It's a special class my coach Pete has crafted for the holiday. My leg has healed enough to start training again. I want to go. How can I possibly go? I can't even move. But if I don't go to class, then how can I ever race again? And it's then, in that humbling fog, that the dimmest of lights turns on in the distance of my brain. *I want to race.*

And then, the same thought from the hospital. *I am a Spartan.*

Lying in a ball, phone still clenched in my fist, I wait, a spectator to my own psyche, while *I want to race* and *I am a Spartan* wage war with the cold, constricted, fear loop running through my body. No one is watching the moment I sit up and slowly swing my two feet to the cool hardwood floor. I pause on the edge of the bed, as I will so many times in the future remembering this precise moment. Our exercise bike is downstairs. If I can stand up, I can get downstairs. If I can get downstairs, I can get on the bike. If I can get on the bike, I can pedal. If I can pedal, I can go to class tomorrow. If I can go to class tomorrow, I can race again.

I want to race.

I am a Spartan.

Moments pass. And then I choose to stand up.

And I run for my Slip Wall.

The Obstacle: Monkey Bars
(adaptability)

Head to any playground on a sunny afternoon and you'll likely see children flying across monkey bars with seemingly no effort. Their movements are instinctive and fluid—they adjust their technique on the fly. Kids seem rubbery, with a wide range of motion in the shoulders and, often, an even distribution of weight that makes carrying themselves in this way a natural movement.

You might still recall the feeling of floating from bar to bar from your own childhood. But attempt the monkey bars now in your grown-up body and you may find you can't hang on for more than a couple of rungs—at best. We're no longer as limber. Our weight distribution has shifted to our midsection and below. Our grip strength has waned. But equally important, we've lost the muscle memory and mental flexibility to fly through the air with the greatest of ease.

Monkey bars are a staple of most obstacle races, no matter how long or short the race. But forget about the red and blue playground rigs of your youth—the ones with those small, thin bars. In a Spartan race, at least, these are grown-up monkey bars, spaced much farther apart than at the playground. The bars are thick silver aluminum. And sometimes their height is staggered. If you hit this obstacle early in the morning, the metal may be wet from dew. Or if it comes after a barbed-wire crawl, the rails could be slick with mud from previous racers' hands. You only get one attempt at the monkey bars and you must ring the bell at the other end or be prepared for burpees or a penalty loop.

Monkey bars forced me to remember what it's like to adapt on the fly. To not get so fixed in one way of doing things that I'd automatically shy from a better one. When the bars are dry, swinging from arm to arm is a beautiful, relaxed way to travel. But if the metal is slippery, then matching hands with both on the same bar or going underhanded (palms facing toward you) and sideways can offer more security. At my strongest, I will learn to change my technique midway through if needed.

Watching packs of grown-ups tackle this obstacle feels like being back at the playground. Few obstacles bring out the consistent whoops of joy upon completion in a race that the monkey bars do, as adult bodies intuitively summon movements from decades past and fly across space and back in time.

In fact, that's exactly what it took for me—a trip back in time on a playground—to finally crack the code to this obstacle.

11

LEARN, UNLEARN, RELEARN

"Lady, you're doing it ALL wrong!"

The child is clearly fed up. She's been watching me take my turn at the monkey bars on the playground of Haldane, one of our local schools. It's a chilly Saturday morning, and I'm out here with a handful of kids, standing in the mulch while their amused parents watch from the sidelines. Pete's floating monkey bars are still too high and tricky for me. Hence, I'm leveling down here on the playground. Over and over I've attempted to make it across, only to have my grip fail on the cold, red second bar. It's getting embarrassing. Clearly, it's also getting annoying for the kids to watch my pitiful attempts. And one of them has decided to act.

"You—need—to—SWING. Like—a—MONKEY." The staccato instructions are firm coming from this exasperated redheaded tyke who can't weigh more than thirty pounds. She stalks up to the staircase behind the bars, puts a tiny elbow in my hip to push me over, and climbs up beside me. Technically, she's cutting in line, but I decide not to call her out since her mom's watching.

"Like *this*."

The little girl catapults her legs back and forth to gain momentum and then moves from bar to bar, hiking up her hip before she releases her back grip for more power in her swing. I'm simultaneously annoyed, impressed, and envious. I've been out on this playground in the cold for the past few weekends trying desperately to improve my technique, but to no avail. Like a lot of women my age, the weight I have is more concentrated in my hips and lower body, and let's just say that moving it all through the air is not a natural motion anymore. While I've improved on the floating rings, the monkey bars have proved far more vexing.

"I weigh more than you," I tell the little girl grumpily. She stares at me through orange curls dangling into her eyes. I try framing the situation in terms she can understand. "You're flexible and proportioned evenly, like a French fry, and I'm like a, uh, well, I'm more rigid and shaped like a carrot." More staring. Clearly my metaphors are not resonating. "Fine," I tell her. I step up the rungs, grab the first bar, and attempt a halfhearted swing.

"Swing HARDER!" the French fry cries behind me. And that's when I feel two little palms press against my rear end and start pushing me. Oh my God, she's going to knock me off. . . .

And then it happens. I instinctively reach out and grab the next bar, and the momentum generated by the French fry causes me to swing backward and then forward again as I grasp for the next bar.

"Keep going, lady!"

And somehow I do, hitting a rhythm and making it almost to the final red bar before plopping down into the mulch and rubbing my palms. My effort is rewarded by a smattering of applause from tiny, pink, bare hands and a few gloved grown-up ones over on the benches.

"See, lady? I told you so."

In the months following my melanoma surgery, before meeting this pint-sized, redheaded teacher, I continue to crave something to focus on that feels forward-looking, a way to wrest back a sense of ownership of my body. As my leg heals, I set my sights on a big upcoming February race in Jacksonville, Florida. It's double the length of the two races I've already run—somewhere between six and eight miles, a length Spartan calls a Super. (Back in these days, Spartan was fuzzier with the actual lengths of races, whereas today the Sprint, Super, and Beast races are more or less fixed to the 5K, 10K, and 21K standards.) It's also part of Spartan's U.S. National Series, which consists of five key races that will determine series champions for both the Elite and Age Group racers. With my own sense of urgency amped up, I decide to race in the Age Group category to see how I truly stack up against competitors in my bracket. This means I'll be held accountable for all penalties, and theoretically (ha ha) be in contention for a top-three podium slot. Even on a National Series competition weekend, only about 20 to 30 percent of racers compete in the Spartan Race Elite and Age Group categories, so I'll be running with a smaller and more formidable crew.

In late February, Lisa and I fly to Florida, leaving the frozen grounds of New York and landing in the balmy South a few hours later. It's the first time I've left town since the unraveling, and a residue of worry still clings to me like mud from a race. I've begun leaving my running shoes out where I can see them when my eyes open in the morning. Something about the image cues me to get up and move. Often, I go for a run immediately, knowing that as soon as I begin to leave footprints in the frosty dirt the knots in my chest will loosen. Like I said, my parents aren't wrong about nature as medication.

On race day, I awake groggy in the hotel room, feel my chest tighten, and then remember I'll soon be out on the course. I dress quickly and eat, and we arrive at the WW Ranch Motocross Park around 6:30 A.M. Race organizers hand me my first red Age Group racer headband, #1766, which distinguishes me from Open category racers, who wear black headbands. The usual rock music is booming, and I struggle to tamp down a headache and my nerves while watching the who's who of obstacle course racing Elites warm up, jogging around the festival area.

From Instagram and my YouTube studies, I recognize a few of them, including a small, dark-haired racer named Faye Stenning, who reportedly has the most podium finishes of any Elite female racer right now. She has an active Instagram following and is known for her blunt language and her habit of balancing social posts that feature her scaling obstacles with ones of her lying on the beach in bikinis, sipping cocktails. (My kind of racer, though I suppose that now means doing it with that floppy hat.) I notice Faye stays out of the starting corral until the very last minute, when she jogs up, launches herself over the starting wall, and makes her way to the front of the pack, staring straight ahead like some predatory animal.

When the heat for my age group of 45–49 begins gathering, I borrow a page from Faye and hang back, studying the other women. They look a lot stronger than the Open category racers and are programming what look like fancy racing watches. I look down at my own wrist, which sports an old plastic Swatch watch I've thrown on, and immediately feel imposter syndrome. At the last minute I climb over the wall, but I don't have Faye's confidence to move to the front of the pack. And it's a good thing, because the moment the race begins, the others are so far ahead of me that I realize I'd probably have been run over. These women are fast, and this will be the last I see of most of them until we're back in the festival area.

I'd wanted an opportunity to benchmark my abilities, and today is a wake-up call. I fail the monkey bars and the rings, which are wet from morning dew. There's also a new obstacle called The Box, where a rope with some knots tied in it dangles over the top of a slippery eight-foot-tall square. You must use the rope to hoist yourself up high enough to grab a horizontal bar on top of the box and then pull yourself up onto the box. It's difficult to climb the rope, because it's lying flush against the slick box. I watch racer after racer turn themselves upside down, collapse on the mat below, and finally give up in frustration. Then I take my turn and do the same. Staring up at that slick eight-foot wall, I cannot fathom ever being able to summit this obstacle, and with a sinking feeling, I walk away to perform my penalty.

For more than two hours, I slog through woods with muddy riverbanks and slither with other racers on our wet bellies, across sand and under barbed wire. Once again, I'm strong on the heavy carries. The Rope Climb also goes smoothly, and in a moment of redemption, I hit my spear throw. But none of it can make up for how sluggish my running is, or the fact that I'm still doing a lot of things wrong on the grip-intensive obstacles.

After I cross the finish line, Lisa and I check the results. I'm twentieth in my age group.

That's twentieth out of twenty-three racers.

In fact, had I not hit my spear throw, I'd likely have rolled in dead last. We stare at that ranking for a moment together, each of us processing the results differently. I can't remember a time in recent memory when I've been among the lowest performers for anything I attempted. Also, though it's still early days, I'm falling in love with this crazy sport. And when you love something, you hold yourself to higher standards.

Lisa sees it differently. "Hey, I think it's amazing you even finished," she says, putting a hand on my muddy back. "And it's a National Series race, and you weren't last!"

I nod and swallow hard. *Not last* will have to be medal enough today. That and the fact that not once during the two hours, forty-six minutes, and forty-nine seconds I was out on the course did a single thought about aging or dying or loss of control enter my brain.

What I think at that moment is: I still have so much to learn. But there's more to it than that—a key secret that needs to be unlocked. Which finally happens when that little red-haired girl gives me the literal and metaphorical push I need on the monkey bars.

When we're younger and taking up new activities, it's mostly about learning and acquiring skills. We don't know much, so there aren't a lot of bad habits to undo. Conversely, by middle age, we know a lot more and have acquired a *lot* of habits—some of them good, some not so much. We've also forgotten things we once knew instinctively (such as how to move like we did when we were kids). To progress with something new there's obviously learning to do, but equally important, there's unlearning and relearning.

When the French fry schooled me on the playground a few weeks after the Jacksonville race, it dawned on me that I'd been practicing the monkey bars all wrong. I'd been attempting the same old technique of just dead-hanging from a bar and trying to move to the next one, without really analyzing what I needed to stop doing or do differently to make progress.

There's something called the ten-thousand-hour rule. That is: it takes roughly that many hours of practice, likely along with certain innate talent, to become an expert in a particular skill. This benchmark of mastery gained a lot of attention (and debate) with the publication of the bestselling book *Outliers: The Story of Success* by Malcolm Gladwell. Gladwell's book was an important study of what factors make successful people become "the best" in a particular discipline. *Outliers* cites a body of research by a Swedish psychologist named K. Anders Ericsson and his colleagues. After years studying the nature of expertise and human performance, they concluded that "even the most gifted performers need a minimum of ten years (or ten thousand hours) of intense training before they win international competitions." But not just any type of practice. Mindless repetition in and of itself won't be enough. To advance, your practice needed to be "deliberate," focusing on tasks beyond your current capabilities and comfort level, unlearning bad habits, adjusting techniques, and often engaging with a teacher or coach to provide critical feedback.

In other words, if you wanted to become the best free-throw shooter or tennis player, standing there hurling the ball at the basket or waving your racket around all day wasn't going to cut it. You needed to understand what you were doing incorrectly and rewire your brain to do it better.

Up until now, I'd been practicing just to practice. But after making it partway across the monkey bars, something clicked. I had just unlearned a bad technique I'd been executing for months (hanging without swinging) and subsequently relearned a motion I'd known instinctively as a kid. That realization was like a light turning on in the shadows. "Just doing" might have been a great mantra for getting started. But to truly improve, I needed to move beyond just try, try again and figure out what I was doing wrong.

Being around younger people, it turns out, is a good way to start. Just down the hill from the playground at Haldane is a football field and a running track. Thankfully, the high school boys turn out to be as gracious about sharing their turf as the little ones up on the playground. Or at least they are after a few solid laughs watching me attempt to flip their enormous tire. I've been out there tugging at it to no avail while they run drills in the background. Spartan has included tire flips (two hundred pounds for women and four hundred pounds for men) as obstacles at some of its races, and I'm flummoxed.

Finally, one guy walks over to help. "Stop trying to do it with only your arm strength," he instructs. "That will never work. And"—he looks at me rubbing my lower spine—"you're going to throw out your back."

The trick, this young man with shaggy dark hair and a massive chest explains, is to get the tire slightly off the ground by wedging my fingers under it. Then, bending deep into a squat, I can use the power of my legs to hoist the tire to chest height before flipping my hands to get underneath the tire and push it over.

It takes a few tries, but sure enough, once I get low enough, everything he says is true. I finally flip the tire and receive a sweaty high five. "Hey, we're looking for a new quarterback this season," my teenage teacher jokes.

With this type of practice, it's not so much about forgetting the old way of doing things as getting the brain's circuitry to fire differently as we learn a new and better way. And that involves something called myelin. Even if you're not a science geek, stick with me for a minute because this gets interesting. When we learn a skill, our nerve fibers carry small electrical impulses, and this stuff called myelin wraps around the fibers like insulation to keep the signals from leaking out. Myelin is so important that it's a key character in a book called *The Talent Code: Greatness Isn't Born. It's Grown. Here's How.* In the book, author Daniel Coyle gracefully dissects exactly how ability can be created and nurtured in all of us if we train in the right way.

With deep practice, Coyle's version of deliberate practice, we encourage the growth of myelin around the nerve fibers, which helps us improve a skill. The thicker the myelin gets, the better it insulates, and thus the faster and more accurate our movements and thoughts become, Coyle writes in his book. While myelin grows most rapidly in childhood, apparently, we continue to experience a net gain until around age fifty. And even though we then start tipping toward a myelin loss, we still "retain the ability to myelinate throughout life," according to Coyle's research. That means we can still learn, unlearn, and relearn all sorts of things—playing the piano, golfing, fly fishing, speaking Japanese, traversing monkey bars—even if it requires more time and effort as we age.

Over the next two months, I concentrate on creating an environment where I can consistently engage in a better type of practice. I purchase an inexpensive climbing rope and hang it from a tree limb outside our kitchen window. During a visit to our house in New York, my dad helps me construct a spear throw stand. I pay Pete twenty dollars for one of his spears and buy a bale of hay from Home Depot to complete the apparatus. (To state the obvious: it's a *very* understanding spouse who turns a blind eye to a spear throw stand and a climbing rope in the yard when there are no children in the house.) I also pick up one of Home Depot's orange five-gallon buckets for $4.48 and fill it with forty pounds of the salt crystals that we use in our home's water softener tank. This way, I can practice different methods of the bucket carry: on my shoulder, centered in my midsection, behind my neck—tweaking my technique to figure out what works best depending on how taxed my grip is or how tired my legs are. An Amazon holiday gift certificate from my boss, Leonora, funds a small pull-up bar that clips to the frame of our guest-bathroom door downstairs.

The proximity of this gear, which costs less than $250, means I can better control what task I work on and for how long when I'm not at Pete's gym being coached. For instance, I'm still not able to complete even a single pull-up without resistance bands to support my weight. After studying a lot of videos about proper pull-up technique (*Sitting! Screens!*), I deduce that I'm not engaging my stronger back muscles and shoulder blades correctly. Once I correct my technique and stop pulling with just my arms, it slowly gets . . . well, less impossible. Each time I go downstairs for laundry or to take out the trash, I do a few pull-ups, trying to reduce my dependency on the resistance bands, and record the progress in my notebook.

Similarly, every day before work, I leave my backpack on the lawn and quickly squeeze in five spear throws, wiping grass and mud off my dress shoes in my office. Each time I land a stick with the spear, I take careful note of which way my body is positioned, precisely how far back my arm goes, what the proper balance of the spear feels like in my hand, how close my hand comes to my face when throwing.

Even my running mechanics, something I've never thought much about (one foot in front of the other, right?) get carefully tweaked after I start feeling twinges in my hip. A bit of research online suggests it might be due to overstriding, and that I should try to land more in the center of my body mass. I make a switch, and after a few weeks of feeling like a gangly newborn calf on the run, the pain disappears.

Learn, unlearn, relearn.

In mid-April, I rejoin Pete and the Epic crew to race at Citi Field again as a team in an Open heat. It's been one year since my first race, and the experience is completely different. My running still has a long way to go, but I'm able to keep up with the group. At the Rope Climb, I shimmy up and down the rope three times—just for fun— a far cry from last year's epic fall that left me in a crumpled heap under the Coca-Cola sign. And after I nail my spear throw, I realize I'm just one obstacle away from a clean race with no obstacle failures: the "Multi-Rig," with the floating red rings. Even though I completed this at the West Point race, I still wait nervously for everyone else on the team to take their turn. And then, with a deep breath, I start across, relying heavily on momentum from my swings (thank you, little redheaded girl) so I don't dangle like a fish the way I did here last year. Moments later, I tap the bell. The Epic crew congratulate me, and we knock out a few last easy obstacles and cross the finish line together.

I'm so buoyed by this obvious payoff of my deep practice that I decide to try my hand again racing competitively in my age group and sign up for a 21K (13.1-mile) race—the length known as a Spartan "Beast"—in the mountains of New Jersey a few weeks later. In some ways, it's crazy for me to even attempt this venue. This race is roughly twice the length of the Jacksonville race (where I nearly placed last) and among the hardest Spartan courses in the United States, winding up and down ski slopes in unpredictable terrain and temperatures. But I feel like I'm in a hurry—a hurry to improve, a hurry to outrun the anxiety, a hurry to move my body in these new, powerful ways before something bad happens and I can't. And the race is nearby, so I don't have to get on a plane. Plus, I'm a little drunk on my own Kool-Aid from Citi Field and tell myself, How bad can it really be?

So it is that I head straight into an event that will put in place the final piece for me to advance to the next chapter of my obstacle course racing journey.

But, spoiler alert: first, I'm going to crash and burn.

12

DIPS AND TURNING POINTS

The Beast race at the Mountain Creek ski resort in New Jersey ranks as Spartan's fifth-hardest U.S. venue by one tally. It's not so much its peak summit, which clocks in around 1,480 feet and is reasonable compared to other venues such as Mount Ogden peak in Utah. It's more the wildly unpredictable and unrelenting nature of the course. There are tricky, rocky trails that can roil the surest-footed racers. Equally vexing is the wily weather, which rarely seems to cooperate.

This history holds true on the Saturday in late April 2019 when I show up buzzing with the anticipation of racing competitively in my age group for the second time. It's a gray day, with temperatures stuck in the low forties and winds blowing around fifteen miles per hour. Lisa is back in California helping her parents, so Erle accompanies me to the course. Milling about in the race festival area, I spy a young woman in her early twenties, Cali Schweikhart, who lives near me in the Hudson Valley. Cali took the gold medal in the Elite women's category here last year. She's often at the Haldane School track working out when I am, lapping me as we run. (She clearly doesn't need coaching from the high school football team or little girls on the playground.) Cali went to school with the kids of some friends of Lisa's and mine, and we've been introduced via email.

Right now, she's jogging around warming up, with her father

watching intensely nearby. When she waves at me, I notice she is wearing these strange, giant black mittens on her hands. It's my first clue that today is not going to unfold as I'd hoped.

"What do you think those are?" I ask Erle.

He shrugs. "Beats me. They look like big oven mitts."

I contemplate the thin, mildewy cycling gloves with open finger-tips I'd grabbed from our garage that morning. They seem pathetic compared to the monstrous weapons on Cali's hands. Sensing my doubt, Erle weighs in optimistically: "I'm sure you'll warm up fast once you get started." It is very cold just standing around staring at my gloves, and so I start darting back and forth between the starting line and the porta potties, where doors keep slamming behind nervous stomachs. A few other racers are wearing big mitts like Cali's. They also have waterproof shell jackets, something else I don't have.

When my start time comes at 8 A.M., we take off up a giant, steep hill that's more of a power hike for me than a run. Erle is right. I do warm up fast, settling into a rhythm as we climb a lot during the first two miles. The slower pace and uphill slog suit me. Suddenly I'm competing not so much on speed but on stamina and willpower. One of the early obstacles is something called the Tyrolean Traverse: a long rope suspended horizontally in the air which you must move across either by hanging upside down underneath it and walking your legs and hands atop the rope, or by balancing your chest and belly on top and pulling yourself forward. The catch is, you can't touch the ground until you reach the bell suspended farther down the rope. I've watched a few videos about this obstacle, but it's my first time touching it. I opt for hanging underneath, and soon enough I'm halfway across with my forearms burning. But I can hear the bell clanging behind me and keep pulling and walking my legs, and suddenly I'm there. I swat it and drop to the ground. I can't believe it. Excited, I clap my hands a few times.

Buoyed by this success, I move past mile three and soon find another tough obstacle I've never encountered called Stairway to Sparta. It consists of a high wall with some red rock-climbing holds to grip. I've also watched a bunch of videos about this obstacle. A lot of people are failing to get up the wall, so I figure I'll give it one shot and join them in the burpee pit. I rush for the wall, jump high to grab the first set of holds, and grip tight. I summon my basement pull-up practice and manage to reach a hand up to the next hold and pull up again and reach the third. One more pull and I realize that, with my long legs, I can just reach the first hold, plant my toe, and use it to propel myself up. And then just like that, I can climb up the rest of the wall. This success is so shocking to me that I literally yell to nobody (since I don't know anyone): "Oh my God, I'm going to do this."

And then I'm off and running again.

The disbelief is still banging around my brain when I nearly face-plant after a girl in front of me twists her ankle hard coming down a hill. (That rocky terrain.) She moans while racers carefully run around her. We aren't supposed to help one another as Age Group competitors, but I stop, since I'm literally almost on top of her.

"Can you move?" I ask. She shakes her head and holds her foot, grimacing.

"OK, hold on," I tell her. "I'll go get someone." I climb back up the hill, retracing my steps until I reach Stairway to Sparta, and tell a volunteer there what happened. "I'll call for a medic," she says. Then I run back to the girl, who now has managed to roll herself to the side of the race path to get out of the way of the herd.

"They are sending someone," I tell her. "Do you have any friends racing with you out here?" She shakes her head no.

"I can sit with you until the medic comes." Even in her pain she looks at me like I'm totally crazy. "No, oh my God, go. You're going to be so far behind."

This fact has not occurred to me. Clearly, I am missing some key competitive gene. "Um, OK," I say. Years of being imprinted by my mother's good Southern manners are colliding with the realization that the girl is right. "If you are sure?"

"Thank you, but go!" she says. And so I do, running faster now. I still feel strong and am even starting to pass a few people. A tingling begins to creep over my skin like electricity. This course is hard. And I am passing people.

These next two miles are the calm before the storm. Erle is waiting at the bottom of a steep hill where we careen back down toward the spectator festival area for a few obstacles—specifically, the Rolling Mud, Dunk Wall, and Slip Wall—before heading back up the mountain. He later confesses that he couldn't believe the look of ease and joy on my face as I approached. "I almost didn't recognize you."

The electricity coursing through me lasts through the cool, gooey Rolling Mud, my body still warm and sweaty from the first five miles, and lingers a few blissful seconds longer. We climb up and slide down a couple of soupy mud pits and then plunge into the water, where the floating black Dunk Wall awaits. And in that moment, everything changes.

The water is so cold I almost can't breathe. I feel for the bottom of the Dunk Wall underwater and then, taking a deep breath, submerge myself to duck under the wall and over to the other side. My face goes numb as I crawl through the rest of the cold water in my now-soaked wool-blend shirts, cotton pants, arm sleeves, and hydration vest and climb up the embankment right before the Slip Wall. Erle is shooting a video of me, and in it you can see me standing on the muddy ground, ponytail dripping down my back, studying the Slip Wall as if I can't remember what I'm supposed to do. Finally, I make a run for it, grab the rope with my numbing hands, and climb up and over.

On the other side, my mind goes blank, and I stand there shivering like a sad, wet puppy who doesn't understand why she just got spanked.

Until now, I've been mostly climbing the mastery curve—with nowhere really to go but up, since I was starting at the very bottom. But this steep rise of improvement—it ends here after the New Jersey

Dunk Wall when I hit my first real "dip," as George Leonard dubbed it in his book *Mastery*.

Even if you never attempt an obstacle course race, these next few paragraphs might keep you safe and are yet another reason why we must fight back against the midlife assassin.

Water, it turns out, can carry heat away from the body much faster than air—some twenty-five times faster—which means you can lose a great amount of heat very quickly when wet. I should know this after nearly half a century of feeling the shock of chilly ocean water or unheated swimming pools. But somehow that wisdom has eluded me on this spring morning up on a mountain. And today, I don't have a towel. The sun is hiding behind the clouds. And I'm stuck in these wet clothes for another eight miles.

To understand precisely what happened to my body that morning when it encountered the environmental trifecta of cool temperatures, water, and wind, I reached out to Robert Kenefick. Kenefick is an extraordinarily accomplished researcher focusing on the body's cardiovascular, thermoregulatory, and performance responses to exercise and environmental stress. He was a principal investigator for many years at the U.S. Army Research Institute of Environmental Medicine and helped oversee its Thermal and Mountain Medicine Division. Equally notable for this story, Kenefick has years of experience as an endurance athlete, having competed in numerous marathons and ultramarathons. He's also a veteran Spartan racer who participated in the grueling Death Race, that hardcore precursor to Spartan Race. That includes a winter Death Race where Kenefick helped carry a giant beam out of a freezing river and then waded back and forth across the river, performing one hundred burpees on each side, with the goal of reaching one thousand. In other words, this is a guy who *truly* understands the impact of temperature on the human body—both professionally and personally.

Our bodies, he explains, are wired to maintain a stable temperature of about 98.6°F (37°C). When the temperatures around us fall, the thermoreceptors (tiny sensors) in our skin start feeding information back to the hypothalamus, deep in our brain. The hypothalamus functions like a central command center, managing temperature, hunger, thirst, and other factors to ensure our body stays in a stable state called homeostasis. When conditions change—e.g., the temperature falls—this command center begins sending out signals for our body to adjust.

As I stood there on that muddy embankment like a shocked wet puppy, the warmth in my skin was trying to move toward the cold air, because generally heat moves toward cold. To stanch that heat loss, my blood vessels started clamping down on the periphery to reduce blood flow, which subsequently made my skin temperature decrease. The technical term for it, Kenefick explained, is vasoconstriction. And that's when the shivering began.

"What your body is trying to do is to say, 'Well, if I can get my muscles to contract, then I can generate heat,'" Kenefick says. "'And if I can generate heat, then I can try to maintain my core body temperature.' And that's why we shiver."

Muscles and tendons also have optimal temperatures for flexibility and length, he adds. And—as I'll learn in another mile or two—in colder temperatures, when our muscles are not at the optimal temperature to make movement, they shorten and tighten, and we can cramp. Being wet just makes things a whole lot worse. First, there's the moment of submersion in the cool water. Because water is denser than air, it will start pulling the heat from your body. "You are now dumping heat into the environment, which is water. Once you get out and your clothes are all wet, then the wet clothes are still pulling heat out of your body," Kenefick says. Wind doesn't help either. As the airflow goes over your skin, even at a modest five miles per hour, it also pulls heat away. This would help if I were racing on a hot day in June, but not up here on this chilly, breezy mountain.

Bottom line? Stay in these conditions long enough and you risk tipping into hypothermia, a dangerous condition where your body temperature starts dipping below that optimal 98.6°F (37°C) down to 95°F (35°C). Confusion and lack of coordination can set in, followed by a weak pulse or slurred speech. While hypothermia is generally a risk at very cold temperatures, according to the Centers for Disease Control and Prevention, the condition can occur even at cool temperatures (above 40°F) if a person is chilled from rain, sweat, or submersion in cold water.

As for age? Being older doesn't typically help. While every person's body will behave differently, there are circulatory and cardiovascular changes that can occur as we age that may negatively impact our ability to adequately regulate our temperature. If muscle mass is declining too, that can impact our ability to generate heat, and this can be of concern regardless of whether you're an endurance athlete. (Say, if you fell overboard on a winter boating expedition, or your car broke down in a snowstorm and you had to hike for help.)

All this science is still foreign to me as I start climbing slowly back up the mountain into mile six, soaked through to my skin. All I process in the moment is a growing sense of misery because I can't warm up. I'm noticing with envy that other racers seem to be putting on warm windbreakers and wondering how they kept them dry. My wool and polyester shirt and cotton pants, where Dolly's dog tag is stuffed in one pocket, are holding water. The sluggish pace makes everything worse. (Kenefick tells me that pausing to knock out some push-ups or burpees might have helped.) We crawl through the earth under barbed wire. My soggy cycling gloves are useless, and my fingers numb more as they press into the damp dirt. There's a rock in my shoe pressing into my heel, but when I attempt to untie my laces to remove it, my fingers can't work the knot. I trudge on, rock digging into my heel, until I come to an obstacle called the Atlas Carry, where you hoist and carry a large, heavy stone weighing approximately seventy to ninety pounds (lower weight for women) around a set of flags. It's not a hard obstacle, and I get through it, but at the end, my right groin muscle seizes up and won't loosen.

We enter a long stretch of wooded trails for mile seven, and there is no sun. Soon I can no longer raise my right leg over fallen trees and instead use my hands to lift it over. I push up the sleeves of my soggy, long-sleeved race shirt so my skin can dry a little and notice my fore-arms are purple. My hydration vest is wrapped tight like a wet blanket around my chest, pulling heat out of my body. For a while, I'm walking alone in the woods, praying for the sun to come out. But by the time I reach the Bucket Brigade (where you carry heavy buckets of gravel through the woods), I'm shivering so hard that I can barely lift the load. Every step sends a surge of pain through my groin. I stop multiple times to rest and clearly look off-kilter, because when I finally complete the obstacle, a burly male volunteer asks if I'm OK. There are multiple UTVs lined up on the road, pulling people off the course to take them to a medical tent. A line of miserable-looking racers sits on the side of the road, wrapped in the silver Mylar thermal blankets you see handed out after a marathon. Looking at them, all I can think is, Someone is going to make me stop racing. I can't stop racing.

Then a crazy thought hits me: I can't get a DNF like that filmmaker I read about in *Outside* magazine.

"I . . . can't . . . stop . . . my . . . teeth . . . chattering . . . don't make me quit . . . will be OK." This is what I manage to spit out. The volunteer removes his coat and pulls me into an embrace so his body heat pushes into me. Then he wraps the coat around my shoulders. As he holds me, I can feel my jaw chattering against the razor stubble of this stranger's neck. How did I get here?

"Are you sure you want to keep going?" he asks me after a few minutes. I don't want to keep going. But I also don't want to show up at Epic and face Pete and the gang not having finished this race. Every well-worn pathway in my stubborn forty-seven-year-old Virgo brain pushes the only refrain it knows: "Don't be a quitter." So I nod my head yes and reluctantly let him go, regretting the decision the second I exit his warm chest back into the damp, cool air. He hands me one of the silver blankets to wrap around my shoulders while I trudge on.

As I start down the hill, my right leg is so locked up that I weave back and forth across the trail. "I'm sorry . . . sorry," I mumble repeatedly to racers trying to get around me. I try hard to focus on the stationary mile eight sign in the distance. Just make it to that sign, I tell myself. Then the sign starts to go fuzzy. I rub my eyes again, see spots. I stop and stand still. There are another five miles ahead of me. How am I going to make it five more miles like this? But how can I quit? I can't go on. I can't quit. The internal battle goes on as I stand still, getting colder and colder. Finally, my body makes the decision my mind can't. It turns around and carries me back up the hill to the warm-bodied volunteer, who wraps his arms around me again, hails one of the UTVs, and places me in it.

As we hurtle down the hill to the medical tent in the festival area, we pass the mile eight sign I never reached. I close my eyes at the sight of it, every rut in the road sending shoots of pain through my groin, head bouncing against the hard metal UTV frame, trying to hold on and not fall out the open side before we reach the bottom.

Racer #2325—DNF.

Did Not Finish.

There is no medal or finisher T-shirt when you end your race in the medical tent on a gray, cold day in April. No glorious fire jump or cheering crowd. No banana, can of Fitaid, or cheery volunteer to cut the timing chip off your wrist. Instead, there is hot broth in a Styrofoam cup, a big tube blowing warm air on you, and a lot of paperwork and questions: "Are you telling us that you decline to go to the hospital?" *Yes.* "Is there anyone here at the race with you?" *Yes.* "What is his number so we can call him?" *I can't remember.*

Erle has been my friend for twenty-six years, but I can no longer recall his phone number. Or Lisa's. The only number I can remember at the moment is my mother's in North Carolina. I call, leave her a garbled message saying I'm OK, but can she call Erle to come find me in the medical tent? And then I sit at the rock bottom of my "dip" and wait, still shivering, the misery of the moment and all its trifling insults clouding any perspective I might have. Right now, I'm unable to understand that what happened today is a gift. Right now, all I can see is short-term, myopic gloom, which leads to a childish loop of negative thoughts.

I did not finish.

I will not get to wear the Beast finisher T-shirt to Epic tomorrow.

Maybe I really am not cut out to be an obstacle course racer.

Before we leave, the medics tell me the Dunk Wall was eventually closed due to the low temperatures. I don't even care. The ride home is quiet. While Erle makes a fire, I take a shower and assuage a very worried Lisa by telephone. Then I curl up on the couch under a pile of blankets and watch Marvel movies while feeling decidedly unlike a superhero. Before I go to sleep, I take a pair of scissors and cut off a piece of the foil blanket from the Spartan volunteer and place it beside my bedside table in lieu of a finisher medal.

I do not dream.

The next morning, I doomscroll through my Instagram feed, gorging on posts from actual finishers of yesterday's race, including my pals at Epic. Keith made it through the Dunk Wall misery. Then I notice a new Instagram message from Cali, who has placed third in the women's Elite heat. It's from late last night.

"How did it go today? I was so happy to see you (even if briefly) before!"

It's a generous note. So I choke back my pride, congratulate her on her race, and tell her I'll send an email. Once I start writing, it's like therapy. I'm old enough to be Cali's mother, and yet here I am seeking her counsel about WTF just happened.

Soon a kind but matter-of-fact digital tome arrives back to me. "My first thought was that you were not the only one I know of who struggled with the cold and had to pull themselves/be pulled off of the mountain. I hope you're not beating yourself up about that. Even many pros I know still struggle to find the right combination of gear to wear in hopes of staving off getting too cold. The Dunk Wall can be the straw that breaks the camel's back too, especially with races like the Beast this past weekend, when it was followed immediately by a slower uphill climb that doesn't allow you to get moving fast for warmth and only takes you up to colder/windier conditions."

Then she launches right into instruction mode as she unpacks more racing mysteries. (Wear a windbreaker and put it into a plastic bag before you get wet. Those funky oven gloves she wore are called Bleggmits and are made from neoprene and come from Australia. Choose thin, long-sleeve compression shirts that shed water quickly.)

I'd reached out to Cali seeking empathy. But she's just given me a much greater gift.

Information. And clarity.

Because I'd done OK in the race up until I hit that Dunk Wall. My own lack of knowledge is what did me in. It's now, wallowing in my first big dip, that I realize getting better isn't just about getting stronger or faster. It's also about getting smarter.

I'd gotten this far with Pete and the Internet. But what would it take to go to the next level?

Cue the music, please, for the Canadian Crusher.

13

EDGES AND EQUALIZERS

The week following my DNF in New Jersey, my first order of business is to track down the cocktail-sipping Elite racer Faye Stenning, whose pre-race coolness I tried unsuccessfully to emulate in the Jacksonville, Florida, race. Faye runs an online training business called Grit Coaching. My new young mentor, Cali, knows her and thinks we'll hit it off. "Faye is amazing," she says. "She'll get you to another level."

I know a little bit about Faye. Recently she'd been tapped to appear on a new national obstacle course competition reality show called *Million Dollar Mile*, produced by NBA star LeBron James. She was one of Canada's superstar runners in her youth and is counted among the best female obstacle racers in the game. Hence her TV show nickname: the Canadian Crusher. Faye's business partner is a Canadian Olympic runner named Jessica O'Connell. The duo post photos of their students on Instagram, and I'm heartened to see that in addition to a lot of young, hyperfit racers, there's a handful who look my age. And their fees for personalized coaching are less than some gyms charge in the New York area. If I'm looking for information and edges to become a smarter, better racer, these two seem to check a lot of boxes.

On a gray Tuesday, while I'm wolfing down another lukewarm bowl of soup and salad from the Consumer Reports cafeteria, I shoot off a message to their online portal. The intake form asks for goals, so I write:

1. *to improve my obstacle proficiency and shore up my weaknesses to run the cleanest races I can*
2. *to hone my all-around fitness and work to avoid injury so I can be a functioning athlete for as many decades as possible*

Then I think for a moment and decide to add a more ambitious "stretch goal" (a term we use at work) even if it seems audacious given my twenty out of twenty-three placement in the Jacksonville race and my recent DNF.

3. *to one day place in the top 10 of my Age Group in the Spartan Races.*

A few hours later, I'm staring glassy-eyed at a big monitor projecting slide thirty-three of an eighty-plus-page presentation on our organization's marketplace challenges (clearly, we have quite a few) when my phone notifies me there's a new email message. I look at it surreptitiously under the conference room table. It's Jessica from the Grit team: "Sounds like you have some solid experience, and I love your specific goals—they are holistic and definitely priorities of our training programs. We would love to work with you!"

I book a call for two days later and then refocus on the monitor, where we've now advanced to slide thirty-four.

My soon-to-be new coaches' physical journeys are about as different from mine as you could imagine—as if we'd lived our lives in reverse. You know my story so far. Theirs is about the early discovery of a true gift, the gift of speed, and how that powerful revelation shaped them into adulthood for better and for worse. Both Canadian, they were born in 1989, the same year I graduated from high school. Early on, Faye was a wunderkind in Calgary and throughout the country, her talent having been identified when she was a young girl. "Before gym class started, we had to do one lap around the school, and I'd come back minutes ahead of the rest of the class," she recalls. "My teacher called my parents and said, 'You gotta get your daughter into track and cross-country. I've never seen anyone run like that before.' So, my mom put me in some track meets, and I remember driving up to these events, and I would just win, win, win."

The discovery of an early gift is both a privilege and a curse, because it must compete with all the other pastimes and temptations of growing up. Even as Faye was written up in the newspapers and dubbed one of the best runners in Canada, she felt the lure of a teenager's social life. "I was really conflicted, because I was a party girl," she says. One day her coach asked her to run with a new girl at school named Jessica, whose own running prowess was gaining attention. Faye balked at first. "I was like, I don't run with girls." But the coach insisted. And on a sunny spring afternoon, they met up for a forty-five-minute run near the river by their high school. Jess remembers being so nervous that she almost didn't show up. "Faye was a child phenom from the early days. People were like, 'Faye Stenning is the fastest person ever.' She was very popular, and I was very insecure."

They started running, and Faye recalls cockily chatting up Jess, thinking she'd fall behind quickly. But that didn't happen. "I kept pushing the pace, and she kept pushing the pace, and then we were running really fast and neither of us was breaking." They ran each other so hard that Jess says her coach wouldn't let her train the next day. "I knew at that point, there was another stud in town," Faye says.

In contrast to Faye, who was confident, brash, and deeply aware of her physical gifts, Jess was shy and recalls being "fairly useless at sports" as a kid (save a respectable stint at Irish dancing). She began to run track just to stay fit and because she idolized athletes. But she got faster. And then faster—clocking 1,500 meters (almost a mile) in

4:37. It wasn't long after their initial running date/duel that Jess beat Faye at a state meet in the 1,500-meter race. She hid from Faye, nervous about her reaction to this dethroning. But Faye found her, wrapped her in a hug, and said, "This is so exciting. You're good now." The friendship and competition, Faye recalls, helped stabilize Faye at a time when the pressure to be thin and fast had driven her to become bulimic. At the worst point, her five-foot, six-inch frame had shrunk to eighty-seven pounds. "I also was getting in with a bad group of people who were into alcohol and drugs. Being with Jess and her circle helped pull me out of that."

After college, their athletic roads diverged. On a whim, Faye competed in a Spartan race with a now-former boyfriend. She won the Elite women's heat by twenty minutes, she recalls, and went on to become one of the top female racers in the sport. Jess eventually qualified for and competed in the 2016 Rio Olympics. But they stayed in touch and eventually launched their online coaching business as a side hustle while training for their individual sports. Grit Coaching was a professional hedge in many ways. As they approached their thirties, they were acutely aware their days of physical glory were finite, even as Jess trained for the 2020 Olympics. "You give up a normal life and don't know it at first, because it's such a grind and you are so all in," says Jess. "If the most incredible job in the world came up, or if I wanted to start a family, then all of a sudden the benefits of being a professional runner become challenges—the cons outweigh the pros."

And so, while they were looking at probably the tail end of their "best" athletic performance days, I was just getting started. Before our first call, Jess tells me, she googled me to see what they were dealing with. "I thought, this is a Boss Woman, and that the thing about high performance is that you are a high performer. You don't half-ass a sport if you are a high-performance person. And I knew you were going to be very analytical and motivated, so I would treat you differently than someone who needs more motivation."

Understanding my fundamental wiring and attributes would

allow them to tailor my training so I could compete more strategically. "You kept saying to us in the beginning, 'I'm not an athlete,'" Faye says. "But at the same time, you came across as someone who was driven, not afraid of doing the work and was type A and would stick to a plan. That's better than having someone who's like, 'Oh, I played Division I softball,' but you're having to pull teeth to get their training done."

As it turns out, attributes such as discipline, resilience, openmindedness, and humor sometimes can be even better indicators than skill of whether we succeed or stumble in an endeavor. At least, that's the conclusion of a former Navy SEAL and officer named Rich Diviney, who wrote a book called *The Attributes: 25 Hidden Drivers of Optimal Performance*. He arrived at this notion based on his experience training candidates for a premier special-operations unit. Anytime we achieve something new or hard and then think, "I didn't know I had it in me," Diviney suggests that's our dormant attributes rising to the surface.

In the months and years to come, I often felt Jess and Faye had their hands on a secret knob controlling my attributes. And they knew when to turn up the heat or lower things to a simmer to get the best outcome. What surprised me most was that my age was simply another data point. From the moment we first spoke, neither of them would let me use it as an excuse or a limitation for my performance. (And, boy, there were times I tried.) And that shift in mindset became one of the first edges they gave me.

Our first goal is a June half-marathon Beast race in Ohio to get the New Jersey DNF out of my system. This way I'll know I can psychologically and physically handle that distance. Jess and Faye talk me out of racing competitively in my age group and into running once again in the more relaxed Open category. Instead of immediately gunning for speed or lifting heavy weights, they structure my workouts to be more strategic by laying down a foundation that will allow me to tolerate more intensity and speed in subsequent months. It's back to the "plateau" phase of my mastery journey, but I trust them. A week mapped out includes two classes with Pete, a run/core day, a strength/grip day, a run/glute/hip day, an off day, and a long run day.

Part of this reset is the, at first, *boring* exercises to activate and strengthen my glutes, as well as mobility and stability work for my ankles, shoulders, and hips. Then there's rolling my feet with a nubby little rubber ball to release tightness and stretching my big toe against a wall.

"Nonoptional," Jess says firmly when I protest, telling her these exercises seem kind of wimpy next to pull-ups and bucket carries. "At least they are if you don't want to get hurt. Trust us, this will make you a more durable racer."

At her suggestion, I buy a ten-dollar set of resistance minibands, and before many workouts, I pull them around my knees and ankles for toe taps or weird movements called "monster walks" that make Lisa laugh each time I amble like some prehistoric reptilian creature across our living room. This is just one of many small exercises designed to stabilize my movement patterns and improve my range of motion. It's tedious stuff, but because it's in my program and because I am so deeply married to box checking, I never skip the exercises. So it is that this small acquiescence to monotony becomes a key edge. I will go for years without a serious strain or avoidable injury in racing—and when I finally do get a small tear in my foot, it is likely due to slacking off on using that nubby little rubber ball. Soon, the real-life benefits of being "durable" will become clear. Hip stability and balance help me stand on one leg and pull a sock onto the other foot without needing to sit. My glute strength allows me to rise to a standing position from sitting on the floor without using my hands or knees for leverage. I can reach behind me in the car to grab my bag without taking off my seatbelt and turning around, thanks to my shoulder's range of motion.

Journalist Jeff Bercovici spent three years interviewing professional and elite athletes, including Super Bowl champions, big-wave surfers, and Olympic medalists, as well as coaches, geneticists, sports psychologists, and doctors. His goal: to understand how some athletes seem to defy the limits of physical aging. In his book *Play On: The New Science of Elite Performance at Any Age,* he talks about their secrets. I reached out to Bercovici and asked him, what was the number one thing he believed the rest of us mere mortals could learn from the pros?

"So, I think by far the biggest enemy we all have is injuries," he explained by phone from California, where he was working as business editor for the *Los Angeles Times.* "And the secret to being able to compete fully is to avoid injuries. Especially when you are older, you feel like you want to just push through something so badly, because you feel like your time is limited. There is something about the way elite athletes take care of their bodies that we can all learn from. They treat it like a piece of equipment that can always be optimized."

Optimizing my hydration and fueling is another edge Jess and Faye begin to school me on. Plain water won't cut it, Jess tells me. I need electrolytes to replenish my sodium, magnesium, and potassium (she uses a brand of tablets called Nuun, which I buy and still use). They instruct me to hydrate well in the week prior to the race—not just the day before, as I've been doing. When I ask them about various supplements people post about on social media—beet powder for endurance or pickle juice for muscle cramping—they caution me never to experiment with a new food, drink, or supplement on race day or risk stomach issues. Clearly, this is a problem for many racers, judging by the lines at the Spartan venue porta potties, so I take them at their word.

These edges—or equalizers, as I come to think of them—make me feel for the first time that my age could work to my advantage while learning something new and hard. After all, one of my key equalizers was that I already knew how to learn. I'd been learning for a long time. Fundamentally, my job as a journalist was to research things and learn. I *liked* to learn. In middle age, any hubris about relying on a body in its prime to power through and perform miracles—well, that was long gone, if indeed it ever existed for me. I needed intel.

Intel on gear, clothing, weather, hydration, food, sleep, terrain, could all help. Even the order of the obstacles in races and how those obstacles were positioned on the course might matter. I sign up for a Spartan workshop where we spend the day walking a course and getting tips on how to be a better racer. Choose the lane of the monkey bars with the most sunlight so they'll be drier, the instructor tells us. Before jumping on, take a moment to study the Z-Wall—that series of walls where you move horizontally across using wooden blocks for your feet and hands. Which way is it positioned and leaning on a hill? Pick the wall where gravity works in your favor. Methodically, I study and file all this info in memory, believing that ultimately, all the little edges might add up to something.

"When you're older, you can see the bigger picture more than you could when you were seventeen," says Alex Hutchinson, the author of *Endure*. "A word that pops to mind is 'patience.' It's really easy to get excited about big goals, but to actually achieve them requires patience to take care of details, patience to stay on track when obstacles arise. Older people are more patient."

On my drive to the Ohio race, Faye and Jess give me last-minute encouragement over the phone. My longest training run so far has been nine miles, but Jess assures me that the energy and excitement of the competition will get me through the final three to four. And she's right. Throughout the morning, my body carries me steadily through the woods and over the walls without protest. When we climb hills with the heavy sandbags, I feel my glutes kicking in, thanks to the tedium of those miniband activation exercises. I hit my spear throw, which I've been practicing over and over in our backyard. When I see the marker sign for mile eight, the one I never reached in New Jersey, I trot across the road to pat it with my hand.

And sure enough, as the end nears, I speed up and start passing people.

The last half mile is a gauntlet of obstacles, including the Tyrolean Traverse, where, despite having nailed it my first time in the New Jersey race, I now slip off at the last minute before the bell. I look for the burpee pit and can't find it. Maybe they got rid of burpees for this obstacle? I finish the race and jump over the fire, and they hang the finisher medal on my neck. I'm elated at finishing, but the lack of burpees at the failed rope traverse is nagging at me. I track down a Spartan Race official and ask him why there aren't burpees required there.

"There are," he says, pointing to the burpee pit on other side of the obstacle from where I had landed when I fell off. Clearly, I just hadn't looked hard enough. My heart sinks, and my head drops. I know it doesn't matter—this is an Open race, where nobody is counting your burpees and I'm not competing for the podium—but it feels like I cheated somehow.

He's still standing nearby when I put down my banana and start doing thirty burpees in the festival area.

"You're crazy," he tells me as I press my already filthy face into the dirt, arms shaking. *Eight.*

"Yes," I grunt, spitting out a blade of grass in the direction of his feet as I speak. *Eleven.* "I . . . think . . . maybe so." *Thirteen.*

Now that I've checked a half-marathon-length Beast race off my list, my new coaches agree I can return to more competitive racing in my age group. But they want me to start small, with a 5K Sprint in the woods of Tuxedo, New York. Pete and the gang are coming, so I plan to run competitively in my age group in the morning and then do a second loop with them in the Open competition later that afternoon—a feat I thought Pete was crazy to do during my first race at Citi Field. Erle, who's been taking a few classes at Epic after work to keep me company since my melanoma diagnosis, also decides to run in his age group.

In the days leading up to the race, both Faye and Pete separately give me more tips on monkey-bar technique. I have yet to complete the obstacle in a race, despite the little redhead's schooling of me. Pete implores me not to wear gloves. "Trust me," he says. "Bare hands are better." Faye adds: "Before you get on the bars, find a tree or dry grass to wipe your hands on."

Erle is seven years older than I am, so I hit the course fifteen minutes before him in the 45–49 age group. He's in good shape and tells me, "I'll try and catch up with you." I still don't think of myself as athletically competitive, but from the moment I cross that starting line, all I can think is "I can't let Erle catch me." When I reach the monkey bars, I find the sunniest lane and nearly jump right on after looking over my shoulder for my friend. Then I remember Faye's and Pete's counsel. I step off the bench, take off my gloves, and run over to a tree to wipe my hands.

When I grip the first bar, I swing my hips hard and reach out for the second bar with my left hand. Then I pause, swing my hips back again, and let go with my right hand to move forward. And somehow my hands both stick. This happens again, and then again, and I try not to think about the fact that the bell is getting closer and closer, until suddenly I'm at the opposite end and the bell is in my face, and *clank*, I smack it and drop.

Oh my God. I completed the monkey bars.

French Fry, where are you now?

For the rest of the race, it's as if there's a parrot lodged in my skull—*Oh my God. I completed the monkey bars.* When I jump over the fire at the end, I'm still looking over my shoulder for Erle. He's not too far behind me, which is impressive. We accept our finisher medals, stretch for a while, and eventually go check our race stats. I refresh the screen twice to make sure I'm not mistaken. It says I placed eighth out of sixteen. I've only been working with Faye and Jess for six weeks, and already I've met my stretch goal of a top-ten Age Group placement. Granted, there were only sixteen people my age in this race, and it was a short distance. But I was in the middle of the pack, not at the end. And I didn't fail a single obstacle.

Maybe it was a fluke.

What if it was a fluke?

Oh my God. I completed the monkey bars.

A few days later, an email lands in my inbox from Spartan. The subject line says: "You qualified." I click open the message.

"Congratulations, Gwendolyn! You qualified for the 2019 Spartan North American Championship on August 24 in West Virginia, USA." The message includes a password for me to enter a gated heat in the Age Group division for the race, which is a half-marathon Beast. I call Erle, baffled, thinking the email might be a mistake while hoping that it might be real. "Yeah, I got the same email," he says. He'd finished ninth in his own age group. "It's real. I looked online. It's because we finished in the top ten of that race."

He pauses, reads my mind, and laughs. "No way. I'll go with you to West Virginia if you want, but I'm not running thirteen miles."

August 24 is only two months away. Faye and Jess double down with my program, carefully crafting a path that will get me through the course in West Virginia, which Faye says is no cakewalk. My long runs gradually increase to between ninety minutes and two hours, followed by intense sets of core work, including planks and maneuvers that put me in strange positions like the bird dog, where I'm on hands and knees and extending my leg and opposite arm. I splurge on a sixty-five-dollar pair of thirty-pound kettlebells so I can walk short distances with them. (It's called "farmer's carry.") And then there are these crazy hip taps they want me to do off the Amazon pull-up bar I bought with that gift certificate from my boss. With this move, I hang with both hands, then let go with one of them, tap my hip, regrip the bar, and then do it on the other side. And more mobility work, more stretching, more glute activation.

As I get better at something hard and once seemingly out of reach, the sense of empowerment permeates the rest of my world. For the first time in my adult life, work is no longer the first and last thing on my mind when I awake and go to sleep. After I close my eyes at night, I replay different foot techniques of rope climbing in my mind instead of chewing on the annoying thing my colleague said in a meeting. I make my points to co-workers with increasing confidence, including that guy who always interrupts. (Dude, I can climb a seventeen-foot rope!) My decision-making sharpens; I answer emails when they land in my inbox and don't punt until later. Maybe it's a byproduct of making quick choices like where to place my foot on the rocks while running. Or maybe, with my training, I simply don't have as much time to waste.

My body is changing too. T-shirts once loose in my shoulders no longer fit comfortably. At night I sleep so hard, I barely wake up to use the bathroom. The baby calluses stop peeling off and become permanent grown-up calluses. I begin to track my resting heart rate at night with my watch and note that it has dropped to a low of around forty-nine beats per minute from the high fifties. My physical energy levels are the most robust I can remember since my early twenties. The long stints of sitting around conference tables during meetings at work make my body increasingly restless. I start standing behind my chair, trying to ignore the perplexed looks from our chief financial officer. Soon, I notice, our chief digital officer stands up too. And then our head of testing as well.

One day, I ask Lisa to look at a photo of me swinging across the red Multi-Rig rings during a race that I've uploaded onto Facebook.

"Does my hydration vest look like a pistol holster?" I ask her.

"What are you talking about?" she says, squinting at the screen. "Pistol holster?"

I point to a comment where a former *Wall Street Journal* colleague has written, "Nice guns!" She squeezes my bicep, laughing. "He's talking about your arms."

* * *

The real test of "was the New York race a fluke" comes in late July when I fly home to North Carolina for back-to-back races in Black Mountain, near Asheville. My parents drive up from the coast to cheer me on for the first day's event, which is a 10K Spartan Super. It's by far my favorite Spartan Race venue yet, with a mix of elevation and flat runs amid trees fat from the summer sun.

I comfortably place seventh in my age group out of twenty-three contenders.

The next morning, I return alone for a shorter 5K competition and take fifth out of fifteen, gunning it hard until the very end. Afterward, I'm sitting on the ground trying to get the mud out of my ears and nose when a kind-looking young man with a black beard approaches me. I'd met him earlier that morning, before the race started, and we were both huddled near the fire jump obstacle at the finish line trying to stay warm. His name is Cory Edwards, and he's a registered nurse with a master's degree working in a cardiac lab in Chillicothe, Ohio. Eight years younger than I am, he's broad-shouldered and super muscular. We'd bonded over a common affinity for pickup trucks, Texas Pete hot sauce, and Waffle House.

"Hey," he says with a grin, dropping down to sit next to me on the ground with his gear. "How'd you do?"

"Eh," I tell him. "I'm sitting here licking my wounds. I got fifth. Would have done better but I fell off the Multi-Rig at the last minute." I look at him for a moment. He's got mud all over his beard. "You want a face wipe?"

He laughs and reaches out his hand. "Sure, thanks." Then, while carefully wiping off his chin, he says slowly, matter-of-factly, "I'd say fifth is pretty good if you ask me."

We chat a little more and then do the modern-day version of keeping in touch, which is to start following each other on Instagram. Like me, Cory was small growing up and so didn't play competitive sports; like me, he's filling a void inside himself with OCR. He becomes my first official race friend—someone I'll see every few months or so at different Spartan venues while staying connected in between through thumbs-ups, messages, and comments on social media. Much like regular patrons of a pub, our physical world together will begin and end at these races. Our sense of each other will be limited to the race tights and hats we wear, our speed or lack thereof on any given day. And yet, over time, a sense of closeness will develop, a familiarity born of deeply needing this "third place" that isn't home and isn't work to make us whole.

Driving back to the hotel, I think about what Cory said about fifth place. He's right. Five months ago in Jacksonville, Florida, I finished almost last in a race. My stretch goal when I signed up for coaching with Faye and Jess was to one day place in the top ten for my age group. Today's race makes three top-ten finishes now, and I'm working my way closer to the front of the pack. That can't be a fluke. All these little edges and equalizers I've picked up are working.

I'm off the plateau and back on a rise.

The Obstacle: Spear Throw
(take nothing for granted)

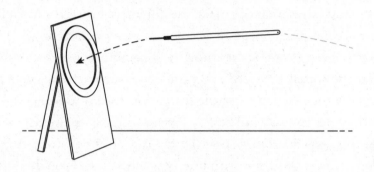

One of the most exciting, if polarizing, obstacles in Spartan races is the Spear Throw.

Competitors get one shot. Standing from roughly twenty-five feet away, each racer hurls a wooden pole with a metal tip at a rectangular target roughly the size of a big hay bale. The spear needs to stick in the target without falling out to count as successful. It's the single most failed obstacle of all time, according to Spartan. And watching racers make their attempts, it's easy to see why.

Some people attempt to throw their spear like a baseball, and it arcs up and over the target or falls short. Others toss downward, merely stabbing the dirt in front of them. Many hurl the spear across their bodies instead of straight ahead, and it sails past one side of the target. Occasionally you'll see someone grab a spear with two hands and loft it underhanded into the air. (To be fair, I saw that work once. Anyone can have a lucky day.)

A more successful technique is to stand with your nonthrowing hand outstretched and aimed at the target, legs slightly apart. You then lean back, push through your rear leg, and throw forward so the hand holding your spear tracks past your ear. Eyes should be always on the target.

Some racers love the Spear Throw. But others hate it. Because even on a day when everything else is clicking and you're feeling fast and strong, missing your target is a possibility. For Elite and Age Group racers, that can make the difference between a first-place and a second-place finish, or it can mean no podium finish at all. ("I missed my $*%@! spear throw" is a common post-race refrain/explanation/excuse.) Speed and pure power aren't the key determinants for success. This obstacle forces you to slow down, get your breath under control, and be very precise with your movements.

In this way, Spartan's Spear Throw is a great equalizer. Almost anyone can get good at it with proper practice. But if you don't take it seriously, it can ruin an otherwise great race. It's a reminder to take nothing for granted. And for a late-in-life athlete trying to merge her old world with a new one, this made the Spear Throw perhaps the most important obstacle of them all to master.

14

DON'T FORGET
THE PREVIOUS VERSE

The moment the FedEx truck pulled into our driveway, I knew I'd messed up.

When you plunge headfirst into something new, there's an inevitable ripple effect on others, be they spouses, partners, friends, or parents. And by middle age, we've established a certain dynamic in our relationships, a set of patterns each participant knows and expects from the other. When one person deviates wildly from those patterns, it can shift or even upend that dynamic. Inevitably, there will come a moment of reconciliation of "what's new" with "what exists."

Here's one of the best pieces of relationship advice I can give. If you decide to buy a giant 146-pound steel pull-up station to install in your garage, it's probably best to check first with the other people living in the house to see how *they* feel about it.

Because at our house, Lisa didn't see that one coming. Notably, because while plunging down this new racing rabbit hole, I neglected to tell her. But in a way, the pull-up bar was just a metaphor. In fact, she never saw my obsession with obstacle course racing coming to begin with. She'd been a natural athlete since her youth, first picked by the boys for the kickball team, strong and agile enough to throw a baseball with precision, and always loaded with ribbons from Olympic Day at her summer camps. Being pretty and athletic was a powerful combination even at an early age; in fourth grade, little boys had competed for her affection, calling at night and walking around the classroom saying, "I love Lisa." We'd laughed when a male friend from her elementary school had reached out on Facebook after she'd turned fifty, writing, "I remember in third grade that you beat me in arm wrestling." Hard physical things didn't unnerve her. She believed in her body and had trusted her life with that sensibility at age twenty-nine, when she was diagnosed with breast cancer and underwent a then cutting-edge nine-hour surgery in which the surgeons removed tissue from her abdomen to reconstruct her right breast after a mastectomy. Her mantra, "I'm young, I'm strong, I can beat this," was the refrain lifting her from a paralyzing haze of biopsies, bone scans, chemotherapy, and lymph node dissections.

That I would wake up after a dinner party unsettled by a little girl's innocent ramblings, so dubious about and still so detached from my own physical strength in my midforties, and then go google "What are the hardest things you can do?"—it was baffling, she would eventually confide. And it was also unsettling. She assumed after the first Citi Field race that I'd have scratched whatever itch was vexing me and check obstacle course racing off my list. She'd cut together a short video from all the pictures she took at the race to commemorate the event, and then assumed everything would go back to normal. When that didn't happen, questions naturally surfaced. "The intensity of what you were doing snuck up on me," she recalls. "It's one thing to be athletic and another thing to put your body through the brutality of these races and to go to this level of extreme fitness. Sometimes I thought, 'Is she crazy?' But then, I also couldn't help but wonder, was there something missing in our relationship?"

There wasn't, and I was fortunate enough to know this clearly and without reservation. But there was something missing in me, this hole to fill from my youth, and now this growing fear of leaving the earth that had begun to consume me. Yet, as I was filling that emptiness week after week, month after month out on the racecourse, I never communicated why I was doing this to the most important person in my life. Partly, this was because I didn't fully understand all the drivers of my motivation at the time. But partly, if I'm honest, it was because I didn't want her—or anyone, for that matter—to ask me to stop. I knew that to most people obstacle course racing seemed insane—the intensity and occasional ferocity of it. "Why did you choose this sport over tennis or swimming or just trying to run a marathon?" they inevitably asked.

Always, I sort of hemmed and hawed and deflected. Because I couldn't yet articulate that it was precisely the sharp edges of the sport that were protecting me from the demons of time I felt closing in, with their incessant whispers . . . *It's no use—eventually you will go.* That out on the racecourse, rolling across rocks, briars, and roots, under a stretch of barbed wire, those demons couldn't catch me. To feel that strong, to be that free of worry, to be in that much control of my body whether for an hour or four hours, it was like stopping time. And that elixir was so powerful that, selfishly, it terrified me to think of having to give it up because it might not seem normal for my age or was inconvenient or disruptive to some existing life pattern.

So I pushed ahead, never processed my feelings out loud, and imagined maybe I could make this all happen without much interference in the existing fabric of my life. But of course, that was blind. My training consumed my weekends and off-hours. At night, I'd be too tired to finish a movie. Our vacation locations, increasingly, would come to be planned around race venues, some admittedly more desirable than others: Jacksonville, Florida; Palmerton, Pennsylvania; San Luis Obispo, California; Glen Jean, West Virginia; Lake Tahoe, California. I was standing up during meetings at work and climbing the back stairwell up to the Consumer Reports roof to do push-ups; of course, my colleagues noticed. The photos I shared with my parents featured me scrambling through mud pits, always to the horror of my well-kempt mother. My Instagram feed was filled with new racing friends Lisa hadn't met. There was a spear throw stand

and a climbing rope in our backyard. And my body was changing, so I didn't even look the same.

Going back to our musical metaphor about midlife for a moment, the bridge of a song isn't meant to stand on its own. It's part of a larger story. The bridge needs what's come before it to have context and meaning and to set the stage for what comes after. It's true that some people may feel their previous verses never felt or sounded right. And indeed, it sometimes seemed as if more people our age were getting divorced than staying together—many of them talking about being lost, needing someone new to make them feel found, and wanting their next chapters to take them in a vastly different direction.

I understood this and supported them. But it wasn't how I felt—or what I wanted. If I was lucky, the verse after this bridge would include the same cast of characters as the previous verses. And yet, I was mucking it up a bit by not communicating that more clearly.

But you really can't pretend nothing has changed when an enormous steel pull-up bar gets unloaded into your driveway.

Lisa was unlocking her car and about to drive to the train station when the FedEx truck pulled up and started unloading boxes, in a procession that suggested a whole set of new living room furniture had arrived. Which, now that I think about it, probably would have been preferable, since ours was well-worn from years of Dolly rubbing against it. I ran outside, excited. But one look at Lisa's face made me remember that in my chase for edges and equalizers, I'd somehow neglected to mention this purchase. The logic seemed clear at the time. I'd been making do with the small makeshift bar that I would attach to our guest-bathroom doorframe. But I always had to tuck up my knees when using it. If there was a real pull-up bar in the garage, I could improve more quickly, and hang attachments like ropes and balls from it to strengthen my grip.

However, I'm not sure I'd looked so carefully at the dimensions, which added up to a footprint of four feet by five and a half feet and a towering height of almost eight feet.

"Um, I forgot to tell you," I stammered in answer to the obvious question: *What is this?* "I ordered a pull-up bar for the garage."

Lisa just kept looking at me.

"I think you'll like it," I attempted, before adding, weakly, "Maybe hanging on it will be good for your back?"

We said our goodbyes for the day, but I knew I'd messed up. I also knew that I hadn't necessarily just forgotten to mention this purchase. Once again, I'd kept quiet because I didn't want to risk her asking me to *not* make the purchase. Not that she'd ever given me any indication that she would. But my own insecurities about what I was attempting were still so deep-seated that I was trying to reach my end goal, whatever that might be, without attracting much attention and then would say: "OK, done. See, isn't this great?" Like I said before, awareness of your own addictions and weaknesses is critical to fixing them. And here I was again, operating under the false sense that I was in control and could ultimately make everything with this adventure of mine OK, if everybody just gave me enough time.

"We are everything that ever happened to us."

These words were spoken to me many years later during some interviews with external experts we were conducting for a new project at work. They came from a Florida relationship therapist and licensed mental health counselor named Tracey Johnson. Several colleagues and I were interviewing Johnson about trust, and I could see how this one statement impacted everyone on the call, regardless of their age. Our ultimate professional interest was in why people do or don't trust the news, but we were digging deeper to understand how trust manifests itself across experiences, including our interactions with other individuals. Johnson was stressing how much past experiences shape our future and how we behave in relationships. Identifying what those past experiences are and talking about them is critical to preventing conflict or misunderstanding. "The more honest discussions people can have about where they came from, the better."

The problem was, I wasn't having honest discussions with anyone who really mattered to me. That included my parents. It doesn't matter how old you are; you still can crave approval from your mom and dad. For them, I sensed that the metamorphosis of this skinny, unathletic little girl they'd raised seemed bizarre in its timing. Like, really, *now*? Now, when you're well out of your physical prime and technically old enough to be a grandparent? *Now* is when you decide to start scaling eight-foot walls and putting yourself at risk for hypothermia?

Their benchmarks of my athletic accomplishments still included the one-point basketball game from junior high, the worried calls from our head of physical education about my low body weight and lack of athletic aptitude, the soccer game championship in high school where we were so far ahead that Coach Yohman, guaranteed a victory, allowed me off the bench. My moment of glory ended abruptly after I darted onto the field, only to immediately hear the referee halt the game with a fierce blow of his whistle. I'd been warming the bench decked out in my teenage jewelry, assuming that I wouldn't see any playing time. Thus, gold necklace, little hoop earrings, and a matching bracelet all accompanied a very excited me into the action, causing the violation. And my tired teammates had to wait for their victory while I stripped all the bling off—just to jog back and forth for another sixty seconds, far away from the ball, before the clock ran out. (My mother, who doesn't go to the grocery store without jewelry and makeup, does admit to thinking, "That's my girl.")

As for Erle, for the twenty-six years we'd been friends, our athletic adventures had mostly been intertwined. Living in Pittsburgh and working as reporters in *The Wall Street Journal* bureau there, we'd swim together on weekends and spend the last part of the workout treading water before eating tacos and watching *Party of Five* on Fox. (We even convinced an editor at *WSJ* to let us write a story about *Party of Five*'s devoted fan base when the network was considering canceling the series. It got one more year.) Together we tried to up our physical game after we both moved to work in New York City in the mid-1990s, our paths generally intertwined like siblings. When

I joined the gym across the street at the World Trade Center towers, Erle did too. When Erle got to know the chiseled, tough-talking financial journalist Charlie Gasparino, who worked out there, I did as well.

To give you a forty-five-character-count sense of Charlie, his X (formerly Twitter) bio, as I write this, reads: "God, Country, Pullups and Vodka in that order." Out of the corners of our eyes in the gym, Erle and I both watched Charlie, who then wrote for *The Wall Street Journal* but would go on to be a well-known personality on the Fox Business channel, as he moved with confidence and a deserved swagger through the free weights and machines. One day, an investment banker type made the unfortunate move of jumping in on the lat pull-down machine Charlie was already using but not setting the weights back to Charlie's heavier load. It was poor gym etiquette, but Charlie nicely asked him to reset the machine. The investment banker, who must have stupidly assumed that a thick paycheck trumped a thick bicep in this setting, gave him some lip to the effect of "How about you do it yourself?"

Charlie looked at him for a moment. Then he stepped closer, put his hand on the lat pulldown bar, and suggested that if the banker didn't do the right thing, Charlie might do something to him with the bar that he would never forget.

That Erle and I never forgot this tale of gym bravado underscores the fact that neither of us possessed any ourselves. Like me, he'd been a skinny kid who was sometimes teased for his own slow physical development. He possessed more natural agility than I did and played on the basketball team for a few years in high school. But surviving unscathed as a super-thin boy was hard anywhere in the 1970s and '80s, and particularly in the Deep South of Vidalia, Georgia, where football was the king of sports and bestowed a powerful social pecking order on males. And so, he too was dogged by demons about his physical self. When he took up boxing, I also followed him there—literally—running behind him past stockbrokers and bankers in the early-morning light to a small gym nestled in the bowels of

Wall Street, where we'd train before work. Our coach, a seasoned boxer named Tony Canarozzi, had generally already knocked out sixteen rounds of work on a heavy bag before we even arrived. For months, Tony put us through the paces, teaching us to punch and eventually spar wearing mouthpieces and headgear; my arms would be so tired afterward that I could barely shampoo my hair. With Tony, we both tasted a glimpse of the strength we ached for. The first time Tony hit me, I instinctively hit back—so hard his eyes widened. And there was something about it that made me feel terribly alive.

We also worked out some Saturdays with Tony at the historic Gleason's Gym, where Muhammad Ali and Jake LaMotta threw jabs and hooks. Then came my first white-collar fight, against a girl named Ruth. She'd fought seven times before in amateur competitions, which Tony neglected to mention until right before I stepped in the ring. I survived three rounds and landed a few punches, but Ruth struck me so hard in the eye and forehead that I couldn't wear a baseball cap for two weeks. After that, the fear of getting hit hard enough that my brain wouldn't work began to scare me more than not being tough. And so I looked elsewhere for whatever salvation I was seeking. Erle kept it up a while longer, but eventually he too stopped. But we moved on to new adventures together, including submitting applications to the FBI to become special agents. This was prior to the 9/11 terrorist attacks, but I had vague, dreamy ideas about working in counterterrorism. And while we passed a difficult written exam that had meant weeks of studying algebra after work, we eventually got put on a waitlist, because the agency wanted candidates with advanced degrees, and our bachelor's degrees in journalism apparently didn't cut it.

All of which is to say that for roughly half my life, Erle had been the person I'd been attempting challenging things with, including a polar bear plunge into the Atlantic Ocean one frigid February morning. So when I started racing, it seemed only natural to assume we'd do it together. And yet, as the months crept by, I realized this wasn't a road I wanted to travel with someone else, even my best friend.

Obstacle course racing felt like my secret, albeit one I shared with thousands of strangers. The solitary nature of racing, of being on a course where nobody cared who I was outside of that venue, was part of what drew me to the sport. It made me feel like finally I could depend on the body I'd been born in, and that body alone. Racing with Erle was fun, but the more serious I grew, the more I wanted to go at my own pace and not feel like I was following my metaphorical older brother into the ocean or the boxing ring or over an obstacle racing wall. Or that he'd be there to help me if I needed it.

When I told him this, we were standing outside of a conference hall waiting to attend a panel on the future of audio and podcasting. It was only the second time in our long friendship that I recall feeling awkward around him. The other was a night in the mid-1990s in Pittsburgh when we'd first started hanging out as fellow *Wall Street Journal* reporters and he asked if I'd ever considered us being more than friends. His face had gone white to the degree that I'd asked him if he was anemic right before he got his question out.

The truth was, I had considered it. Back then, I'd dated mostly men and had just recently ended my first relationship with a woman, a beautiful, confident artist I'd met in college. Where things were going to end up for me on the romantic front, I still was unsure. But instinctively, Erle felt like family to me, a sibling I might have wanted but never had. Dating would have changed our dynamic irrevocably. And in what I now believe was the greatest stroke of maturity of my twenties, I opted not to screw things up. Instead, I fumbled around for the right words to explain what I was feeling without hurting this person I was coming to care so much about. I ended up rambling on about how I was flattered but just wanted to focus on work, hoping the underlying answer was clear, knowing it probably was not.

Now, so many decades later, that strained moment a distant memory in our shared rearview mirror, I attempted to explain my desire to race alone. This was right at a turning point in my training, when I was starting to notably improve. He'd been, understandably, eager to join me on the Spartan ride and had started sending links to training tips and Instagram posts of racers and talking about what future competitions we might run together. Suddenly, I felt pressure. Doing a couple of races together was one thing. But now I felt like my secret journey was getting co-opted. Plus, what if he suddenly became a lot better than I was? Would I get demoralized and quit? It was incredibly insecure of me to think this. But I wasn't confident enough yet in what I was doing or my own abilities for this not to be a possibility. None of the adventures we'd had together meant anything close to what obstacle course racing already meant to me. I couldn't imagine not having this experience, and I wasn't sure I could share it with someone else without it changing. As I attempted to voice this highly unorganized mash-up of emotions, we were rushing to get back into the podcast conference, and my delivery was once more, as it had been so many years ago, a flood of imperfect words. To his credit, whatever disappointment he might have felt he simply hid. "I just want you to be happy," he said. You can't ask for more than that from a friend. And so, again, we moved on.

We don't get do-overs, but if I got one, I'd try to do a better job of what Tracey Johnson recommends by identifying sooner that my need for obstacle racing was a reaction to everything that had happened to me. My physical insecurity. The fear of having no control over how I'll leave the earth. And I'd try to explain it clearly to everyone I loved. My silence was a risky gamble. Had my family and friends been different people, they could have made incorrect assumptions— that I was seeking a new life, a new set of friends, a verse to my song that didn't include them. And those assumptions might have led to a series of reactions and repercussions we'd all have regretted. "Trust is not so hard to build, but once you lose it, it's almost impossible to get back," Johnson told us during that initial interview. "People are afraid to tell each other how they are feeling. They are afraid of how others are going to react. But if you are thinking something, you need to say it."

The pull-up bar, which still stands in the garage thanks to Lisa's generosity, remains a constant reminder of that risk. We never talked about the bar again, I'm embarrassed to say, until years later when I started to write this book. She came home from work the day it arrived, we made dinner and moved on. It was up to me to explain, and I knew she was waiting. But I never did.

"That pull-up bar, it just showed up," she later told me. "A lot of times you do stuff and are so quiet about it. I had no idea you had googled 'What is the hardest thing you could do?' I didn't under-stand that at the time. But I wanted to understand."

Fortunately, those around me also began signaling back to me what *they* needed in return for their implicit acceptance of my head-over-heels obsession with this sport. A vacation that didn't include a Spartan race. A promise to my mother to not take unnecessary risks on a course and to clean the mud out of my ears. Pictures on Insta-gram of my real family, not just my race family. A hike, a weight-lifting session, or, occasionally, a race with my friend. All of it truly so easy, none of it close to "Stop doing this."

And then something unexpected happened. The tables got flipped on me.

Perhaps it's impossible to watch someone you care about go through a metamorphosis without also examining your own path. Perhaps they were destined to test their own limits. Regardless, the people around me began changing too.

Lisa, for her part, took up acting and voiceover training. At first, it might not have seemed such a stretch from her current on-air work as a journalist. But in truth, all of it—talking on camera to millions of viewers, reciting lines before a crowd—was the evolution of a woman who as a little girl had felt utterly unconfident with her ver-bal self, even as she physically could hurl a dodgeball or baseball with the best of the little boys. Her father, a successful advertising writer and director, held the mic literally and figuratively in her household. He directed commercials with celebrities including Ringo Starr,

Loretta Lynn, and Michael Douglas. It was her dad's stories that often dominated family gatherings. His jokes, his ideas, his opinions, seeped into Lisa's. She revered him and sought his counsel on every career move. "There goes Alan and Little Alan," a family friend once joked when she saw Lisa commuting to work with her father.

"He was the fastest brain in the room, the one who made everybody laugh" is how Lisa remembers her dad when she was growing up. Photos of him with his celebrity clients and framed gold records covered walls of her parents' home and later his room in the assisted-living facility where he resided for a while poststroke. "I, on the other hand, was always insecure about what to say and how to say the right thing," she says. "My dad spent hours coaching me about my confidence, trying to build me up, but I was always so worried I'd say the wrong thing or that I wouldn't be as clever as he would be."

Then came the morning in the early nineties with Regis Philbin and Kathie Lee Gifford. Lisa was working as an editor for *Us* magazine and was invited on Philbin and Gifford's ABC talk show to discuss the publication's story "The 10 Sexiest Bachelors." She stayed awake the entire night before her appearance, worrying that her mouth would open and nothing would come out. Sitting in the hair-and-makeup chair before going on air, she told the publicist for the magazine the appearance would be a disaster. She believed this while walking on set, believed it sitting down beside Regis, and she believed it up until the very moment the red light of the camera came on and they went live to the world. Lisa's mouth opened, she expected nothing to come out, and instead . . . the words flowed. After more than twenty years of formulating her opinions based on those of her father, these were *her* words and ideas, and people out there (millions of them) were listening to what she had to say. It would mark a turning point in her career, but more profoundly, in her confidence.

Anyone who grew up alongside a parent with a strong personality can probably relate to this moment in some way, even if their own moment didn't include two celebrity talk-show hosts. The parental decoupling process would take decades, and acting was yet another method of keeping at bay the shyness and insecurities that still sometimes tugged at her. Once a week, she'd rush over to the Barrow Group Performing Arts Center from Times Square, after her day job at Reuters finished. Then she'd spend three hours learning in the same space where Anne Hathaway honed her craft. "I couldn't have done this earlier in my life because I didn't have the confidence," she says. "When you feel so insecure, to be able to break out and expand to be another person, it's totally exhilarating."

For his part, Erle had spent years driving by a sign posted on the garage where the Long Beach fire trucks received maintenance. The sign solicited volunteers for the fire department. He'd been tempted to call but just never got around to it, never fully believed he could succeed in that physically demanding environment. But as I'd moved deeper into the obstacle course racing world alone, he finally made the call. At age fifty-five, he became one of the oldest probies (short for probationary firefighter) in the department, carrying and deploying heavy equipment alongside guys in their twenties. He attended drills on weekends—learned to move and crawl blindly through smoke-filled rooms without panicking, and to carry a 150-pound dummy out of a burning building. In a sign of respect for his age and his effort, the other firefighters informally called him Captain, and four years later he rose to second lieutenant. Being a firefighter instilled a physical confidence in my friend he'd lacked since his days as a skinny boy in his small Georgia hometown.

It also offset a growing disenchantment he felt professionally, as his role in journalism had shifted from the creative thrill of chasing individual stories to more of a managerial function, rife with the monotony of meetings, PowerPoint presentations, and politics.

"I never thought I could do this," he says about firefighting. "The mental part would be hard at any age, but now the physical part is probably the hardest. There are times when everything hurts the next day. But I love it. It feels like I'm doing something with a higher purpose, which is sometimes hard to feel in your regular job."

Now it was my world that needed to adjust to them. To Lisa's late nights in the city. To Erle not being as available on weekends if I wanted to hike or schedule an impromptu dinner. To both having their own tight-knit communities of fellow actors and firefighters, people they shared experiences with that didn't include me. Yet, their adventures balanced our relationships, and as time passed, the new passions made our lives feel fresh again. Lisa's bedside table filled up with books on acting methods, a counterbalance to mine on endurance and fitness. Erle's table held a pager to listen for fire calls. I attended plays at the Barrow Group and read lines with Lisa at night to help her rehearse. Erle and Lisa continued taking turns accompanying me to races. Now all students again, together we rolled back the fog of midlife monotony in our individual and collective worlds. And by doing so, we held the line. We stayed together. And we evolved and wrote our bridges. Together.

Meantime, my parents also began pushing back against a slow physical fade-out. They'd been active all their adult life, snow- and waterskiing, scuba diving, hiking, hoisting sails and pulling lines on their boat. Yet, some of that activity had naturally wound down in their seventies, in part just due to general wear and tear, including a knee replacement for my mother on the leg she primarily used to stop while skiing. They were hardly sedentary; they still fished, tended to their five acres of land, and were in motion much of the day. But watching me run around their property, attaching a car tire to a chest harness and pulling it down their driveway, must have made an impression somewhere.

My mom put on a fitness tracker, got a personal trainer, and joined a gym again for the first time in three decades. My father took things a step further and underwent a brief stint of coaching with my Canadian trainers (yes, *my* trainers, Faye and Jess). He then joined the local chapter of an exercise network called F3 Nation, filled with men young enough to be his sons or grandchildren. For several months, he hauled himself out of bed early in the morning to work out with the group in a nearby municipal park until the T-shirt and sweatpants my mom laid out for him the night before were soaked with sweat. Already fit from his manual labor mowing, weed whacking, and splitting firewood on their property, he strengthened himself more.

And so it was against this evolving backdrop that I approached the 2019 Spartan North American Championship, my life remarkably still filled with the people so critical to my earlier verses. We were all changing . . . pushing ourselves and pushing each other to believe that some of our boldest moves might yet be to come. Not every day was inspirational. Most days we lived on the plateau. Occasionally we disappointed each other by not listening or by taking more than we gave. And we disappointed ourselves with our inevitable stumbles. A bad week of slow running. A drill where the anxiety of a claustrophobic smoke-filled room led to panic. An acting class where the distractions of a father's poststroke health needs were simply too much, and the monologue fell flat. A cold gray morning when the realities of a seventy-six-year-old body made walking the dog feel like a chore, not a privilege.

Still, stronger than all of that was the flicker of hope. Hope that we aren't done yet. Hope that even though we all are most certainly grown up, we might still find more to be. A text one morning from Erle captured the essence of what we felt, the flicker visible in his final exclamation point.

"Good morning. Big fire last night. Came in at 2:15. I helped throw a ladder to a second-floor window, climbed it, broke the window out and went in. I got home about 6. Exhausted!"

15

DO WHAT YOU CAN, WHEN YOU CAN, WHILE YOU CAN

Three races in two days.

That's the goal that Faye, Jess, and I have set for my West Virginia race weekend. The big race for the Spartan North American Championship will unfold on Saturday, a 21-kilometer/13.1-mile Beast. Age Group athletes will take the course right after the Elite racers (including Faye) plow through and do the rest of us the courtesy of breaking down brush and thorns and tamping down the trails with their fast footprints.

My goal for the championship itself is modest: finish and don't be last. It will be only my third attempt at a race this length, the first one having ended with me shivering in the medical tent. My stretch goal is to also complete the Super and Sprint races the next day, Sunday, earning what's known in Spartan racing as a Trifecta Weekend medal. A "Trifecta" for Spartan Race means completing its three mainstay distances (Beast, Super, Sprint) in a single year. Knocking them all out in two consecutive days gets you a special medal for running almost the equivalent of a 26.2-mile marathon over forty-eight hours ("Spartan miles" tend to run longer than a standard mile) with nearly ninety obstacles. In the annals of distance running, this is a drop in the bucket. Many ultra-endurance racers run 100-plus-mile distances. Rich Roll, who wrote the book I devoured right after my father-in-law's stroke, completed five Ironman-distance triathlons in under a week. (An Ironman race consists of a 2.4-mile swim, a 112-mile bike ride, and a 26.2-mile run.)

But for someone who a year ago had never competitively raced more than 3.1 miles and couldn't hoist her own body weight, completing these three races would be a significant notch in the belt of impossibly hard things with a little *i*, as Steven Kotler, author of *The Art of Impossible: A Peak Performance Primer*, so eloquently describes in his book. There are, of course, those capital-*I* Impossible feats that have never been done before. "Paradigm-shifting breakthroughs," Kotler writes. "Four-minute miles. Moonshots." Equally important for most of us, however, are the lowercase-*i* impossible triumphs— the feats that "no one, including ourselves, at least for a while, ever imagined we'd be capable of accomplishing," is how Kotler puts it.

Lisa can't make the trip due to work, so Erle plays my race wingman. We make the best of the nine-hour, 565-mile trek by alternately blasting country music and listening to podcasts on longevity while passing through what feels like half the states in the eastern end of the Union.

The morning of the championship race, I awake around 4:30 A.M., quickly shower, and tug on my long racing socks and racing compression pants before forcing down my now-standard pre-race meal of Greek yogurt, berries, granola, and a piece of multigrain bread with almond butter. Eating this early is its own act of willpower, knowing I'll need the fuel later but wanting nothing to do with food at such an unnatural hour.

Erle navigates the dark roads to the race venue clutching a mug of black coffee. He's not a morning person, so we don't talk much. Instead, I play "Countdown" by Beyoncé and "Over When It's Over" by Eric Church on repeat.

"How do you feel?" he finally asks.

"Not great," I tell him, staring out the passenger-side window into the glaring lights of a strip mall with a tattoo parlor. "I don't know what's wrong. My stomach is a mess. I want some of your coffee but I'm afraid of what will happen."

"You'll be fine once you get on the course," he says.

We drive a little more. Eric Church fills our silence.

Now it's over when it's over.

Ain't it, baby, ain't it?

"Why am I doing this?" I say, not really expecting an answer because it's not a real question. "We could just turn around, go get breakfast. I could have coffee and go back to sleep."

He laughs. "Yeah, and then you'd regret it and hate me. No way."

A few more moments of Eric Church and strip mall lights.

Erle looks over at me. "Remember, you're doing this because you love it," he says gently.

The course is spread out over a Boy Scouts of America training campground in Glen Jean called the Summit Bechtel Reserve. The dewy field where we park is adjacent to an expanse of tents for the scouts, and bathrooms, where the inevitable lines are forming. It's a gray, cloudy day with moisture in the air, meaning the obstacles will be wet and slippery. West Virginia's reputation as a "wild, wonderful" state will be on full display as the course takes us through undulating terrain with elevation, wet rocks and roots, water, thorns, and moss and leaves that disguise holes waiting to turn ankles. Indeed, a trip and fall in a final slippery trail section of the race will be one major factor separating the first and second female Elite finishers today. My own coach Faye will nearly mow down a small black bear that runs across her path during the race. That she doesn't slow down earns her the accolade of "badass" on YouTube, where the moment is captured on a race video. (Time code: 54:14 and link in the book's Sources and Notes section if you're interested.)

The Elite racers are queuing up to start when we arrive, and I see Faye at the front of the women's pack in her bright-blue sports bra, shorts, and no shirt. Shirtless racing is the default for many of the best racers, male and female alike. Given their sculpted abs that look like they came out of a 3-D printer, I can't blame them. Like a seasoned baseball or football fan, I now can recognize the real contenders. That includes the two women who will battle for today's top title:

an American named Nicole Mericle and a Canadian named Lindsay Webster. Lindsay is married to one of the best male Elite racers, Ryan Atkins. With two Spartan World Championship titles under her belt, she arguably is on her way to becoming obstacle course racing's G.O.A.T. (greatest of all time)—men and women included. There's also a newish, intense twenty-seven-year-old dark-horse racer named Rebecca Hammond, who earned her Harvard Medical School degree this year. Along with Faye, Rebecca landed herself a spot on the CBS show *Million Dollar Mile,* with the nickname "The Harvard Hammer." Catchy.

I'm glad to see one of the oldest male Elite obstacle racers also at the starting line—a chiseled forty-year-old chiropractor named Ryan Woods (aka "rjwoodsy" on Instagram) whose LinkedIn profile says he attended the same university as my dad, North Carolina State. That Ryan, who is only seven years my junior, can still give the scrappy twenty- and thirtysomething guys a run for their money is inspiration for every older racer. There are a handful of these seasoned athletes who still hold their own in the Elite ranks. In the women's field, a five-time Ironman champion named Heather Gollnick, who is one year older than I am, is often a contender for the podium in women's Elite races alongside Faye, Lindsay, Nicole, and others. Although Ryan Woods and Heather have been competitive athletes for a while, I still feel a loose connection, knowing they too are out there running on joints that have seen decades of wear and tear and navigating treacherous terrain with eyesight that's maybe not as sharp as it once was.

As has become my habit, I stand in the back of the pack and quickly touch my pants pocket to ensure Dolly's dog tag is zipped up safe. We chant the Spartan opening speech, shout our three *Aroo*s, and take off. The first two miles of the race are heavily taxing on the upper body, which immediately puts me behind in the race. I slip off the dewy monkey bars and the Olympus obstacle, where you traverse a nearly vertical wall with only hand grips. The eight-foot Box foils me yet again, and I can't quite nail the Stairway to Sparta today—the contraption where you must pull yourself up a wall by rock-climbing grips. It's not even 9 A.M. and already I've bought myself 120 burpees as other racers surge ahead of me and am thinking longingly about Erle's hot cup of coffee.

At some point, I feel someone pat me on the back. It's Cory, the cardiac lab nurse from Ohio whom I'd met in North Carolina. He started racing after me and is now passing me, his bare chest already plastered with mud. "Go get 'em!" he says.

Seeing my new friend go by is just the jolt I need, and I finally start to find a groove. Carrying a heavy log through water and mud lets me gain back some confidence as I pass some racers. So does the sandbag carry, which plays to my strengths with an uphill climb that doesn't require speed or bicep strength. For a while, I'm all alone running in the woods, which is in equal parts unnerving (am I off course?) and intoxicating, with the smell of wet leaves and that now-familiar hum of control beginning to course through me. Here I am in a championship race, less than a year from my surgery, still on this earth, still able to make my own choices with my body . . . where I plant my foot, how I leap over a fallen tree, how fast I run.

This oneness with the universe lasts about fifteen minutes.

At which point I hear the screams.

They are faint at first, in the distance, but growing louder. I jog up a hill and see a crowd of racers congregating off to the side of the course, looking downhill to where the race continues back into the woods. There's a harried-looking race volunteer there too, murmuring into a walkie-talkie. Down below us, yelps continue to ring out.

"What's going on?" I ask no one in particular, taking a sip of electrolytes from my hydration vest.

"There's a bunch of wasps or hornets or some kind of bee shit down there on the course stinging people as they go through," a sturdy, balding, shirtless guy who looks to be in his early forties answers. Like Cory, he's got mud splattered across his chest and a few scrapes. "A bunch of people had allergic reactions and are getting pulled from the course."

My brain starts doing quick calculations. I'm also allergic to bee and wasp venom; have been since I was a kid. While it hasn't been life-threatening yet, I generally need an antihistamine and sometimes a steroid because the swelling is so severe.

No one's going to give me a steroid shot or a Benadryl here in the woods of West Virginia

"Is there another way around the nests?" I ask the guy, who is knocking mud out of his shoes while sucking on an energy gel.

"Couple of folks are trying to find one over there," he says, gesturing to some racers slowly winding their way off course through the thick trees.

I weigh my options for a few seconds. Quit and drive home nine hours, having DNFed again. Go off course but increase my likelihood of finishing last. Or just plow ahead and take the risk of being stung. The prudent choice is option one or two for sure. But the months—no, the years—it's taken me to get here, to be standing in the middle of these West Virginia woods beside this muddy, shirtless stranger, are like a hot iron searing against my judgment. I don't know for sure that it's now or never. Never requires a nonexistent crystal ball. But knowing your days of opportunity are closing lends a kind of clarity for decision-making.

Which is to say—do what you can, when you can, while you can.

"What are you going to do?" I ask the shirtless man.

"I'm going to run really fucking fast," he tells me.

My answer comes quicker than my brain processes it. "OK. Me too."

He plunges down, with me right on his heels. Secretly, I'm hoping whatever stinging army is down there will get him first and not bother with me. We try to steer to the edges of the white tape that marks the course, assuming the other racers got stung more in the middle. No such luck. Five seconds later, I hear him yelp and start slapping his chest wildly.

"Oh my God! My nipple, my nipple. They stung my NIPPLE!"

It's too late for me to course-correct, and suddenly I feel my right thigh burning like someone is jabbing a needle in it repeatedly. Looking down, I see at least five wasps attached to my racing tights. I'm instinctively reaching up my hand to swat them off when a piece of wisdom restrains me: I remember once learning that certain wasps can sting more than once. If I get a sting on my hand, I won't be able to grip any of the next obstacles. Instead, I let them have at my leg a few moments more while I dash to a creek bed and kneel in the water. One by one, the wasps detach. There are still maybe seven or eight miles to go; I'm slightly unsure of where we are on course. The swelling will start soon. I could climb back up the hill and try to get a UTV to take me to the medical tent.

Then, still kneeling in the water, I have a sudden flash of feeling this kind of pain as a kid, except from a jellyfish who'd gotten wrapped around my body while I was swimming off the side of my parents' small live-aboard sailboat. I'd climbed out of the water crying and pulling its tentacles from my arms and thighs. We were far from shore, so my parents lathered my welts in a wet compress of baking soda and water to alleviate the pain. I obviously don't have any baking soda right now, but there is a ton of cool mud around me.

That memory is another edge kicking in right now, an equalizer, even if I don't realize it through the stabbing pain in my leg. It's part of my crystallized intelligence. As humans we possess both "fluid intelligence," which is associated with short-term memory, and "crystallized intelligence"—those learnings accumulated over a life span. Fluid intelligence is often affected by aging, disease, or injury, while crystallized intelligence can increase through our sixties and seventies and maybe not start declining until our eighties.

Recalling that jellyfish moment and our jury-rigged medical treatment on the boat, I now dig into the creek bed and start pulling out globs of wet dirt and pressing them inside my racing tights on the stings.

And then I start running again.

The rest of the race is fuzzy in my memory. I remember swimming in a lake. It cools off my leg and lets me make up some distance, because swimming was considered a table-stakes activity for a Southern kid growing up around lakes and oceans. There are another thirty burpees at some point, which forces me to repeatedly press my stung thigh into the hard ground. Still, the excitement of the race gets me to the finish line. After they cut off my timing chip and hand me a banana, I head to the wash area, which is just a bunch of low-pressure hoses with cold water. There's an array of stings, all of them swelling. Erle accompanies me to the medical tent, where they give me Benadryl.

Then we check the race results.

I'm sixteen out of thirty-five.

"Hey, that's pretty good," Erle says.

I let the information sink in. I wasn't last. And I've moved to the middle of the pack in my age group in a national championship race.

"Yeah," I say, "It's not so bad."

There's a guy standing behind us waiting to check his own results. "Did you make it to Tahoe?" he finally says politely, clearly trying to move us along.

"Tahoe?" I ask him, misunderstanding. "No, we came down from New York."

"I mean, did you qualify for Tahoe?" he says. "The world championship?"

I do know there is a world championship race for Spartan, but I don't really understand the Byzantine qualification rules. Even my coaches, Faye and Jess, couldn't explain them, with Jess saying the intricacies are "worse than our Olympic team selection criteria!"

"I sincerely doubt it," I tell the stranger, moving out of his way.

"How do we find out?" Erle asks.

"There's a tent over there where you can ask and register." He points to a long line of people behind us, near the entrance to the festival area.

We move away from the results line to give him space. "Look, there's no way I've qualified," I tell Erle. "Let's go back to the hotel so

I can shower. My leg hurts." Translation: I also don't want to get my hopes up.

"You don't know," he says. "Maybe placing somewhere in the middle of a big race like this counts more or something. Let's just find out."

Reluctantly, I follow him, and we stand in line with a bunch of muddy people who've clearly raced at Tahoe before and are swapping war stories about the intense elevation and some horrific cold-water swim.

When it's finally my turn, I tell the red-shirted woman at the computer my name.

"Spell that?" she asks.

"G, w, e . . ." I finish spelling my first name and then blurt out defensively, "I don't think I qualified, but I, uh, well, I'm just checking. . . ."

"OK . . . Gwendolyn . . . let's see, sixteenth today," she says, nodding, looking at the screen, and then smiles. "Yep. Congratulations. You've made it to the world championship for Age Group competitors. Nice work. Do you want to sign up now? There's a discount."

Erle is already reaching for his credit card, since mine is in the car. "Yes," he says. "She does."

After I register, we sit on the grass in some shade, drinking a beer and watching the Elite finishers take the podium. Various renditions of the song "Take Me Home, Country Roads" blare from the loudspeakers. Lindsay Webster, the GOAT, has pulled out a win in a tight finish against Nicole Mericle, while "The Harvard Hammer," Rebecca Hammond, takes third. My coach Faye places fourth after failing The Box (like me) but outrunning a bear (not like me). And in a big score for the older crowd, Ryan Woods, the forty-year-old chiropractor, places first among the Elite men.

Tomorrow I'll complete both the 10K Super and 5K Sprint races and earn my first Trifecta Weekend medal. Then we'll need to hit an urgent care clinic on the nine-hour drive home for my leg, which at this point sports a big, fluid-filled welt from the stings. By Tuesday, I'll be back at work on steroids—staring at the same screens, sitting at the same scuffed conference-room tables. There are chores, laundry, and bills to be dealt with. My next dermatology appointment looms; with it will come another biopsy, and waiting and worrying until we hear "benign" on the other end of the phone. Amid it all, I'll need to train for Lake Tahoe, which is just five weeks away.

But none of that exists at this moment. At this moment, I'm a few days before my forty-eighth birthday and have just learned I qualified for a world championship endurance race. And maybe it's because of the lyrics looping incessantly around us, but amid all these tired athletes lounging in the sun, I do feel this might be the place I belong.

The Obstacle: Cargo Nets
(perspective)

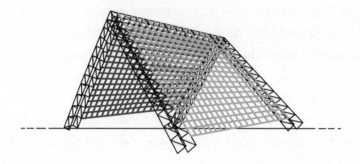

One of the most deceptive challenges in obstacle course races is crawling up and down a cargo net. A Spartan version of this obstacle is called the A-Frame Cargo. It's an enormous metal contraption, almost nineteen feet high and shaped like the letter A, where you climb up black netted webbing on one side and down the other. At first glance you might think, "Meh, what's the big deal?" Until you start climbing. Then you'll find the webbing can be loose and wiggly, and the mash-up of bodies makes it possible someone might accidentally kick you in the face. And once you're at the summit, you might suddenly think, "Oh, wait, am I scared of heights?" At which point it's too late if the answer is yes.

Even if you aren't unnerved by heights or the prospect of tasting someone's shoe sole, honing your A-Frame Cargo technique is a good idea. Because often, this obstacle is one of the last before the Spartan finish line. And if you're neck and neck with a competitor, how fast you get up and down it can be the deciding factor.

For many people, myself—eventually—included, the key is a flip. At the top of the frame, instead of reaching one leg over the crest to tentatively climb down the other side like a ladder, you grab the netting on the other side with both hands, engage your abs, and then flip your entire body over the apex. From there, you can either roll or slide-walk down the netting to the bottom. It's a lot faster. And honestly, flipping just makes you feel like a badass.

But if the pressure's not on, if you can spare a few seconds, then at the top it's worth a pause. Because often there's a spectacular view spread out before you of the racecourse, and sometimes of the topography: mountains, wildflowers, streams, forests—a note of awe to absorb while the familiar hum of competition drums below. If there's a meditative moment to be found in a heated, dirty sport like this, the top of a tall cargo net is where it can happen.

16

AGE IS A SECRET WEAPON

"**Oh my God. Wendy, this is crazy.**"
My coach Faye is standing in my house analyzing the gear sprawled across my dining room table. We're a week out from the Spartan World Championship in Lake Tahoe, and she's driven up from the city with her boyfriend to practice her spear throw technique on my makeshift target. Ever since West Virginia, I've been on a strict training program titled "Road to Tahoe!" The program is designed to build my tolerance for the long, steep climbs so I don't unnecessarily tax my hamstrings or groin. Mondays and Thursdays find me doing multiple sets of step-ups on boxes, squats, and reverse lunges, all while holding dumbbells. Then there are nearly a dozen different activities to isolate my hip and glute muscles, including single leg squats with minibands. I've got longer runs three times a week accompanied by intense core work, foam rolling to open my spine, and rolling my feet on the small nubby ball. The upper body doesn't get a pass, because the obstacles can be harder in a championship race. So I'm also in the garage performing pull-ups, dead hangs, and push-ups with claps in between and carrying thirty-pound kettlebells by towels around the property to build grip strength. One day a week I go to class with Pete and work on obstacle simulation, after which I spend some time hauling my Home Depot bucket up and down our dirt road past the neighbors' houses.

All told, on training days, I'm putting in two or more hours of effort, including recovery and stretching. The commitment puts all my time-management systems to the test. I'm ruthless about meetings beginning and ending on time. I'm also ruthless about my own diet and stop drinking alcohol altogether leading up to the race. Every spare moment is spent fine-tuning my gear list for Tahoe so I don't face a repeat of my cold blowout in New Jersey. Now that I've got my coach here in person, I've asked her to assess my collection.

Which she is doing.

And she is laughing.

Faye is a racer who shows up at the starting line in shorts and a sports bra, trusting her speed, athleticism, and sheer grit to endure whatever conditions a race brings. Spread before us on the table is what, through her eyes, must seem the racing equivalent of a hazmat suit. One of the other edges I've worked on is to learn everything I can about competing in cold, wet conditions. What to wear. How to move. I've read everything I can find online (*Sitting! Screens!*) about thermoregulation. Based on my research, I've amassed what seems like the right stuff to give me a shot at finishing.

Cotton is a no-go because it holds water. Wool is better but also can get heavy when it's wet. Synthetic weaves that shed water generally work best. Neoprene will create a boundary layer to hold heat in and insulate the body even when wet. I need to protect my extremities at all costs; the specific cylindrical nature of fingers means the air surrounds them and makes them at risk for a cold injury. If I can't move my fingers, I can't grip the obstacles. "Leverage the technology that's out there" is how Kenefick, our temperature expert from a previous chapter, puts it.

Laid out before Faye are the results of my exhaustive research. Frogskin neoprene socks and pants with quick-dry fleece lining. The special neoprene oven mitts (Bleggmits) I spotted Cali wearing in New Jersey for my hands. To keep my core warm, I've purchased a shirt from this company called Neptune, stitched with six pockets around the stomach to hold these waterproof "Inferno pouches," containing air-activated body and hand warmers—the kind people take to football games or snow skiing. There's a tight-fitting fleece cap for running, a swim cap for the lake to keep my head dry, and an ultralight waterproof windbreaker made of Gore-Tex I pick up on sale at my local REI store. And of course, my hydration vest with electrolyte tablets, energy gels, and some nut butter packs. I've also pulled out a small dry bag we use for water sports and plan to stash a lot of clothing inside it during the dreaded swim, because technically, everything racers bring on course must accompany them through the Swim obstacle.

"I, uh, think you're going to overheat," Faye tells me, fingering the Frogskin socks for a moment and then dropping them like they've burned her. I nod, my face reddening a little. She is the expert, after all.

"Well, maybe I'll take some of it with me to Tahoe, just in case." I hedge, knowing full well I'm going to bring every single item on the table.

The thing is, normally Faye would be right. But I've been tracking the temperature forecast for the area where we'll be competing with the intensity of a storm chaser. Generally, September would be perfect for racing in the Olympic Valley, California, area, with highs hovering at almost seventy degrees Fahrenheit and lows in the high thirties to low forties. But that's not what's coming. Instead, I'm reading about the possibility of temperatures around freezing on race day, and even snow. And the Tahoe race apparently is infamous for this short but cold alpine swim midway through the competition. My gut tells me to trust my instincts and prepare accordingly. We're all going to face the same harsh conditions, whether we're twenty-eight or forty-eight years old. Gear and preparation are equalizers.

Gear is something I can control.

Lisa and I arrive in the North Lake Tahoe area three days early to help me acclimate to the 6,200-foot surface elevation. During the race ascent we will be climbing to an elevation of around 8,300 feet, according to Spartan, and then running up and down the Olympic Valley mountains, home to the 1960 Winter Olympics. At night I study the race map, noting the obstacle placement to see when I'll be most gassed and when I can run faster. But mostly I practice my clothing tactics—primarily, how I will remove multiple layers before the swim and stash them in my dry bag to carry with me into the water. Lisa picks up a pair of sturdy bright-blue hiking boot shoe-laces in town so I can use them to tie the dry bag tightly to my back while I swim. I write down the order in which I'll remove my gear on a hotel notepad and then rehearse, sweating in the warm hotel room, until I can remove and pack it all into the bag in the correct order without thinking. Now that we are physically here at the race site, I can see for myself just how dramatically the weather is shifting on the mountains each day.

"Remember, plan the dive and dive the plan," my mother tells me by phone from North Carolina when I check in with her the night before the race. While I've heard this phrase often from my parents—because they'd had it drilled into them by their dive instructors—it never really registered. But it does now.

My plan is yet another equalizer.

As the weekend of racing opens, Spartan holds a Friday Parade of Nations, its version of an Olympics opening ceremony, in which competitors from around the world march through the town bran-dishing the flags of their countries. There are reportedly fifty-nine different countries represented, including India, China, Denmark, Guatemala, Malaysia, Belgium, Mexico, and Canada. It's a surreal moment as I take my place behind the American flag, which is whip-ping hard in the stiff wind. I'm not a reporter watching this event from the sidelines; I'm one of the athletes in this parade, represent-ing my country. Following the drum-beating procession, I keep half expecting that someone will soon tell me I'm in the wrong place. But they don't, and as our English-language chants collide with others being shouted in multiple languages, one common word occasionally surfaces: the Spartan starting-line chant "*Aroo!*" Together, we make our way to a main stage area, where Spartan founder Joe De Sena waits to greet us. As usual, he doesn't mince words.

"Listen, it's going to be really hard tomorrow. It's going to be cold. It's going to be really hard on Sunday. But that's the way we like it." He grins and raises his arm in the air while people cheer. "I just made a phone call and asked them to lower the temperature twenty degrees for you. And I know you like that."

Joe's prediction isn't wrong. On Sunday, the day of the Elite and Age Group world championship races, I awake and learn via text, email, and Facebook that the race start will be delayed by two hours so course organizers can deal with the snow and ice that's been accumulating. A delay wouldn't be such a big deal ordinarily, except that with my group now starting at 12:15 P.M., it means we could be up against darkness if it's a particularly slow slog. Which I'm expecting for me, given the elevation. And the rules say that without a headlamp, you will be pulled from the race for safety reasons if you don't reach a certain point by a certain time.

I've planned my gear with meticulousness bordering on the maniacal. But I don't have a headlamp.

Lisa immediately starts calling outdoor-gear stores in town and locates one with a few lamps left; she gives the clerk her credit card number to hold it and heads into town. While she's gone, I exchange a few texts with Pete, who is back in New York and, for the first time since I've known him, isn't 110 percent gung ho about a race. "Be safe," he says. "We're cheering you on back here but watching those temps. Remember, you have nothing to prove out there."

His words give me momentary pause. But I know Pete is wrong. I do have something to prove. And that clarity is what's going to get me to the starting line and up that long, gray mountainside trail. Intrinsically, I want to finish for reasons that run so deep in my psyche that they outweigh whatever discomfort might lie ahead. There is no prize money when you don't run the Elite category. The official race-day videos won't focus on the Age Group competitors today, even though we compete by the same rules. When ESPN broadcasts the race two weeks later, our non-Elite obstacle triumphs and burpee failures won't be center stage. However, at forty-eight, I've got other reasons to get up that mountain—reasons that are more motivating than a prize or a cameo on TV.

All of us generally know what it's like to be motivated by something extrinsic—money, a promotion, power. It feels different from intrinsic drives—which are more psychological in nature and satisfy our fundamental drives—such as curiosity or a search for competence or security. When we are intrinsically motivated, our purpose generally is tied to the "process" of participating in an activity, and our main reward is the sheer satisfaction of engaging in the activity and seeing it through. I've since learned that this kind of intrinsic motivation is formidable because it's potentially stickier than the more fleeting lure of a medal or cash prize. "The great adult athletes don't tend to be the ones who were the best in their early teens," says Jeff Bercovici, the author of *Play On*. "That whole phenomenon of winning a championship in your first season or becoming MVP can lead to a crisis of meaning. When you come to a sport later, it forces you to be intrinsically motivated, because you have to pay that much more attention to process."

Indeed, there is absolutely no extrinsic motivation for many of us to leave our warm hotel rooms and hurl ourselves into hours of cold physical punishment on a mountain. Every driver comes from somewhere else. And for me, it's a mental folder of Polaroid-snapshot memories: a little girl cowering behind her best friend during dodgeball; the one-point basketball season; a hand holding my throat against a junior high school locker; the half-dozen "I'm sorry but the pregnancy test came back negative" calls from my gynecologist's office; the "So, what I'm telling you shouldn't take years off your life, but . . ." diagnosis from my dermatologist.

The final test of these memories' grip comes when a Facebook post from Spartan confirms that despite the temperatures and snow, the Swim obstacle is still open.

I tell Lisa, who watches me neutrally for a moment before offering one more graceful way out of what lies ahead. An offer that would be impossible to turn down absent a heart of certainty. "We could just stay here, get a bottle of wine, and watch the snow fall."

I smile. "That sounds amazing," I tell her. But the look on my face answers the question for both of us.

She nods. "We'll do it after you cross the finish line." And without another word, we gather up my gear and walk out the door.

Hypothermia.

The word begins to worry my mind, a mental splinter. Air temperatures are hovering in the high twenties, and we're about five miles into the race with snow and ice on the ground and occasional wind gusts of around twenty miles per hour. We've got another eight to nine miles left. Coming into view now is a frozen landscape roughly a quarter of a mile away with bobbing bright-red dots scattered across it. As I jog toward them, I recognize the dots immediately for what they are: humans clad in life jackets moving across a small lake, the jackets a precaution in case their legs cramp or their hearts falter when they hit the cold water.

And in about two minutes, one of those bobbing bright-red dots in the water will be me.

If this were a normal September day temperature-wise, I'd be filling up with confidence right now because so far, my race has gone better than expected. In the starting corral, I'd chatted with a forty-year-old high school history, government, and economics teacher and mother of three named Molly Starr, who also is a student of Faye and Jess's. An experienced Spartan racer, and someone who has completed hundred-mile races, she put me at ease. "All you have to do is just keep moving. Don't let the cold make you stop or slow down." And then the race announcer began cracking jokes about our 40–44 and 45–49 age groups. "I call it the grown-and-sexy crew," he shouted through the microphone. "Grown and sexy. Bills are paid. Credit's OK." That broke the tension as I joined the women around me in granting him a small laugh. Some fiddled with their watch timers. Still wearing my old analog Swatch watch, which I've become oddly fond of, I fiddled with my hat and gloves instead. *Say what you will,* read the collective thought bubble above us. *We're the ones about to climb that mountain.* (Plus, he wasn't wrong. My bills *were* paid, and my credit score was excellent. If that's what being grown and sexy was, so be it.)

During our long first climb out of the starting line, I held my own in the middle of the pack and tried to stay right behind Molly. Racers already began stumbling on the second obstacle, which was a six-foot wall positioned in the middle of a steep incline, so you had to fight against gravity to get over it. I succeeded and then also nailed the monkey bars, which were staggered in height. (Hat tip, little French fry girl.) Later I passed people during the bucket carry up and down the mountaintop, thanking my neighbors silently for putting up with my weeks of practice on our dirt road. I even hit my spear throw, which spared me the indignity of burpees in pools of icy water covering the ground. There have been a few setbacks, including a tricky moment where I got caught up in the barbed-wire crawl and ripped through my jacket and shirt and down to my skin. And only minutes ago, I was hunched over, lower back screaming, lugging two wet forty-pound sandbags up a steep incline. The double sandbag carry turned out to be one of Spartan's world championship obstacle alterations. Usually there's only one sandbag to lug, but with two, the total load was almost two-thirds of my weight. Foot by foot, I slowly, steadily crept forward, remembering Molly's advice to just keep moving. Later she'll tell me this was the only moment in her racing career when she seriously considered quitting. Men, their bags sixty pounds each, cursed. One stopped, bent over, and wept, tears frosting his whiskered face. Our private pain finally gave way to voice when a woman's knee buckled behind me and she collapsed. We yelled up the mountain, even as we kept moving, "MEDIC, MEdic, medic"—a verbal sports-stadium wave—so a race volunteer would hear and call for assistance.

Still, overall, this first leg of the race has gone much better than I'd expected. The Bleggmits have kept my hands toasty. And I've stayed warm—so warm that at one point during our initial climb, I unzipped my shell jacket and tied it around my waist, wondering if Faye was right and I was going to roast myself from the inside out.

But now the true test is here: the Swim.

Watching Spartan's race recap later, I'll learn that the race orga-nizers were waffling most of the night about whether to keep the Swim obstacle open. Was it too dangerous? Officials apparently fol-low something called the "eighty rule," which means the air tem-perature and the water need to add up to at least eighty degrees to keep a water obstacle open. Today we're hovering right around that mark, with air temps around twenty-eight degrees and approxi-mately fifty-degree water. Given that it's a world championship race, they've opted to let people get wet and opened an additional medical facility directly across from the swim obstacle.

The purpose of the swim isn't to exhaust racers. The purpose is to chill them to the bone and then see how they respond to that adver-sity. "You need to almost go into a meditative state when you are hitting that water," the announcers will explain in the race recap video. "Because if you are not mentally prepared and in the right place, it will absolutely crush your soul."

Reaching the lake, I try not to look at other racers, many of whom are standing on the frozen, snowy banks, clearly deciding how to approach the water. Molly is coming out of the water now. "Keep moving!" she tells me, gritting her teeth. And she's right. Speed mat-ters now for executing my plan. First, my top layer of clothes comes off—windbreaker, insulating vest, long-sleeve race shirt, the Neptune shirt with pockets for heat warmers—until I'm down to my sports bra and otherwise bare upper body. My bottom layer of race shoes, neoprene race socks, and pants stays on. At the last moment, I remove my warm running cap and tuck my ponytail inside a rubber swim cap. My bare stomach is turning pink, but the cold keeps me focused.

I pack everything, including my hydration pack, inside the small dry bag that I've carried in my pocket the entire race just for this very moment. Then I tie the dry bag to my back with the pair of bright-blue hiking boot laces. My plan is to swim freestyle, fast, and hope this bag stays secure and keeps my upper layers dry.

At the lake's edge, a handful of race officials carefully monitor the splashing competitors. I thank them while fastening my own life jacket. Hooking it around my neck and cinching the straps across my bare stomach, I plunge into the lake.

Submerged, my lungs seem to shrink into a burning pair of prunes. It's worse than the New Jersey Dunk Wall that sacked me. The only time I've felt anything similar was the winter morning I followed Erle into the Atlantic Ocean during that polar bear plunge. That day I was back on dry land in seconds with warm, dry clothes waiting on the shore. Now I've got several minutes of paddling out, circling around a buoy, and heading back to shore—all while hoping not to get kicked in the face by another swimmer or feel my legs cramp. Many racers are moving slowly and sticking to the inside lane. To get around them, I choose a longer outer lane path where I can swim faster. Once I'm clear of flailing arms and feet, I deploy my own long limbs to power me through the water. It's awkward and not pretty. The life jacket forces my head up. The dry bag presents a constant drag. Still, I'm moving relatively quickly, and soon I've rounded the buoy and am moving past the spotters in yellow kayaks, who are ready to assist any racer who cramps or falters.

As I reach the shore and start emerging into the cold air, one of the race monitors checks in. "How do you feel?"

I spit out some lake water and step onto the lakeshore. "Never . . .

better," I tell him, teeth chattering. "Thinking . . . about . . . going again."

He chuckles. "Good for you."

I run up the hill, untying the dry bag as I go, and find a spot clear of racers in the snow. It feels worse out of the water with the wind blowing. I know the clock is ticking. Opening the dry bag, which mercifully didn't leak, I unpack my clothing and put it back on in order, glad I rehearsed because right now my brain is stuck on an unhelpful loop that goes something like: "It's cold . . . it's cold . . . it's so cold." A woman next to me is coaxing another female racer to move. "You've got to get going. You can't just stand here." But the girl is crying and shaking, her clothing soaking wet, knees slightly bent as she hugs herself in a futile attempt to get warm. Her eyes are shining with something approaching animalistic fear. She has nothing dry to put on.

"FUUUCK," I hear a guy scream as he comes out of the water. "My balls are totally gone."

Well, I think vaguely, there's one thing I don't have to worry about. Hat on, shirts back on. I take a moment to unwrap a couple of the hand warmers so they activate and then stuff them into the pockets of the Neptune shirt. I'm quickly losing feeling in my exposed fingers and even my toes, despite the Neoprene socks. I fumble for a few moments with the zipper on my jacket but don't have the finger dexterity to fasten it. So I leave it open and stick my arms through the hydration vest, which I also can't fasten. I pull on the Bleggmits using my teeth and start running.

Everything will come down to the next five to ten minutes and whether my gear performs as I've planned and warms me up. I'm wiggling my toes in my shoes and my fingers in my gloves, trying to coax them back to life. But mostly I just run. I run as hard as I can, looping through the snowy, rocky trails down the mountain, heavy, gray clouds looming above me. A few times I pass racers sitting on the side of a hill, trembling and waiting for medics to come get them. Some are wearing shorts. Most are completely covered in heavy, wet clothes. I offer a few words of encouragement, which I know will land flat. I've been where they are.

At some point, I begin noticing the native plants and pick up my head to look around. Being from the East Coast, I've never seen a scrubby, wild, raw beauty like what's spread out before me. I wish Lisa were here to see this. "God, it's amazing out here," I say, passing a guy with his hands stuffed down the front of his pants. Out here, I give him the benefit of the doubt and assume he's simply keeping his fingers warm.

"Can't look," he says, warm breath coming out in white wisps. "Don't want . . . to . . . trip." Well, that is an issue when running with your hands stuffed in your pants, I muse silently.

And suddenly it dawns on me.

I'm not thinking about being cold anymore.

In fact, my toes no longer hurt. There's a warmth spreading through my core from the heat packs in my shirt. I can grasp the zipper on my jacket and pull it up. We're about six miles in at this point. There's still another seven or eight to go. But now all that's left is to keep moving and not get hurt. Even if I fail every obstacle before me, which I know won't happen, I can still finish.

It might have taken me forty-eight years, but I can finish a world championship race.

This knowledge is like fuel. Fuel that powers me through the next couple of hours. Of the final seventeen obstacles, I will fail three. It's far from perfect, but the burpee pits are crowded, so I'm not alone. My running training program from Jess is paying off, and my legs are strong heading down into the village for the final mile. It's still light outside, so the headlamp goes unused. I turn over my two-hundred-pound tire easily (silent thanks now for my young Haldane football mentors) and climb the A-Frame Cargo net. We're too close to the finish for any view gazing, so I flip quickly and then sprint through the streets of town toward the last obstacle. Even though the Elite racers are already long finished, spectators are there cheering for the rest of us. A few even stretch out their hands for a high five as we run by. And for the briefest of moments, accepting their hand smacks, I drink the Kool-Aid that Faye, Lindsay Webster, Ryan Woods, and Ryan Atkins sip so regularly.

Lisa isn't at the finish line when I cross it. I wander around the village looking for her and for Faye until I finally hear a voice calling, "Wendy? Wendy!" Turns out Lisa's been hanging out at the medical tent looking for me. "Oh my God," she says, pulling me into a hug. "You finished! So many people got pulled off the course from the cold. I've been so worried. Are you OK?"

I wipe my face with my dirty Bleggmits and stare back up the mountainside. I imagine those Polaroids of my past lying scattered amid the scrubby plants and cold earth. "Yeah, I am," I whisper into her shoulder. "Can we go have that wine now?"

It's not until I've showered and Lisa has graciously used her eyebrow tweezers to extricate what appears to be a piece of barbed wire lodged in my abdomen that we check my race results.

"It doesn't matter if you are dead last," she says to me, pouring me a second glass of wine. "You finished. A lot of people didn't. You're a rock star no matter what."

My time is five hours, twenty-three minutes, and four seconds.

My age-group placement: eleven out of thirty-two.

We both stare at the computer screen for a moment.

"Wendy," Lisa says, pulling her eyes away from the screen. "This is amazing. It's the world championship. Not only did you finish but you did well. In the top half of finishers."

My cellphone rings. It's Faye. I haven't checked the full slate of Elite winners yet, although I had heard while on the course that American Nicole Mericle had bested the unbreakable Lindsay Webster for the top spot. (Nicole, it turns out, also used a dry bag to stash clothes during the swim; Lindsay chose what looks on the race recap video like a black garbage bag.) And another American, a for-

mer U.S. Army Green Beret named Robert Killian, took home gold
for the men after grabbing the lead when he nailed his spear throw
and the other top contenders missed. (Take nothing for granted.)

"Hi, Faye," I say, releasing my gaze from the statistics on the laptop. "I looked for you after the race. How did it go?"

"Oh God. That race. That was so brutal," she says, talking a mile a
minute in her typical fast Faye-speak. "You were right about the cold.
I had to quit at the double sandbag carry, and they took me to the
medical tent. I started falling asleep, and they think I was mildly
hypothermic."

She goes on to explain how her gear wasn't right. How she'd been
so focused on her fitness and relying on that gift that she'd raced in
shorts and borrowed a jacket from the male Elite winner, Robert
Killian, just before the race started. But the jacket was so big on her
that there was no insulation. And once she got wet, up on the mountain, she couldn't get warm again.

"Anyway, it was awful and so hard. I just wanted to call and tell
you not to feel like a piece of shit if you didn't finish because I didn't
either and to me that was an impossible race and it broke me."

I sit down on a chair by the fire, trying to process what my coach
is telling me. "I did. I mean, I did finish," I tell her finally.

The briefest of pauses. "That's amazing. I'm so proud of you," I
hear Faye say, her voice cracking slightly. "You were really smart with
how you prepared. I lost my motivation during that race. I was one
hundred percent focused on my placement, and once I got so cold
and knew I couldn't make the podium, I had no motivation to get
me through. I was just toast."

I can tell Faye is crying. I do not know what it is like to be twenty-
nine years old, weighted with the blessing and the burden of physical
greatness since youth. But I do now know what it's like to not finish
a race, and the haunting questions that come, about whether you
tried hard enough. More importantly, I know from decades of experience how critical it is in moments of failure to not feel that your

entire sense of self is wrapped around a single identity, be it athlete, journalist, parent, or spouse. Faye is an Elite obstacle course racer, one of the best in the world. But she is more than that.

"Faye," I tell her gently, "you are a class act to pick up the phone and call us. Those of us who finished, finished because of how well you trained us. You're an incredible coach."

She is quiet for a moment. "Thank you. But you all finished because you love this sport. It's changed my outlook on racing. I have to figure out why I want to keep doing this."

Later that night after Lisa is asleep, I crawl out of bed and sit alone for a while by the gas fireplace in the living room of our suite. Sprawled on the floor is my gear, bearing its scars from the day's work: pants knees caked with mud, jacket with its abdominal barbed-wire tear, shoes damp and stiffening. When the race results are finalized, I'll be twelfth out of thirty-three racers my age—a showing I'd have believed was impossible a year ago. In the morning we'll leave Tahoe and drive to San Francisco, where the reality of Lisa's father's stroke one year ago is setting in. She will be with him when he awakes, the mornings often an unbearable loop of rediscovering he cannot move or speak the words that once flowed so freely. We will take her mother, Stella, to dinner and try to find words we all believe that hint at a future not full of today's despair.

With just the low light of the fireplace, I write myself a letter on a postcard. It's my A-Frame Cargo moment. I tell myself to remember how this day felt and to summon the hope and awe of that raw, rugged mountainside in the moments of fear that will surely return. To recall what it feels like plunging down a rocky slope with a sandbag on my back, sure-footed and alive, next to other athletes. To believe, the next time I feel doubt about what is possible, in the power of moving from a near-last-place finish to today's results in the span of seven months. And what such an act can mean for the time I have left. I write all this down because I know how fast these feelings will recede.

Before going to bed, I quietly place my championship finisher medal to rest beside my water glass. Once my head is on the pillow, I expect to fall asleep immediately. But that doesn't happen. Instead, it's like any other race day, and I start replaying where I struggled, making mental notes on how I can do better. *Grab with both hands to make it through the ropes at the end of the Multi-Rig; get foot placement right on the confounding eight-foot Box; running descents were good, but I'm still too hesitant. . . .*

And just like that, the ink still drying on my letter in the other room, today's accomplishments and challenges begin sorting themselves into learnings and receding into the background. But I don't mind. Because I know what it means.

I am not yet done.

PART THREE

17

WHEN THERE'S
NO BELL TO RING

"**T**his is your year. It's all coming together now."

I'm on a pre-race call with Faye and Jess while driving to the airport. It's February 2020, about five months after the Lake Tahoe Spartan World Championship, and I'm heading south for the first major Spartan race of the year. As I pull into JFK International Airport, my coaches are rattling off a list of last-minute reminders: Run in a straight line; pick up a sandbag closest to the course so you carry it the least distance; jog for ten minutes before the race with some short, fast sprints so you are warmed up. Go out hard.

My ears still ringing with their guidance, I board a plane to Jacksonville, Florida, not knowing this will be my last race for fourteen months.

The event is the same U.S. National Series venue where I had placed a lowly twenty out of twenty-three a year earlier. This time, however, I am in a different headspace while driving to WW Ranch Motocross Park. Last year, I'd slunk to the back of my age-group pack with a stomach full of doubt after watching my future coach Faye launch herself over the starting wall at the last minute for the Elite women's heat. Now I'm excited. Like I want to try to compete. It may seem like a ridiculous thing to say; what else would you be doing in a race? But until now, that's never been something I really thought was in my DNA, at least on the athletic front. In my first obstacle race, all I wanted to do was not die. After that, I just wanted to get good enough to not fall off a rope or embarrass myself. And as I improved, I wanted to take on longer, harder challenges—including the recent world championship—with the goal of simply finishing and not being last.

But after September's Lake Tahoe competition, I had raced the next month at a location connected to Fort Campbell, a U.S. Army installation astride the Kentucky-Tennessee border that is home to the 101st Airborne Division. Usually, as the pain from running hard would set in, I just slowed down to protect myself, thinking, Well, it's good to just be out here. Doesn't matter how I place. But that day, I could tell I was among those in the lead in my age group. And something shifted. I ran hard with the sandbag, climbed the rope as fast as I could, chased people down. For a "nonathlete," it was a very different kind of feeling.

There was no Internet connectivity at the race site that day, so Spartan couldn't share the results immediately. Instead of heading back to the hotel immediately, I opted to run a second lap of the course in the relaxed Open category, wearing one of the weight vests being handed out as an extra challenge for this particular venue because it was connected to an active military installation. I didn't fail a single obstacle with the vest on, and it weighed somewhere around fourteen pounds. It was only later, while stopping for gas on the way back to meet Lisa, that I checked the Age Group results from my first race on my iPhone and nearly dropped the pump after seeing I'd secured the bronze medal.

Standing there with drops of gasoline dripping onto my muddy race shoe as I stared at my screen (albeit not sitting this time), it dawned on me that I might be able to expect more from myself than not finishing last or in the middle of the pack. That I might become an actual contender. The thought simultaneously terrified and elated me. It was one thing to go out to race and just get through it the best I could. It was an entirely different matter to go out and say, I want to try to win. On the one hand, the uncertainty was incredibly disconcerting to me. On the other hand, if I could change this part of me so late in the game, what else might still be possible?

It was here, the smell of fuel wafting around me at this Southern filling station, that the tide of battle against the midlife assassin took a major turn, ripping the "stick with what you're already good at" security blanket out of my hands for good. And, as I eventually would discover some seven thousand miles from home, the ultimate outcome would have nothing to do with podiums or medals at all.

Four months later in Jacksonville, Florida, as I travel alone on Interstate 10 with Jess's "this is your year" assertion ringing in my ears, everything feels familiar. Eric Church's gravelly voice intoning "Over When It's Over." The almond butter and multigrain bread I'm eating with my right hand while steering with my left. Especially the venue with its scent of dewy morning grass mixed with smoke from the fire jump and its blaring rock music.

I am nervous. But I am not clueless. With nineteen races logged, my body knows this place and its ways now.

Following my coaches' guidance, I dutifully perform my ten-minute warm-up jog and sprints. I'd spied Faye lined up at the bathrooms a bit earlier. "Go out hard," she'd told me. "Remember, this is a Sprint. You don't have time to catch up."

When they call the 40–44 and 45–49 age groups to the starting line, I weave through the other men and women to make my way to the front. Given that this is one of five key races making up this year's Spartan U.S. National Series, I know the best competitors are here. But my confidence grows once I spy Cory Edwards, the cardiac lab nurse from Ohio I'd become Instagram friends with. He is grinning and exudes a sense of "I'm ready." After he hugs me, I start to settle down, stretching my limbs in this human cattle pen of other anxious racers bouncing on their toes. The announcer starts his spiel—now so familiar that I answer without thinking.

"Who am I?"

"I am a Spartan!" Cory and I yell it in sync, shaking out our arms.

"Spartans, what is your profession?"

"Aroo! Aroo! Aroo!" we cry.

"Let's race!"

I placed fourth.

It's unclear exactly how many racers were in my age group that day. Spartan's online count puts it at twenty. Another sports tracking site at twenty-two. Regardless, I'd moved up—by a lot—from pulling in nearly last a year ago and was less than two minutes away from the podium at one of the year's most important Spartan races. For the first time, I'd come out hard, just like Faye coached, and endeavored to stay as close to Cory as I could for as long as I could—not easy, because he was much faster. By trying to pace him, I kept within striking distance of the front of my age-group pack, not stopping once for water, until I missed my spear throw. Instead of the dejection I expected, my tired legs flooded with anger at my error and started cranking on their own through the penalty loop. "You go, girl," another female racer said, patting me on the shoulder as I brushed past her panting the now-familiar words, "On your left." I jammed up a hill on my hands and knees under barbed wire like a predator was chasing me—knowing my heart rate was at an unsustainable level, but also knowing there wasn't much farther to go. My mind froze into a single loop of thought: "Do not stop running. Whatever you do, don't stop."

And I didn't, until I crossed the finish line breathing like I was in a crowded room that only contained enough oxygen for one person.

Suddenly, there was my name, Gwendolyn Bounds, listed in the results among those women my age who were at the top of their game in this sport. Names I would soon see again and again as we ran, sweat, chatted, and followed each other into the next age bracket: Kim Cole of Idaho, Angelina Borisov of Tennessee, Angela Murphy from South Carolina, New York's Jody Musolino. I'd soon come to recognize many of their faces, and to know they were the ones I was trying to keep up with or beat. Some of the women I would chat with during longer running stretches of a race—about their work, their families, and how and where they trained. I learned from them, both on the course and off. After running neck and neck in the 45-49 Age Group at a race in San Francisco's Oracle Park with a woman named Robin Legat, we followed each other on Instagram, where I picked up training tips from the impassioned and at times humorous videos she posted. And there were moments of unexpected generosity, such as when South Carolina's first female captain of the highway patrol, Tara Laffin-Craig, offered me tips on how to complete the dreaded eight-foot Box obstacle. Tara raced in a skort (combo of shorts and skirt) and had a husband three years younger who'd gotten her hooked on Spartans. Often she would be my closest competitor down to the wire. I liked her. And I admired her consistent presence on the course.

I didn't know any of these women the way you know close friends. But in time, I knew them in a fashion that felt intimate nonetheless. I could sense when they were struggling by a subtle change in their gait or the way they approached an obstacle. Did they pause for a deep breath before climbing the rope, or did they jump right on? Were they jogging with the sandbag or walking? We had a general sense of one another's strengths and vulnerabilities. For instance, nearly all of them were faster than I. But as I got stronger, I could sometimes complete obstacles more quickly. If one of us sensed the other was fatigued, we might draw energy from that like glucose. If a few of us got bunched together mid-race, sometimes we'd verbally push each other as a pack with the mantra "Let's go pass some boys."

I deeply respected them all.

Not just for their physical prowess, which was substantial. Indeed, there were races where the women in their late forties and early fifties who regularly made the podium posted better times than some of those male and female competitors landing in the top ten of younger Age Group heats. Still, what I respected most was that these women were out racing hard and performing well, despite the snarl of middle-aged realities I knew awaited them off course. By now, all of us were probably more likely than not to have gotten a difficult medical diagnosis, lost someone we loved, or faced age discrimination in the workplace. We had kids, partners, dogs, cats, parents, employees, and other people and creatures who depended on us. Many of us were coping with the reality of the approach of menopause and the fatigue, hot flashes, and muscle and bone-density loss that can accompany it. In fact, if I hadn't been taking birth control pills continuously to prevent the endometriosis that had hindered my ability to get pregnant, I might have struggled more with my training. The steady flow of synthetic estrogen in the pills likely helped blunt some of the symptoms women face from hormonal changes as they age.

Matt B. Davis has interviewed many over-forty Age Group athletes for his *Obstacle Racing Media* podcast. There's a perspective and joy the older athletes bring to the sport, he tells me, that's likely a byproduct of this looming sense of being closer to the end of their days than the beginning. "When I hit fifty, I felt that in my bones. I was fucking scared. And then I started interviewing all these athletes who were forty plus. And they are crushing it. They really take pride in it. And they aren't these jacked-up guys who always looked that way. That's when something shifted for me. It's like, you have this job, and you make money, and you're a husband or a mom or whatever you are. And then your body starts to slow down, and it's like, 'What is there in life?' But then by going out there and doing something hard, you get to feel alive again."

I board the plane home to New York, elated to have brushed shoulders with this group of women and already thinking about whether I'll see some of them again at the next race on my calendar, in San Luis Obispo, California.

Maybe Faye and Jess were right, I think. Maybe this will be my year.

* * *

You know what comes next. You lived it. We all did. The trickle of news stories that at first seemed so removed from everyday life. Far, far away, there was a virus causing a respiratory illness that was bad enough to kill people. Within weeks, that trickle of stories became a steady flow of warnings as the disease, this "coronavirus," was detected spreading to other countries, including the United States. Now experts were saying it could jump quickly among humans. And then suddenly, or so it seemed, the dam broke, flooding us for the next two years with the twists and turns, mass confusion, and hysteria of an international health crisis that upended the world as we knew it. We all had to regroup, retrench, and relearn almost everything, from the once mundane task of securing toilet paper to the gravest matters of how to work, school our children, and stay safe among one another.

As for obstacle course racing? Well, it goes without saying that 2020 was *not* to be my year. Or at least not in the way I am envisioning on that elated plane ride home from Jacksonville.

I arrive home and carefully scrub mud from the crevices and laces of my special VJ brand obstacle racing shoes, this act also now familiar and comforting. As the hardened muck melts to a silky orange liquid, I replay the race in my head and say goodbye as my proof of effort runs into the grass. Then I store the shoes to dry on a shelf, where they will sit untouched for more than a year. Soon my race schedule empties as Spartan begins shutting down its events for the year. Sweating, breathing hard, and jumping into mud pits with other people? That's a no, nope, and no way, according to most health officials. Spartan's CEO, Joe De Sena, begins posting his daily training regimens online, and the company launches virtual races. The obstacle course racing community makes the best of things by posting funny videos of themselves competing around their homes: climbing a mountain of pillows on the bed, performing a sandbag carry with the dog or a toothbrush spear toss. But implicit in the jokey ether is the clear absence of one obvious goal for training: races.

There is no bell to ring.

It's my truest test yet of intrinsic versus extrinsic motivation to train. If winning, or achieving some kind of external benchmark or reward for an activity, is the primary driver, then the relationship with that activity is inherently fragile. Because the world is fragile and unstable.

Here, I think, is where age is another equalizer. By midlife, we've experienced fragility and instability before, and survived things that the first time around, individually, may have felt like never-ending misery but, in totality, give us perspective. This is what *Endure* author Alex Hutchinson was explaining a few chapters back: that life has a lot of obstacles that pop up, and when we're younger, it's easier to get thrown off and say, "Oh well, I'm not going to reach my goal, so let's move on to something else." Whereas once you've been around a few decades, it's easier to know that even if something doesn't pan out in the short term, you still can resume it later in some fashion.

There was a book I'd begun reading prior to Covid-19 called *Stillness Is the Key*, by the young modern-day Stoic philosopher Ryan Holiday. I remember a chapter in which Holiday wrote about the ancient Zen adage "Chop wood, carry water." It was in the context of just focusing on what you can control *now*. Not thinking about the past or worrying about what's to come. I'd heard that phrase before, but now the mantra stuck in my brain like a flashlight coming on in the darkness of this shut-down world.

Do the work. The work, not the outcome, is what matters.

And so, without any races, results, or podium placements to think about, everything related to obstacle course racing becomes just about the work. The simple act of practice for practice's sake. I can't worry about the next competition, because there isn't one. All I can do is train, rinse, and repeat. Which I do, even going so far as to set up a mock obstacle course race for myself alone on my dirt road. Standing at a starting line drawn in the gravel with my toe, I ask myself and the birds and squirrels this question:

"Spartans, what is your profession?"

"Aroo! Aroo! Aroo!" comes the lone human voice.

"Let's race!" that same voice commands herself.

And then I take off for three circuits of one-mile runs, a sandbag carry through our flowering gardens, a forty-pound bucket carry up past the tall blue house on the hill, a rope climb in the backyard, pull-ups in the garage (thank you, Lisa), hauling a boulder past our front gates and back. If I fail my spear throw, I do burpees. When I'm done, I drink a Fitaid and hang one of my old Spartan Sprint finisher medals around my neck. Then I recover lying on the driveway, watching the clouds, alone. No blaring rock music, no hum of food trucks. No podium. But it keeps me working. And it keeps me connected to something I miss so much that my nighttime dreams now coalesce around several repeating obstacle course scenarios. The nightmares include getting lost on a poorly marked course, being stuck in a wall of mud, and trying to stay warm in a sudden snowstorm that comes on while racing. But the good dreams, the ones I wish were true when I awake, find me flying across complicated multi-rigs, my grip firm, and sprinting like a cheetah down trails.

This homeostasis lasts for nine months, until just after the New Year of 2021, as the promise of not-yet-available vaccines fills the news. Spartan races begin to appear more frequently on the calendar again. I feel stronger. I feel faster. My me-vs.-me times improve. A few months earlier, I'd tested my fitness at a local non-Spartan obstacle race called the 8 Hour Ultra Viking Championship, where we stayed masked until crossing the starting line. I logged roughly thirty miles that day while climbing a ten-foot wall, crossing balance beams constructed from trees, hauling large logs, and traversing a five-panel series of vertical walls.

I'm ready to see where things stand back on the Spartan circuit.

Then one afternoon, while on a weekly call with my Consumer Reports editorial team, my nose starts to run, and I feel a bit achy. My thermometer reports a low-grade fever of 99.5°F. The next evening, I'm working and realize I can't taste the salt on the popcorn I'm eating. Lisa takes control. "We're both going to get tested."

I protest. Testing positive for Covid-19 is still somewhat unusual at this point, at least among the people we know. And getting tested itself requires an appointment and driving to a big parking lot set up with tents, run by state health officials, and waiting in line in your car.

"We haven't been anywhere," I tell her. "We can't have Covid."

"You went for your annual mammogram and sonogram last week," she reminds me.

It's true. I did travel to New York City for those screenings. But I wore two masks the entire time. Still, Lisa insists, so I agree. She also insists on quarantining me upstairs while she sleeps in our downstairs guest bedroom along with our new puppy—a bubbly twenty-pound Cavalier King Charles spaniel and poodle mix. I like this idea even less than I like getting tested. But I reluctantly agree.

She gets her results first. Negative.

"See?" I tell her. "It's fine." I say this even though my head is pounding, my feet are numb, and I have a rash across my abdomen.

A few hours later I get my phone alert and pull up the link, where the result is in bright red and not green. Red is bad, I think.

Positive.

"Dear Content Team—Last Friday night, I became a statistic. Not one I'd have hoped for, such as 'top 10 female obstacle racers in the world age 45-49.' Rather, an email from BioReference Laboratories relayed that I'd joined the ranks of 80 million+ people worldwide diagnosed with Covid-19.

"People are understandably curious about the virus, so here's what I know. . . ."

I email this letter to my staff and then sign off from work and spend most of the next two weeks alone in our bedroom with a pulse oximeter by my side, sweating and shivering through a fever. My feet are numb, and my oxygen saturation is in the low nineties, which my doctor tells me is borderline to go to the emergency room. (I don't.) Lisa and the puppy stay downstairs; she masks up and leaves food outside my door. A tired state health official calls to take my data; the disease is still new enough to warrant investigating. After he asks if I have chest and back pain, and I answer yes, his response is "That's not good. I don't want to hear that." His voice sounds broken and defeated from the sheer volume of calls he's made, and despite how bad I feel, I tell him to take care of himself. Before we hang up, he implores me not to die.

I expect my anxiety to kick in full force. Lisa does too. But something has shifted. Maybe it's because of obstacle course racing. Maybe the virus itself just doesn't scare me as much as a cancer diagnosis. Regardless, for the first time, I believe in my body—specifically, in my heart and my lungs. That they are strong, and I will recover. And so, to the extent I can, I continue to "chop wood, carry water." On day four, I force myself to walk outside on our dirt road for five minutes. It's the same dirt road I'd been sprinting down in mock races two weeks earlier, and now I can barely make it back to the house. But I do the same on day five, adding on another five minutes. On day six, I start forcing myself to do ten humble push-ups on my knees before bed. Remembering everything I know about muscle loss and bed rest is enough to force me out from under the covers. *Just move,* I tell myself. *Moving is all that matters.*

I find other ways to train. Lying in bed, I devour a book by James Nestor called *Breath: The New Science of a Lost Art.* (More unlearning to be done.) I download apps on breathing and work to control my oxygen intake and carbon dioxide release. I stretch. I meditate. I listen to podcasts about obstacle course racing.

Two weeks after my diagnosis, I emerge from quarantine weak, chest and back aching, and still napping between my meetings. Friends and colleagues begin sending stories about something called long Covid. I wish they wouldn't. I call my coaches, Faye and Jess, cognizant of how much fitness I've probably lost, and we figure out how to create a slow-comeback training plan.

Target date: a June half-marathon race in those rolling, muddy hills of Ohio. It will be 470 days since I rang my last bell. What would that time away mean for my aspirations of being a competent contender?

The Obstacle: Tyrolean Traverse
(faith)

In the longer versions of Spartan racing, racers generally encounter an obstacle called the Tyrolean Traverse. You may
remember I talked about it earlier. It's a long rope suspended horizontally about six feet off the ground. The goal is to start at one end
of the rope and make your way along it for about forty-five feet to tap
the bell hanging at the other end. The key is, you can't touch the
ground or let go until you reach the bell. The obstacle is modeled
and named after a common method used in mountaineering to
cross between two high spaces.

To recap, some people climb on top of the rope and pull themselves toward the bell, belly flat against it, with one leg dangling
toward the ground and the foot of the other hooked on the rope. But
it can take some deft maneuvering, especially if you're tired, to get up
on that rope and not topple off. And so a lot of racers, me included,
make the traverse upside down, headfirst, moving hand over hand,
either walking our legs along the rope as we pull ourselves along or—
in a sometimes faster but potentially more taxing move that can

burn unprotected skin—pulling the legs along the rope with one stacked atop the other.

Regardless of the technique, you can hear the bell jangling at the other end, almost like a taunt. In my early races, I'd pause midway and look to see how far away the bell still was. We all want to know when we'll reach our goal, especially when tired. But that pause just wasted grip strength and time. And so eventually, I willed myself to stop.

Because in the end, there was no point in looking. The bell was there. I'd reach it when I reached it. So long as I just kept pulling.

18

FINDING FLOW AT FIFTY

A week of rain has left the fields and backwoods of this Ohio town called Garrettsville a muddy, treacherous mess. They've just lifted the Covid-19 restrictions, and masks are off. In many ways, it's eerily like 2019, when I first raced here to redeem myself from my New Jersey DNF. Almost as if the world hasn't been shut down for more than a year. What has changed, clearly, are the economy and the job market. Help Wanted signs pepper the grounds of local businesses everywhere Erle and I look as we drive into Ohio. Political signs from last year's presidential election still adorn many properties, touting candidates from both sides of the political aisle.

It's warm and in the high sixties for my early-morning start time. Ohio's terrain is modest in terms of elevation, but the course can be deceptively difficult after a big rain. Driving to the race, Eric Church and Beyoncé accompanying us once again for the ride, I'm unusually calm, my typical precompetition jitters left behind at a Fairfield Inn off Interstate 80.

"You OK?" Erle asks. He's playing wingman for me once again. Ever since the pull-up-bar incident, I've been mindful of how many races I expect Lisa to sit through. And a seven-hour drive to Ohio, beautiful as it is, did not rank high on her to-do list.

"Yep," I tell him, counting the Help Wanted signs silently as we pass one low-slung manufacturer or retailer after another. "I actually am."

We continue for a bit without speaking. We've both been here before. This sleepy ride is now as familiar as Church's race-day lyrics.

"Remember when you did thirty burpees in the festival area here two years ago?" Erle asks.

I laugh. "Yeah, that volunteer thought I was crazy."

Faye and Jess have prepped me as carefully as they can for today's half-marathon Beast competition. Starting in February, once I felt able to run again, they'd begun slowly adding short intervals of faster running, with easy jogs in between, that got longer as the weeks progressed. The first outings were dreadful. My legs felt rubbery, heavy, and detached from my body. The first real slow run post-Covid-19 was only twenty minutes and left my heart rate jacked up even at a glacial 12:45-minute mile on flat terrain. I couldn't stay awake past 2 P.M. and had to block an hour during the day to sleep and then catch up on work at night.

"You're going to have to fight to get back what you've lost," Jess told me after I fretted out loud about my sluggishness and spewed a bunch of doubt into the phone. "But it's always easier to get back to where you once were than to build fitness for the first time—your body remembers. Patience."

And so once again, I turned my brain's central governor over to my coaches and did what I was told. And after five or six weeks, things started to stabilize as they consistently ramped up my workouts with longer runs and increasingly heavier weight to lift, along with regular rounds of burpees thrown in for good measure.

Chop wood. Carry water.

Soon enough, an unfamiliar calm begins creeping into my type A life. This calm, it extends beyond training and seems to open my sight line to the rest of the world. In fact, that which once seemed mundane and routine I now sometimes observe as strangely vibrant. I chop tomatoes and find odd comfort in the sound of my knife hitting the cutting board. An ordinary training session in the woods will send me to my knees at the end, breathing in the damp earth in a moment of respect for my surroundings, skin electrified by the spray of a nearby stream. No doubt, the fresh reminder of my mortality, thanks to Covid-19, is playing its role. But the sound of Lisa and our puppy breathing at night fills me with such peace that each evening before I sleep, I think: Please, just one more day like this one.

I am still bathed in this calm when Erle and I pull into the race venue. As I smell the smoke at the fire jump and hear the booming music and see all the vendors—Mike's Hard Lemonade, Athletic Brewing, various CBD purveyors—all I can think is: I'm home.

This Zen-ness gets immediately tested at registration when the volunteer can't figure out what my starting time is and asks loudly, "What age group are you running?" Suddenly it feels like every head within a quarter-mile radius turns to look at me.

"Fifty to fifty-four," I mumble, almost not believing the words. I'm still forty-nine, but you race in the category of the age you'll turn that year.

"I'm sorry, what? I couldn't hear you," the smooth-skinned young man with thick, wavy hair and zero wrinkles says.

Fine.

"Fifty to fifty-four," I pronounce loudly. Erle grins and looks away. People stare at me for a minute, and so I raise my arms in the air triumphantly—"And now you *all* know how old I am!"

Laughter. And some polite retorts: "You look great!" "Knock 'em dead."

I study my gray age-group wristband, which is printed with some nice, fat numbers representing the ages of the racers who will start together: 50–54, 55–59, 60+. And then I realize: this is the only wristband I'll ever wear again in Spartan racing. They don't group you beyond 60+. Probably there simply aren't enough people who make it to that age and still can, or want to, put their body through this sport's tortures, aka pleasures. Once more, as happened that summer morning five years ago when I woke up and googled, "What are the hardest things you can do?" it occurs to me that I am now closer to the end than I am to the beginning.

I wait for despair to set in. But it doesn't come. Instead, just more of this same calm. After hugging Erle goodbye, I strap on my wrist-band and join the mash-up of unmasked humans taking their warm-up laps before hitting those still-fresh porta potties one last time.

You probably know the concept of being "in the zone."

The late Hungarian American psychologist Mihaly Csikszentmih-alyi described this concept as the experience of "flow." It's a state where actions and decisions move from one to the next seamlessly and effortlessly. Like playing jazz. He believed activities that com-bined hard work and play offered the best chance for flow and subse-quent happiness, so long as you could find the sweet spot between boredom (from something being too easy) and anxiety (from it being too difficult).

Csikszentmihalyi might be credited as the first to popularize the term in his seminal 1990 book, *Flow: The Psychology of Optimal Experi-ence,* but the search for this perfect state of optimal consciousness—when time speeds up or slows down for whatever endeavor is under way—has intrigued humans for centuries. We now know it as "being in the zone" or a "runner's high" or a "peak experience." One key tenet is that your action and your awareness merge; it's a state of oneness with whatever your task. Performance, both mental and physical, surges.

I'd certainly felt moments of being in the zone while writing. But never anything close to it through a physical endeavor—probably because I didn't have the right set of skills to pair with the right chal-lenge. In a sunny Mexico beachside farming and fishing village on the Baja Peninsula, the Modern Elder Academy teaches flow as part of its workshops, which are designed to help people navigate midlife and what comes next. Its founder, Chip Conley, wrote a book called *Learning to Love Midlife.* He tells me: "I believe that flow becomes more important as we age, as we need to move from the weight of the world (which is easy to store up) to the wonder of the world."

Flow is now widely taught in places such as Conley's academy, entrepreneurial start-ups, and corporate boardrooms—all with the goal of enhancing creativity, decision-making, and performance. In my case, though, a classroom wasn't where I'd ultimately find the key to unlocking physical flow and the "wonder of the world."

Rather, it was amid barbed wire, the stench of human sweat, and a whole lot of mud.

Even in the first half mile of the race, I can tell something is different. The first thing I notice is simply how good it feels to be moving again among other people who aren't on screens. Covid-19 bestowed loneliness on most of us in some way. Training without Pete or anyone else to swing, crawl, and groan alongside me has left a hole. The juice I feel from humanity swelling together in the woods is almost overwhelming at the start of these thirteen miles, like a drug putting me on high alert.

In fact, every lime-green leaf, moss-laden rock, bit of mud clinging to my calf, song of birds, seems to register. I identify each approaching obstacle before it comes into view by its unique voice—the squeak of rotating bars at the Twister, where you move across the obstacle using tiny hand grips; the dull hum of palms hitting monkey bars; the continual jangle of the bell at the end of the Tyrolean Traverse rope. Even when I fail The Box, still unable to scale its eight-foot-high slippery face, I am smiling through my penalty.

This race is when I first notice Tara, the South Carolina highway patrol captain, in her racing skirt/shorts combo. I don't know her name yet, so I just think of her as Running Skirt. She is neck and neck with me almost the whole course—like, I really can't shake her—until I trip over a protruding tree root and smack my head on a rock. That separates us. I sit on the ground and shake my brain a few times, then get back up.

The fall is motivational, if only because I *really* want to get some Tylenol. So I start running faster, until I finally catch back up with Running Skirt. At some point I can tell she's choosing her foot placement more carefully, which means she may be tiring just a bit. And that's when I make a move and pass her. It's my first actual moment of specifically marking myself against another competitor, sensing a potential opening and trying to exploit it. Except, honestly, the overwhelming sensation I have is of feeling a little bit rude.

I miss my first leap for the ropes at the Slip Wall; the ropes are often shorter in a longer Beast race like today's. So I take a deep breath and then run as hard as I can, barely grab a rope, land on my belly, and then get up and walk to the top of the wall. From there, it's just a few more obstacles. I hit the Spear Throw, and then I'm over the A-Frame Cargo, leap the Fire Jump, and am done.

It's only after I find Erle, rinse off under the cold hoses, eat a banana, drink a Fitaid, and get a quick concussion clearance (along with some Tylenol) in the medical tent that I check my results.

Second place. The silver medal.

For the first time since this journey began five years earlier—no, for the first time in my life—I am going to stand on the podium at a sports event.

Immediately, doubt creeps in. "Don't text my parents or Lisa yet," I tell Erle. "It might not stick. You know the results sometimes change. Maybe I miscounted my burpees or something."

The awards ceremony starts with the youngest racers, so Erle and I stand around for a while trying to find shade in the hot sun. I'm so nervous about the results being a mistake that when the announcer finally says, "And in second place, from"—and I hear him call out my hometown, I trip trying to make it to the stage.

Classic.

It wasn't a close race, and there were only six of us in my age group today. Covid-19 is still tamping down race attendance. And as I'll come to see in future races, there are generally fewer racers in the age groups over fifty, particularly among women. Sometimes there will be only a single 60+ female contender, or none at all. It's one thing to put a body that age through a road race and another to demand that it crawl under barbed wire and haul forty-pound sandbags through mountains and mud. Part of the secret to victory at this age is attrition: just be the last one standing.

According to the final results today, I'm roughly nineteen minutes behind the first-place finisher, a woman named Nancy Neff from Saint Augustine, Florida, who is so fit and lean I wonder if she's not actually thirty. And I'm about fourteen minutes ahead of Tara (Running Skirt), who takes third. As we stand on the podium together, posing for pictures with our medals, I see Cory, the Ohio nurse, in the crowd, cheering next to Erle.

Remember this moment, I tell myself. You may never stand here again. Just take this in.

Then, despite my headache, Erle and I go back to the hotel and get a bottle of champagne to celebrate. There are two more races the next day, but I'm not planning to race after the fall (or the champagne).

Or at least that's what I tell myself when I go to bed.

I awake at 5 A.M. in the chilly air of the Fairfield Inn, thirsty, and stretch to check what hurts. Everything, I decide. There's a small lump on the front of my forehead, and the time off from racing has clearly taken its toll on my ability to recover. I meditate, drink a lot of water, and fall back asleep so hard that I dream I'm trying to find a bathroom in the house of my childhood best friend, Louise—the one who protected me in dodgeball. My legs twitch in the sheets, and I don't wake up until 7:30 A.M., when I'm falling off a cliff in a race and the impact jerks me alert.

For a moment, I lie there and imagine using the day to rest before we drive home.

Then I pick up my cellphone and call Erle.

His voice is thick and pained, like he accidentally drank Drano. Like I said, not a morning person.

"Good morning," he croaks. "Let me guess. You want to go and race."

* * *

The starting line for the afternoon 5K Sprint race is more crowded than the longer Beast race the day before. Yesterday's winner in my age group, Nancy, is lined up to run again, as is Running Skirt. Both have already completed the 10K Super this morning, which gives me hope, because the way my legs feel right now listening to the opening chants, I'm figuring I'll walk half the race.

Who am I?

What is your profession?

Let's race!

At "Let's race!" something inexplicable happens. My legs take off without my mind telling them to, or, more precisely, my legs unite with my mind in a fusion that feels nuclear at a cellular level. I move so fast from the starting line that I quickly take the lead among the women in my Age Group and soon start passing the men. I hit the monkey bars, which are slippery, and without thinking, switch techniques to keep from falling and hit the bell. My arms lift me over walls without my asking them to. My strength feels limitless, as if all the pent-up uncertainty and loneliness of the past fourteen months is sweating out of my pores, and what's left is clean, pure power.

Call it being in the zone. Call it flow. Whatever this is, I'm in my fiftieth year of life and it's the closest I've ever come to a state of physical grace.

Time folds on itself—we could have been running for five minutes or an hour; I have no idea—until I'm racing for the final gauntlet of obstacles and spy an earthworm struggling in the race path. Suddenly, whatever force has taken over my body abruptly leaves me. And I'm just Wendy again, the daughter of a veterinarian, who as a little girl used to pick up dead birds and squirrels off our neighborhood streets and bury them. I stop in my tracks, turn around, scoop up the cool-bodied creature, and deposit it carefully in the woods so he/she (Maybe they are sexless, I think, watching it writhe in the dirt) won't be trampled.

"*What the hell are you doing?*" I hear my coach Faye screaming. It's imaginary; she's not actually there. But it feels very real. "You're in first place for the first time in your life, and you're *moving an earthworm?*"

On her command, I lock back in and sprint through the final challenges, nail my spear throw, and jump over the fire to cross the finish line in a clean race, having failed no obstacles and saved an earthworm. I look down at my Swatch watch, but the old analog hands have frozen somewhere mid-race. Later I'll learn there are seven minutes between me and my nearest age-group competitor, Nancy, who won the race yesterday and the one earlier this morning.

Right now mind and body separate—mind finding its voice to speak again as I see Erle, who happens to be hanging around at the finish line.

"Oh my God," he says. "You're already back. Are you OK? What happened?"

I tap the screen of my dormant Swatch. After giving me twenty-one and a half races, today it has apparently stopped ticking for good during whatever time-freeze universe I've entered. And then, with a twinge of sadness for my deceased mechanical wrist race companion, I turn to Erle. And the unequivocal words that come out of my mouth are these—words so unfamiliar they are like a foreign language.

"I crushed it."

An hour later they hang a gold medal around my neck.

19

THE FINAL STRETCH

The Facebook post tagging me offers a simple six-word tease:

"Wendy, I have seen your future!"

Below the words, my friend Jo Bass from UNC–Chapel Hill has posted a link featuring a Missouri woman with stark-white hair slithering on her belly under barbed wire in a gooey pool of mud—mud that is plastered across her body and in the crevices of the many wrinkles lining her smiling face. The image links to an article whose headline reads: "83-Year-Old Woman Becomes Oldest Tough Mudder Competitor."

I stare at that photo. I note the woman's flexibility. I study her crawling technique. But mostly I fixate on her smile. I know that look. It's the "Yep, I'm really doing this!" smile. This woman, "Muddy Mildred" as the story dubs her, reportedly holds the distinction of being the oldest person to complete a 5K Tough Mudder, another brand of obstacle course adventure race that generally focuses more on teamwork and camaraderie than the more individualistic Spartan race. (Spartan bought Tough Mudder in 2020.)

Something tightly coiled unwinds in my chest. A loosening, as if I've finally solved a mystery that once seemed unsolvable. Yes, *this*, I think. This is what my eighties could be. *This* is the opposite of the slow decline. *This* makes sense. *This* is a visual of aging that excites me.

A few months earlier, I'd seen a similarly inspiring Instagram post about eighty-year-old Paul Lachance, who recently had completed his tenth Spartan Race Trifecta. In Spartan racing, as a refresher, a Trifecta is that feat of conquering all three of the mainstay distances of the race—half marathon, 10K, and 5K—within a calendar year. Paul, a navy veteran, had done that ten times in a single year. There he was in the photo holding up a fat Trifecta 10x medal, wearing a cap that said UNBREAKABLE, a still-taut, leathery bicep pushing against his sleeve.

He too was smiling.

What struck me most was that neither Paul nor Mildred moved like an old person. I'd been thinking about this a lot after a few minor training injuries landed me in the hands of some capable sports medicine specialists. One of them was a New York chiropractor and certified strength and conditioning specialist named Peter Duggan. The walls of his clinic hold signed photographs and news clippings from Olympic and Ironman athletes as well as MLB, NFL, and NASCAR professionals who are clients—but he regularly treats mere mortals like me.

"Do you move like a younger person or what an old man looks like?" Duggan said to me at one point as he worked on my right foot, where I'd torn my plantar fascia after neglecting that nubby little roller ball. "We all have that friend who is seventy-five and moves like a younger person, and the one who is forty and moves around like an old man." He urged me to practice moving in multiple planes—not just frontward or backward, but also side to side—with exercises including lateral lunges, lunges with torso rotation, and sideways hopping. These sorts of movements, he insists, are key to moving like a younger person, whether for everyday activities or for competing in an obstacle course race.

It got me to thinking: Where did I stand on the road to becoming a Muddy Mildred or Paul Lachance? In the last five years, I'd achieved a level of athletic performance that once seemed utterly off the table. My birdlike frame now carried real muscle definition. And there was no denying that I *felt* stronger and faster than when I was thirty-five. Pushing my limits with obstacle course racing had cleared a view to a future of aging I'd never thought possible. How could I measure and track my progress toward having a chance to move like Mildred or Paul if I ever reached their age?

I turned to science to find out.

Today, an increasing number of tests and tools can measure how our bodies are responding to age. They can track, among other things, our respiratory fitness, muscle mass, bone density, and key blood biomarkers to give us a road map for action.

One steamy July morning, I drive to the Tisch Sports Performance Center at the Hospital for Special Surgery in New York City. There, an upbeat, trim exercise physiologist named Kate Baird straps a tight-fitting mask to my face, making me feel a little like a Top Gun fighter pilot, and directs me onto a treadmill. The mask is attached to tubing that connects to a cart with a computer. Over the next forty-five minutes, this contraption will measure my oxygen consumption and CO_2 production as part of a Metabolic Performance Profile analysis, which includes a lactate profile and VO_2 max test.

The VO_2 max test is considered one of the gold-standard measures of cardiorespiratory fitness, which is correlated with longevity. It analyzes aerobic capacity—the body's ability to take in, transport, and use oxygen to perform vigorous physical activity. My VO_2 max score essentially will benchmark the "size of my engine," as Baird explains it to me. Many factors can influence VO_2 max, according to exercise experts, including genetics, gender, and age. While it's generally assumed that VO_2 max will decline with age, you can train to keep it as high as possible.

Every four minutes during the test, Baird will prick my finger to take a blood sample and analyze something called my lactate profile. That will help us understand how my body is using energy and fatiguing at different intensities of exercise. The more work I can perform (faster pacing, higher power) without a rapid increase in lactate, the better.

I nod as she explains all of this, Top Gun mask bobbing up and down.

We start out slow at a 13:20-minute-per-mile pace, and then after four minutes, I hop off the treadmill for Kate to quickly prick my finger. Then I hop back on, and she speeds up the treadmill a little while, asking me to estimate how hard I feel I'm working by pointing to a level on a chart. We do this nine times, and for the first eight sections, I feel pretty good. It helps that we've got the stereo system pumping Kelly Clarkson's "Stronger (What Doesn't Kill You)" and Kate is cheering me on. Then we drop from an 8:13-minute-per-mile pace to 7:48 minutes per mile, and I start to hit a wall. After that four-minute session, I motion to stop the test with my heart rate hovering near 180 beats per minute.

"I think you'll be pleased," Kate says after I drop my sweaty body into a chair, very happy I'd thought to put on extra deodorant before the test.

From prior research, I know my VO_2 max result generally will fall into one of five categories: low, below average, above average, high, or elite—each category being calibrated for biological sex and age group in ten-year spans. My results land me in the high-performer camp for my 50–59 age group and for someone who is 40–49 or even 30–39. Also, I use about the same amount of oxygen as elite runners when running at the faster end of my range, according to Kate's report, which is apparently a good thing.

But there is room for improvement. The more I can improve my VO_2 max, the larger a buffer I'll have as I age and my VO_2 max naturally declines. My thirteen-page final report from Baird also notes that I clear lactate slowly (or did after this test), which could hurt my ability to recover from the bursts of energy needed for hills, short sprints, and obstacles during racing. I forward the report to my coaches, Faye and Jess, so they can tweak my running training accordingly. After Jess and I note that my running cadence—how many strides I take per minute—is particularly low, which could negatively impact my performance, I download a metronome app and listen to it while running, which makes me feel a bit like the ticking crocodile who swallowed a clock in *Peter Pan*.

(One note: you don't need access to a VO_2 max test facility to get a general estimate of your respiratory fitness. There's a free way to do it called the Cooper test, where you run as far as you can for twelve minutes and then plug your distance into a mathematical formula— search "Cooper test" online—to determine your relative VO_2 max score. Some fitness watches and trackers also provide VO_2 max measurements.)

Now I have a game plan for my respiratory fitness. But what about my muscles and bones—how are things faring on that front?

To start, I seek out a doctor with the necessary equipment to perform what's called a DEXA (dual-energy X-ray absorptiometry) scan to look at my bone density, body fat, and lean mass, which includes muscle. Many people are aware of the importance of bone density, and their physicians may test for it as they age. But muscle, as we now know, really matters as well to protect against the physical assaults of aging. Lose your muscle mass and strength and you're at risk of falling. And that's bad, because falling is the leading cause of injury and injury-related death for adults sixty-five years of age and older. The doctor's written evaluation of my DEXA scan report tells me I am "operating in a peak capacity with a good balance of lean mass and bone density." When we discuss the results later, my physician says with a laugh, "I'm going to tell all the people working in the front office that they should start obstacle course racing."

But there is still room to improve. In middle age, and particularly for women, any extra muscle mass is generally beneficial because it's going to get a whole lot harder to maintain going forward. A year later, after continuing to train and race, I will repeat the scan with my doctor and have added 3.25 pounds of lean mass (which, again, includes muscle) that is well distributed across my body. I hypothesize the improvement might be attributable to the fact that (A) Faye has pushed me to incorporate heavier weights into my strength routine, and (B) I've taken up a pastime called rucking after, surprise, Erle had started doing it. Rucking involves walking or hiking with a weighted rucksack (generally a backpack) and was long a staple of military training before it became a pastime for the masses. It can build both muscle strength and cardiovascular fitness. I now throw on my rucksack to wear while walking our dog, which is a good way to get in an extra workout.

Then there is grip strength, which not only is crucial for everyday tasks such as opening tight jar lids or catching yourself in a fall but has been shown to have a predictive link with all-cause and disease-specific mortality. And holding our screens (whether sitting or standing) does little to help us with grip and might even make our hands weaker. I buy a twenty-three-dollar tool online called a hand dynamometer, which you squeeze for five seconds with as much force as possible. The LCD display readout tells me I clock in straddling the "normal" and "strong" categories on both hands for my age. This is fine, but I set a goal to reach "strong" and double down on some of my grip work. To test your own grip strength, you also can practice hanging from a bar, like I did on the pull-up bar at that North Carolina park with Dolly. Hanging for at least thirty seconds generally is considered OK. One minute or above is better. I was up to just over a hundred seconds when I practiced regularly with Dolly.

These are a few of the tests I use to mark where I am on my fitness journey. There are plenty of others out there, and a good place to start learning is listed in the Sources and Notes section at the end of this book.

And what has this respiratory and strength training done for my overall metabolic health? My blood pressure, which had been elevated before I began racing, has come down to a healthier 106/72 mm Hg. Key biomarkers related to my heart—cholesterol, triglycerides, ApoB, Lp(a)—all check out as very healthy in bloodwork. Some of the results are due to genetics, some to actions I've taken. If you want to find a comprehensive explanation of these biomarkers, as well as a guide to assess and improve your own longevity potential, I recommend the book *Outlive: The Science & Art of Longevity* by the physician Peter Attia with journalist and author Bill Gifford. It's written in a very accessible way for the layperson and can help you set an agenda to discuss with your own doctor.

The one borderline result in my bloodwork is my blood sugar (glucose) levels, which sometimes still teeter close to the prediabetes range, despite a diet that includes no sugary drinks, no candy, and moderate amounts of processed food. This elevation has shown up through the years in multiple different measurements, including for my fasting glucose, hemoglobin A1c, and fructosamine levels. Most of my physicians have shrugged off this slight elevation. "Eat less chocolate" was one common retort. Except, I rarely eat chocolate. And I know that if left unchecked, chronically higher blood glucose can lead to a myriad of problems, such as diabetes, and eventually can damage nerves, blood vessels, tissues, and organs. I don't want to get to that point if I can help it.

"How is this possible if I'm exercising this much and eating so well?" I keep asking my doctors. There aren't many satisfactory answers—even in New York City and even for someone with good health insurance. Apparently, our bodies can react very differently to foods, so it's not necessarily one-size-fits-all.

However, now you can track your own body response through continuous glucose monitoring (CGM) with a little wearable device that measures how different foods, exercise, sleep, and stress impact your glucose levels. I've seen several of the Elite Spartan athletes wearing them at races. So I sign up online for a three-month subscription with a company (there are multiple ones that do this) that ships me the CGM devices directly and pairs me with a nutritionist. I then begin tracking my levels daily in real time on an app, along with everything I eat.

It is eye-opening. Those healthy fruit smoothies I love so much? They spike my glucose with the liquefied fruit. That doesn't happen when I eat berries whole. A bagel—even one covered with healthy salmon—pushes my levels high. Sushi with generous amounts of white rice? The rice turns out to be another culprit. Again, each of our bodies responds differently to foods and the portions we consume. For several months, I experiment with foods and tweak my diet. I learn which grains, such as barley, I tolerate better and how foods high in fat and protein (such as eggs) don't generally raise my glucose significantly. I also discover that if my blood sugar spikes, the surest way to bring it down is to take a brisk twenty-minute walk.

And guess what doesn't spike my numbers? Dark chocolate.

Months later I retest my glucose and all my results are well within the normal range. One measure—my hemoglobin A1c—is low enough now, at 5.0, that my doctor circles it on the report with an exclamation point.

Without the prompt of obstacle course racing, and thus the overall focus on and research about my health, I doubt I'd have ever pushed for this extra information. Maybe I'd have just shrugged off my borderline numbers and chalked it up to the inevitable siege of middle age. And it's possible things might have progressed to a far more unhealthy state. Did figuring all this out take time? Yep. Did it cost money? Some—but ultimately, a few hundred dollars and few months of wearing a glucose monitor may well have saved me a whole lot of problems and money on medical bills down the road.

None of these numbers guarantee anything, of course, but they do put me in the driver's seat of my own health to some degree, giving back a little bit of that control I felt I'd ceded with my melanoma diagnosis. Over time, I've begun to recast the network of people who help take care of my body as a "pit crew." A pit crew is the team of people who keep a car (or human) humming during races, whether by replacing tires or refueling, in the case of a vehicle, or in the case of humans, by providing hydration, food, and motivation during particularly long endurance races. In that respect, I endeavor to think of my pit crew as human mechanics who can optimize, protect, and help fix me when I break. But ultimately, I still must drive. It is a crew with wide-ranging capabilities: cardiologist, gynecologist,

dermatologist, dentist, gastroenterologist, optometrist, chiropractor, psychiatrist, and two physical therapists. I even have an otolar-
yngologist (ENT) who has sucked out dirt lodged deep in my ear
from the muddy dunk wall obstacle in races. Gross, I know. Having
health insurance makes it possible financially. But scheduling the
appointments and not being on autopilot about my health—well,
that is on me.

In his book *Outlive*, Peter Attia makes a list of things he still wants
to be able to do physically in later decades of life. It's something, he
writes, that he discusses with his patients as well. After I first heard
him mention this list on one of his podcasts, I'd started scratching
down my own set of later-life physical goals in my "Don't Let Your
Crop Die" spiral notebook:

1. Stack firewood
2. Take off my socks and pants while standing up (one leg at a
   time, obviously)
3. Get up and out of a chair without using my arms
4. Walk three miles in the snow and ice without falling
5. Lift and empty a 40 lb. bag of water softener salt
6. Carry my 50 lb. dog to the car if she/he is sick
7. *To be continued . . .*

Curiously, my original list doesn't include obstacle course racing.
That's probably because back then I never conceived that someone
in their eighties could still be out on the course, unless someone was
carrying them.

But then I hadn't talked to Muddy Mildred yet.

And I didn't know about the "will to live" research.

Mildred rings me back, still a little breathless. "Sorry I missed
your call. I was out playing pickleball."

She'd completed her first three-mile Tough Mudder at age eighty, she tells me (her most recent being earlier this year at eighty-four) after supporting her son Danny at the World's Toughest Mudder, a twenty-four-hour obstacle course endurance event. After watching him come in from each lap, the Cape Girardeau, Missouri, mother offhandedly told her son, "I sure wish I had done something like this when I was younger."

To which she recalls Danny saying, "Mom, if you want to do it, I'll see that you can do it."

Gauntlet thrown, Mildred signed up for personal training at the local YMCA. She was already walking two miles a day but wanted to build upper-body strength to help her on the walls and heavy carries. She did this for four to five months. She also got checked out by her doctor to make sure he didn't have concerns about her attempting the race. "He clapped his hands for joy," she recalls.

Having worked for a decade at a vending machine company starting at age sixty-five, a job that required her to lift bags of coins weighing thirty to fifty pounds shoulder high to load them into the machines, Mildred says she felt confident about her odds of finishing her first Tough Mudder. And with Danny helping, she did. I ask her about the photo I'd seen posted on my Facebook page of her crawling under the barbed wire. Wasn't it hard to move like that at her age?

"No," she states matter-of-factly. "As long as you stay down low and don't get your hair caught."

Check that.

Last question. Does she believe she can do almost anything, despite her age?

"Most of the time," Mildred answers, "yes."

Will to live.

In 2002, a researcher at Yale University named Becca Levy made a sizable media splash when she and her colleagues published results of research that had reexamined findings from one of the country's most detailed looks into aging in late-twentieth-century America. Starting in 1975, participants had been interviewed about their health, work life, and family, and their thoughts on aging, with questions such as "Do you agree or disagree that as you get older you are less useful?" Levy and her fellow researchers had taken those findings—known as the Ohio Longitudinal Study on Aging and Retirement—and overlaid it with mortality data.

What she found made headlines. Older individuals with more positive perceptions of aging had lived 7.5 years longer on average than those with less positive perceptions. This longevity advantage remained even after accounting for age, gender, socioeconomic status, degree of loneliness, and functional health. And one of the indirect forces believed to fuel this longer life span was identified as "will to live."

Levy, a professor of epidemiology at Yale's School of Public Health, continued to investigate how beliefs about aging can influence our health. In study after study, she found that older people with more positive perceptions of aging performed better physically and cognitively than those with more negative perceptions; they were more likely to recover from severe disability, they remembered better, they walked faster, and they even lived longer. Levy notes that the survival advantage of having positive age beliefs has been replicated by at least ten other research groups worldwide. She chronicles her research journey meticulously in the book *Breaking the Age Code: How Your Beliefs About Aging Determine How Long & Well You Live.*

I've witnessed these findings playing out in my own family. When my father was seventy-seven years old, he was up on the metal roof of my parents' house power-washing it—which he'd done without incident for the past twenty years—when he slipped and fell. For those of you now thinking, "What was your father doing on the roof at seventy-seven?" you are setting up my next point nicely. No offense, but my father is simply not interested in what people think a seventy-seven-year-old should be doing. Neither is my mother, frankly. Both still like to rise at dawn, leave the warm bed unmade with their dog in it, and head out on the sometimes choppy inlet to fish for Spanish mackerel and bluefish in the coastal waters before the day begins. They are just like Muddy Mildred and still believe they can do almost anything. And so up on the roof my father was, and then he turned and slipped and plummeted ten feet to the concrete driveway below.

In the next few hours of chaos, fear, and uncertainty, as an ambulance rushed him to the trauma center at Camp Lejeune, more than one person noted to my mother that my father should be dead. Or have brain damage. Or at least be paralyzed. He'd left a big, bloody imprint of his head on the driveway when my mom, alerted by their barking dog, found him sitting, dazed, on the carport wall. But he was very much alive. He could walk. And he was making sense as he talked to the doctors while they scanned him. Then, with his pelvis and the C2 vertebra of his neck each fractured in two places, he ultimately walked out of the trauma center to my mother's car and went home later that same day.

Throughout his recovery, my dad was itching to get back to his activities: tending to their five acres of property on his tractor, splitting wood, and lifting heavy motors on and off their fishing boat. It took my mother threatening to divorce him after fifty-six years of marriage (she was joking . . . I think) for him to sit still in a neck brace and recover over the summer. He had no interest in the jigsaw puzzles I sent to help keep him occupied.

A year and a half later, a prominent Harvard-trained orthopedic surgeon at the UNC School of Medicine took a CT scan of my father's neck and, with notable astonishment, pronounced him healed.

Will to live. A reason to get up in the morning. An event to look forward to. Levy notes all these forces as possible mechanisms to extend life. Did my dad's good physical fitness help protect him? Of course. Once, over the course of two months, he mixed nineteen pallets of concrete in a wheelbarrow and built a bulkhead to protect their property from seawater erosion. Doing the rough math, that equaled about 798 bags of cement, with each bag weighing eighty pounds—or thirty-two tons in total—that he handled. Same with Mildred's lifting of heavy bags of coins from ages sixty-five to seventy-five, walking two miles a day, and now her sometimes three hours daily of pickleball competition. But both share another nonphysical trait, which is that they think they can do most anything, regardless of their age.

After his stroke, Lisa's father, by some measures, lost many things that once made him *him*. His ability to captivate an audience with a long story, give his daughters career advice, dress himself in his own beautiful wardrobe, drive the cars he loved. And on top of that, he lost the freedom to walk and use his once dominant right hand. Still, he lived five more years—longer than nearly any doctor believed he would. He relearned to brush his teeth and comb his hair and taught himself to eat with his left hand. He sang beloved standards, recalling every word; constantly told Stella, his wife of fifty-nine years, how much he loved her; and wept with elation each time Lisa, her sister, or his grandson, Liam, walked in the door. And he surprised us still with the occasional witty one-liner, even as Stella now took the lead in mealtime conversations. When he finally died, seven months after Lisa's mom underwent double coronary bypass surgery, many people warned Lisa her mother would go downhill fast. "It always happens," they said. But it didn't. At age eighty-three, much like my own mom, my mother-in-law started working out at the gym three days a week, planned an adventurous trip to Greece with her daughters, and began attending local civic association meetings.

Will to live.

Before we close our story in the coming pages, I want to share a final call to action from Mildred for each of us, no matter what hard thing we are thinking about doing, no matter how much it might scare us, no matter how old we are.

"I would say if people were interested in doing something, whether they really can or not, they ought to give it a try and then they know. And just kind of get that out of their system," says the woman who in her ninth decade on earth scrambled over inverted walls, carried heavy sandbags, and crawled through mud under barbed wire.

"I would have hated to have said 'Oh, Danny, I can't do this at my age' and have missed all of this."

In other words, if you question whether you can still do something bold, chances are, it's not too late.

The Obstacle: Fire Jump
(endings & beginnings)

Jumping over fire is a familiar challenge on race-courses, with the obstacle bearing names such as Blazed for Savage Race or Pyromaniac for Rugged Maniac competitions. In Spartan races, because the more literally labeled Fire Jump is usually the last obstacle, it naturally sets racers up for a spectacular final photo opportunity before the finish line, should they so choose. Elite racers are generally subdued—been there, done that—but other competitors make a show of it. There's the kick-your-legs-to-the-side over the logs and flames maneuver. Or the point-one-finger-to-the-sky leap. Some people hold hands with their partners or friends. Others make crazy faces and stick out their tongues. The flames' size varies by venue and weather conditions, but people are generally smart enough to jump high. It is real fire, after all.

We have an inclination as humans to want to mark the end of something hard with an exclamation point. It makes sense, this tribute to our sweat (real or metaphorical), our struggle, and maybe our pain. Plus, while endings signal completion, they also raise the inevitable question, What's next? Pausing to celebrate puts off having to answer that question, if only for a few heartbeats. I'm no different. I'm a finger-in-the-air jumper.

Sometimes, though, Spartan throws a curveball, and crossing the finish line doesn't mean you are necessarily at the end. A volunteer will point toward an extra-mile loop and ask if you'd like to run that before accepting your finisher medal, grabbing a banana, and relaxing. The loop is not required; it has no impact on your race time.

The implicit question is this: Sure, you are exhausted, muddy, and maybe bruised and sore. Everybody is. But are you truly finished? Or are you prepared to push a little more? Do you want to know what it's like to choose that extra-mile loop? Is there still something left in your tank?

I love the extra mile. Because it feels like that's how an ending can become a new beginning.

20

YOU'LL KNOW
AT THE FINISH LINE

There is a moment of silence during which I wonder if she hasn't heard me. And then:

"Wait, I'm sorry. You want to go *where*?"

She heard me.

I clear my throat. The nonchalance with which I attempted to sugarcoat my last sentence has melted quickly in Lisa's ears.

"Abu Dhabi," I repeat nervously. "It's in the United Arab Emirates."

Bad move. My wife works at Reuters, which is an international news organization.

"I *know* where Abu Dhabi is," she says evenly, and more considerately than I deserve. "But let me get this straight. You want to go to the Middle East. Now. While we're still in a pandemic?"

It's October of 2021. Spartan is holding its world championship outside of the United States for the first time, almost seven thousand miles away from New York in these famous epic dunes that have been the backdrop of many movie sets. I've been reading about the venue, which apparently includes one dune—the Hill of Horrors— that Spartan says vectors skyward nearly a thousand feet on a fifty-degree slope. The championship race will be a 21K, half-marathon Beast. I've watched a video of Spartan founder Joe De Sena getting out of a helicopter at the base of the race site (wearing a Spartan sweatshirt in 105°F temps) and approaching this monstrous slope of sand called the Moreeb Dune.

"I don't even know if Godzilla or King Kong could get up this," he pronounces. "It's un-fucking-believable." When the camera turns to this dune, it indeed looks like a vertical wall of red-and-orange pain.

I want to race on this dune.

Ohio, and my moment of flow, wasn't a fluke. I'd gone on to stand on the podium seven times after that gold-medal race and had placed eighth overall for the year in the U.S. National Series for my age group (50–54). I didn't find flow for all the races; during many, I struggled. In Killington, Vermont, home to what Spartan dubs its toughest U.S. venue, I'd labored hard on the long climbs, one of them nicknamed the Death March (horrible moniker, I know) for its 1.12-mile climb up about 1,500 feet of elevation (distance and elevation according to Spartan). There was also a defeating swim out to a bridge for the Tarzan Swing, where you had to climb a loose rope ladder and then maneuver soggily across some individual ropes to smack the bell on the other side of the bridge. (That sound you just heard? That was the splash of me crashing backside into the water and swimming a penalty loop.) I finished sixth out of twelve that day for my division—middle of the pack.

Still, there was something special about each race, and my sense of place and belonging deepened each time I toed the line. In Fayetteville, North Carolina, I raced alongside Pete, who had shut down his gym in White Plains during Covid-19 and moved to North Carolina near where my parents live. We'd crossed the starting line together, and for the first time ever, I'd kept up with my amazing former coach and taken second place for my age group in the 21K Beast and also in the 5K Sprint the following day. In West Virginia, I'd raced a Trifecta Weekend of three races over two days again and celebrated my fiftieth birthday taking third place in the 10K and then in the 5K for my division, alongside the now-familiar faces of Kim Cole (gold) and

Angelina Borisov (silver). At one point, I'd plowed through a barbed-wire crawl so swiftly that three young men respectfully made way for me and cheered: "Go, girl, go!"

Now, that's a sweet fiftieth birthday present.

In Killington, Vermont, after a grueling seven hours, nineteen minutes, and twenty-four seconds of endless climbing in the Beast on the twentieth anniversary of the September 11, 2001, terrorist attacks, I'd woken up refreshed the next day and run the shorter 5K for fun with Erle as we laughed our way through hills together. At the race's end, I attempted to lift the men's weight on the sandbag rope-pulley obstacle called the Hercules Hoist and completed it, which earned me a bunch of high fives from some spectator wives who were watching their frustrated husbands struggle with the obstacle. I did not get high fives from the husbands.

And finally, *finally,* I completed the dreaded eight-foot Box obstacle, in a sweet moment of absolution on the same half-marathon New Jersey course where I'd dropped out of the race from being ill-prepared for the cold and wet conditions. The day I conquered The Box by pinching the knots on the rope with my toes to help me climb it also brought me the bronze medal for my Age Group, which I accepted onstage while staring off across the field at the medical tent I'd landed in that chilly day in April, two and a half years ago. Today The Box stands as one of my favorite obstacles.

Through each of these races I was experiencing the United States—even my home state of North Carolina—in a fresh, hands-on (sometimes facedown) way that made me familiar with my country's land, smells, and topography in ways I'd never have known driving through it by car or visiting the usual tourist sites.

But by far the most special day, the one I've come to think of as The Perfect Race, unfolded in early August in Mill Spring, North Carolina, at an equestrian competition and showground venue called Tryon International in the Blue Ridge foothills. Spartan dubbed it a "Max Race" venue, mostly because of the Southern heat and the advertised 1,158 feet of elevation gain. There, I'd joined Pete for a

10K on Saturday, run out of gas midway through, and taken sixth place among ten racers, trailing in behind Angelina Borisov and Tara Laffin-Craig (aka Running Skirt). Then I'd returned the next morning for a 5K and claimed second place out of eleven competitors in my age group. But getting a medal wasn't what made the day special. In fact, I never even stood on the podium.

Before the 5K race, I'd noticed my father, then seventy-six years old, keenly studying the obstacles near the finish line. This was before he'd slipped off the roof and cracked his neck and pelvis. He was looking at a strange obstacle called the Helix, which is composed of a series of panels made of bars and Plexiglas arranged at different angles in big X's that you navigate without touching the ground. My mom and Lisa were still sleeping back at the hotel, and my father and Erle had driven to the venue with me early that morning.

"What do you think?" I asked him, carefully. He was interested in this. Not just as a spectator. No, I knew my father too well.

He rubbed his face and sniffed. The sniff was his poker tell.

"So, do you want to do the Open 5K with me this afternoon when I'm done with my morning race?" I asked.

He nodded, a single definitive drop of the chin, and said matter-of-factly, "Yeah, I think we should do that."

A pause.

"But don't tell your mother until we're done."

While I race the Age Group 5K, my dad buys a Spartan T-shirt so he doesn't ruin his pink polo shirt my mom had laid out for him the night before. (My father can cut a tumor from a dog, but he cannot choose clothing that matches.) While the awards ceremony goes on without me, we take off in the relentless midsummer sun for the Open heat: jogging some, walking some. My father is fit from all his yard work and years of maintaining his balance while navigating boats through choppy inlets. He crushes the Hercules Hoist. During a treacherous, muddy walk in the woods as he carries his sixty-pound sandbag, a bunch of racers in front of my dad start tripping and sliding, and so down he goes with them, tearing open his knee. When I start to fret, he waves me off and just douses the wound with water and starts moving again. Climbing a steep hill, we are baking in the sun and two twentysomething guys behind us won't stop whining about the heat and the pitch of the climb. Finally, I turn around and point to my father.

"He's seventy-six," I tell them.

The whining stops.

There is a photo of my father and me at the finish line, jumping the fire together at this equestrian center. When I think about this book's title, I think of that photo and my father. He now sleeps with his finisher medal hanging from the lamp beside his bed.

All this has left me with the assurance that I've now progressed a bit further on that Dreyfus model of skill acquisition. I've made it past the novice and advanced-beginner stages into competence and can now, on many days, expect not just to compete but to be a contender for a top spot in my age group. And in some facets of racing, such as throwing a spear or moving heavy things, I'm probably even at the fourth stage, which is proficient. Alex Hutchinson, author of *Endure*, took up rock climbing in his early forties and reflected to me that "it's fun to be bad at something, because it means you can get better." He also noted that it's just a bunch of words until you feel it. And that's what I'm feeling now.

But this Abu Dhabi race and these endless dunes—this is something else. I've qualified already for the world championship based on my podium placements throughout the year. Traveling to the Middle East in a pandemic and racing in one of the world's largest deserts against some of the best international competitors—that feels like I'm pushing my little-*i* "impossible" pin a little further out on the mental map of my racing journey. There's something out there to learn in those dunes—something my gut tells me I won't recognize until I'm there.

Lisa and I sit down and talk for more than an hour. I promise her I won't go if she doesn't want me to. She tells me she doesn't want to keep me from doing something that's important to me, but she's scared for me to go. What would happen if I got Covid-19 again and got quarantined so far away? Or worse yet, what if I was seriously injured, and she couldn't get to me? I admit to her those things make me a little nervous but that I'm more scared *not* to go. This feels like a once-in-a-lifetime moment. She wants to come with me but doesn't want to be so far away while her father is still so compromised. We talk and talk, sorting through options and pros and cons. There is frustration. There are a few tears. Still, it's a long way away from the pull-up-bar moment, where I'd shut down completely and just expected Lisa to read my mind and understand.

Ultimately, we land on a compromise. She will stay here, and I will go to Abu Dhabi—but only if I can convince Erle to travel with me.

He listens to me as I lay out a plan over the phone. I wait while he digests the request and my offer to pay his way.

"Well," he says slowly, "we've already done West Virginia, Ohio, and Vermont. Why not the Middle East? I'll go."

Lisa wasn't wrong. Prepping to travel across the globe with Covid-19 still very much a thing isn't simple. Beyond the normal trip to-dos of booking flights, hotels, and a rental car and finding the right electrical converters and adapters, there's the matter of figuring out how and where we'll get rapid PCR tests forty-eight hours prior to our flight. That's relatively easy compared to uploading vaccination certificates to a special app that will give us permission to enter certain Abu Dhabi public facilities, and purchasing extra insurance, at Lisa's insistence, in case we catch the virus and must quarantine—or in case I somehow get badly injured, and she needs to fly across the globe to get me. There are also cultural details. While its bustling neighboring city Dubai is quite relaxed, Abu Dhabi is still more traditional in some ways. If we want to visit its epic Sheikh Zayed Grand Mosque, for instance, I'll need to wear a head covering.

Meantime, there's my own exhaustive planning for race gear. Now, heat is my challenge. Heat and sand. I research desert running and learn I'll need something called gaiters to cover my shoes and keep the superfine sand from getting into my socks and rubbing blisters on my toes. I spend hours gluing the gaiters' Velcro attachments to the soles of a pair of old race shoes—a complete waste of time, as I'll learn in mile one. (I should have had the gaiters stitched on.) I can't risk letting my skin be exposed unprotected for that long in bright sun, so I research the best sporting clothing with UPF protection and end up with a bright-blue reflective long-sleeve shirt that's advertised for fishing. I also find a white UPF 50 baseball cap, a light-colored UPF 50 neck gaiter (which will double as my mosque head covering), and some thin gloves to protect my hands from the sun.

By the time Erle and I arrive at JFK International Airport to depart on November 25, Thanksgiving Day, I've got a Google Doc with trip notes that is seventeen pages long. At the last minute, the pharmacy performing my scheduled PCR test had canceled the appointment, which sent me scrambling to drive ninety minutes into New York City to a clinic that would turn results around in half an hour. Once our bags are checked in at Etihad Airways, we wolf down some luke-warm turkey, cranberry sauce, and stuffing at an airport bar, call our families to say happy Thanksgiving, and then board the flight for an 8:20 P.M. departure.

The first thing I hear Erle say, about thirty minutes after we take off, is:

"Oh, well, this isn't good."

He's using the plane's Wi-Fi connection and looking at something on his phone. He holds it up and shows me the fat, bold headline from CNN:

OMICRON, A NEW COVID-19 VARIANT WITH HIGH NUMBER OF MUTA-TIONS, SPARKS TRAVEL BANS AND WORRIES SCIENTISTS.

We look at each other as the engines roar and we begin the twelve-hour, thirty-minute journey to the other side of the world. *Too late now.* We don't say it out loud, but that's what we're both thinking.

"Cocktail?" the passing flight attendant asks.

"Yes," comes our simultaneous reply.

* * *

The spectator area at the race site located near the Liwa Oasis is magnificent. There are colorful rugs laid across the sand and flags from every country fielding racers planted in the ground beneath that insane Moreeb Dune that we'll be climbing and descending. Plush beanbag-like chairs in red, white, and green—all colors on the United Arab Emirates flag—dot the spectator area. There's a display of beautiful teapots, and men milling about in the traditional Emirati dress of long, flowing, white ankle-length garments and head coverings. Joan Jett's "I Love Rock 'n' Roll" blasts from the loudspeaker, followed by Arabic music.

There is definitely no mud.

What there *is* is sand. Red-and-gold sand everywhere you look, endless stretches of it. And sun. Cloudless skies where the sun is an only child beaming its gaze upon the sand. I race tomorrow on December 4 with the other Age Group competitors, but we've come to the desert a day early to watch the Elite racers—including my coach Faye, who has been staying at the same hotel as us in Abu Dhabi—take off for their contest.

For the past week, Erle and I have seen everything we can in Abu Dhabi and Dubai, the latter being a playground of the biggest *everything*—buildings, boats, parties, malls, adventure sports. We each observe a prayer session in the Grand Mosque, tour the Qsar Al Watan presidential palace, and watch the sunset at the sprawling Bab Al Shams Desert Resort, where they teach falconry and offer camel rides. At each public location, we must show an app with our green Covid-19 "clear" status to gain entry. The country is so buttoned-up with its precautions, testing, and mask requirements that I figure it's probably the safest we've been since the pandemic began. If there's another practical edge to racing when you're older, it's potentially having the disposable income to take a beat and spend some extra days absorbing the environment around you. I do not know if I'll ever return to the Middle East. And so we rise early and go to sleep late after seeing, eating, drinking, learning whatever we can.

But now it's time to do what I came to do.

That night at dinner, I watch Instagram videos of Lindsay Dawn Webster securing her third world championship alongside her husband, Ryan Atkins, who wins the male Elite heat. Faye comes in seventh. But it's less who wins that interests me. What I'm looking for are more edges. I notice many of the female Elite racers miss their spear throws—except for a woman named Annie Dube, who nails it on the far-right target and then takes the silver medal. That, I decide, will be my target. Erle patiently listens to me dissecting the videos and mostly attempts to restore the calm from this summer, which I clearly forgot to pack.

And then I try to sleep. Which doesn't go very well, because I am awake fielding questions from my monkey mind all night. Have I hydrated enough? Will my hamstrings and Achilles tendons hold in the sand? Will my gaiters work? Can I even run in the sand? Could I be first; will I be last?

About 3 A.M., the monkey tires of swinging pointlessly from limb to limb on my neurons and passes out. And so do I.

Where does it end?

That's what I'm thinking at the base of this dune. It's not even the monstrous, "un-fucking-believable," "I don't even know if Godzilla or King Kong could get up this" Moreeb Dune that Joe De Sena talked about in his Instagram videos several months ago. I've already climbed that, painfully, about a mile and a half back, as a woman behind me, who sounded like she might be Russian, verbally kicked my very sore ass (more on that in a moment) up a wall of sand. "Move, move, MOVE, lady." Maybe she knows French Fry, the little girl from the playground, I thought grimly at one point as I inched my way along the dune, every step a balancing act to avoid tipping right and tumbling down into the festival area.

No, now I am roughly nine and a half miles into the race, standing at the start of an obstacle called the Cliff Climb. The wall of red-and-gold sand stretches about four hundred feet into the sapphire sky. At the top, I can just make out the squiggles of black ropes we need to reach to pull ourselves the rest of the way to the top. I'm watching competitors in front of me sink deep with each step and hearing groans as their hands press into the hot sand trying to gain leverage. A few SUVs wait here at the base with volunteers and staff ready to pull people off the course if they can't make it.

I grimace and unconsciously touch my backside right before I begin to climb. Bad idea. A flare of hurt shoots straight through my tailbone and up my lower spine.

Ugh.

Let me back up for a moment.

For the first six and a half miles, I manage to hold my own, though not without struggle. Running in deep sand turns out to be even harder for me than running in mud. The moment we leave the starting line, I realize how tricky it is to push off over and over on terrain that has no firm base. No amount of beach jogs or snowy trail runs have prepared me for the sensation of this fine, endless sand. My heart rate soars as I fight the ground for the first mile, until finally, giving in to its grip, I find a rhythm that lets me move forward at a slower but more natural pace.

It goes OK, even though at one point I'm looking down and not at the racers in front of me, and I realize I've gone off course. Looking around, I see nothing but identical dunes. No people. No course markers. Everything looks the same. Just the red-and-gold sand. I am disoriented and directionless and suddenly have an overwhelming sense of being lost in the desert in a foreign country thousands of miles from home. Then I see a small flash of red up on a hill—the sleeve of another racer going by. I track up to that point as fast as I can and rejoin the pack. I stop looking down after that.

Around mile six I am feeling decent and almost confident. I'd made the last-minute decision to run wearing my hydration vest with two full seventeen-ounce sleeves of water and electrolytes rather than a belt with one sleeve of water, and it's paid off, because there is zero shade and water stations are not particularly plentiful. I don't know where I am in the pack of my age group but believe I can make some real headway in the next seven to eight miles. It crosses my mind: maybe the podium is a possibility.

Then comes Olympus. And what happens next happens so fast I don't know what happens. I take off my gloves and trot up to one of the obstacle's walls—a slippery black face that is almost perpendicular to the ground, with chains, climbing holds, and holes to move yourself across the wall to ring the bell. Grabbing two of the chains, I plant my feet firmly high up on the wall, heels down to grip, squat, and lean way back.

Then I am just confused. Because I am not on the wall, where I'm supposed to be. Rather, I'm on my backside on the ground. Here, the sand is compacted, as we're in a salt flat area called a sabkha. A searing heat starts to spread from my coccyx down my legs and up my spine to my head. I know this feeling. I'd felt this feeling twenty-five years ago when I'd come off a beer-soaked dance floor on New Year's Eve, hit the stairs in the hard heels of my dress shoes, and landed just like this. Back then, my own inebriation protected me until the middle of the night, when I stood to use the bathroom and fell immediately to my knees. An X-ray and a highly uncomfortable physical exam the next morning (use your imagination) by a young emergency-room doctor had delivered the verdict of a fractured tailbone. And it had taken almost three months of sitting on special cushions at my *Wall Street Journal* desk for running not to hurt.

Now, in the middle of the Abu Dhabi desert, my mind scrambles to put information together. I look at my hands. They are gooey. Someone with sweaty suntan lotion on their palms must have used the chains before me. I need to take my penalty lap. Quickly, so I don't lose any more time. I rise to stand up and take my first step. And in that moment of pain, my race aspirations, my podium hopes, my best-laid gear plans—they disintegrate and waft off to die baking somewhere in the desert.

"Penalty loop is over there." The young volunteer points over her shoulder helpfully.

I nod and grunt something approximating a thank-you.

Limping cautiously around the loop, I start running the numbers and making calculations. There is something approaching seven miles still to go. Could I even make it seven more miles? How can I not make it seven more miles after flying seven thousand miles to be here? I won't make the top-three finishers now, even if I ever had a chance; that much is clear. In this moment, I can comprehend the logic of my coach Faye during the 2019 Lake Tahoe World Championship, when she added up the pros and cons of continuing once her chances of a podium spot were dashed and decided the logical answer was to drop out.

And then another number materializes: 40 percent.

I'd read a book many years ago, just as I was embarking on this obstacle course racing journey, written by a former Navy SEAL named David Goggins. He had overcome grim childhood adversity to become a noted endurance athlete and subsequently a sought-after speaker on discipline, grit, and perseverance. The book was called *Can't Hurt Me: Master Your Mind and Defy the Odds*. At the time, I pored over the pages with something approaching awe and disbelief. Goggins was a person who'd performed physical feats and endured suffering I couldn't comprehend. Achieving what Goggins had was about as likely as me finding a giant ice-cold Olympic swimming pool here in the middle of the Empty Quarter desert to soak my tailbone in. But still, there was one part of his book that had always stayed with me.

The 40% Rule.

When you think you are done, you're only 40 percent of the way toward what you're capable of doing.

If Goggins is right, I think, approaching the penalty loop's end, then my gas tank is still 60 percent full. And if it isn't 60 percent full, then maybe there's at least a quarter or a third of a tank left. And perhaps that is enough so I won't go home with my tail tucked painfully (literally and metaphorically) between my legs with a Did Not Finish, never having crossed the finish line. Plus, I know what it is like to ride defeated to the medical tent, having quit a race. That is not something I want to relive now, no matter how uncomfortable the next few hours might be. If I can walk, I can finish. And I can walk. Had I wanted the podium? Yes. Does it feel bad to know it is now firmly out of my grasp? Yes—worse than I could have imagined, if I am being honest.

Still.

What do you want to be when you grow up?

Five years ago, a gin-soaked man asked a chatty little girl that question at a dinner party, and it freaked me out. Because to some degree, I'd been dialing in my life at that point. Just acquiescing to inertia and a slow, comfortable fade to a chorus whose lyrics said that everything I might possibly be, I already was. I believed my body was just along for the ride on that trip, that it would always disappoint and never amaze me. And that I had little to no control over that fact. As it turned out, there were choices to make—about how to spend my time, what I was willing to learn and unlearn, when to give up and not to, how to grapple with fear, whether to share what I felt with the people I loved. Attempting five weak push-ups on a musty hotel carpet in Québec City beside my dying dog had been a choice. Finding Pete was a choice. Same with getting out of bed to go to his class when anxiety bound my chest to the mattress like ropes. Finishing the first Spartan race after I fell off the rope—a choice. Deciding not to quit obstacle course racing after my cold New Jersey DNF and tracking down Faye and Jess—also a choice. Staging mock races on my dirt road during Covid-19. Staying off social media to train. Learning everything I could about thermoregulation before Lake Tahoe. Going to the dermatologist every three months. Amassing my physician pit crew. Deciding what I eat and drink and how long I sleep. All choices. I may not have total control over my fate. I am fifty years old and most likely won't live another fifty years. It's inevitable that I am going to die. We all are. But until that day comes, I have some control. We all do.

And now there is another choice to make.

Reaching into my shorts, I pull out the two grimy Tylenols I'd jammed into my pocket earlier that morning, spit on the tablets to wash off the sand and lint, and swallow them. In that moment, I recalibrate my goal: finish and don't be last.

Then I glance into the dunes, shoot the midlife assassin a metaphorical middle finger, complete my penalty loop, and get back on the course.

Three miles later.

Now, crawling up the Cliff Climb, I notice the woman next to me has removed her shoes and is climbing in her socks. I understand why. The hours I spent gluing my gaiters' Velcro to my own race shoes back home were a waste. The force of the deep sand has rendered the Velcro useless, and the gaiters are flipped up like visors on my feet. As a result, there's so much sand inside my shoes now that I've had to stop every half mile and empty them to relieve the pressure on my toes. When I finally remove my socks at the race's end, my toes will be covered in bloody, purple blisters. Yet that will be a modest indignity compared to the visit to the colorectal surgeon back home to have my tailbone injury examined.

Still, I'm here. I've fast-walked or slow-trotted the course since Olympus and made it through seven more obstacles, even nailing my spear throw after choosing the far-right target as planned. I'm well hydrated, so don't need to stop often for water. And now I am hellbent on just making it to those black ropes at the top. Putting my head down, I try not to think about anything other than pulling one foot out of the sand and placing it a little farther up the hill, and then doing that again with the other foot. If I reach the top, then the hardest part of the race is over. The last four-ish miles (as I said before, they call them Spartan miles for a reason) will be doable.

With each step, my mind separates a little from the discomfort in the rest of my body. This separation of self from pain is a different kind of flow than what I experienced in Ohio, but it's powerful nonetheless. I also know that a lot of people out on this course probably hurt in some way. I've seen some racers just walk past certain obstacles, not even attempting to complete them. It's cheating, yes, but the volunteer race monitors are hot too, and it's hard for them to keep up with everyone. Or maybe they figure those of us who are this far behind don't really have a shot at the podium anymore, so who cares. Step by step, I finally reach the black ropes, grab one, and haul myself up to the top of the dune, where I ease myself to the ground and start emptying my shoes once again.

The rest of the afternoon is mostly a rhythmic blur. I chat with anyone who can speak English and complete every obstacle left on the course, including carrying a sandbag weighing somewhere between forty-five and fifty pounds (same weight today for men and women) up and down a dune loop. Then suddenly I'm back atop the Moreeb Dune, looking down at the festival area and the finish line. What we'd climbed up earlier—me with that woman behind me yelling, "Move, move, MOVE, lady"—we now get to plunge down. People are doing so and screaming with joy; it looks like they are bounding through clouds. I step off the edge to join them and then stop myself, step back up, and instead stand off to the side.

Look at where you are, I tell myself.

From here, with the meringue-like dunes still glowing in the midafternoon sun, there's a sight line to the past. To all the choices it took to make it here. It feels far—both literally and figuratively—from the small North Carolina gymnasiums and green soccer fields where a skinny, scrappy little girl struggled to find a place in the world of sports. Dolly's dog tag is with me, as it has been for every Spartan race I've run. Only now, it's zipped in my pants' pocket instead of tucked inside my sports bra the way it was during my first race. Runners leap over the summit to my right and lope gleefully to the finish. When the results are tallied, I'll be sixth out of seven female racers my age who finished the course—not last. And I'll be only about twelve minutes away from third place, which is secured by the five-time Ironman champion Heather Gollnick, and the podium. Knowing I might have had a shot without the fall and my terrible gaiter attachment will be something I consider only briefly. I've raced long enough to know everyone has good and bad days, including all the souls on this blazing course today. I could have chosen a different hand grip on Olympus. And injuries are a real possibility in this sport; you know that when you sign the waiver. No excuses. I tried and didn't win—but that doesn't mean I won't try again in another world championship on another day. There is still more to reach for, something I couldn't fully grasp when I woke up panicked after that dinner party five and a half years ago. Tonight, I will sleep soundly with my finisher medal on the table beside my hotel bed.

I'm not thinking about any of that now, though. In fact, I'm not even thinking about obstacle course racing. What I'm thinking about is where Erle and I will eat tonight. I'm thinking about the time difference and when I can call Lisa and have her send me another picture of the puppy. And what I'll say to my parents in an email about this race—particularly how I'll explain the coccyx situation to my mother so she won't worry. And I am wondering about how the construction is going in our garage, and whether the electricians finished their work. There's also that person who contacted me about a possible new job. I need to call them back.

Just the normal life-chorus stuff. Much of it was there before I ever googled, "What are the hardest things you can do?" And much of it, thankfully, is still there waiting for me at the bottom of this dune. But now something has shifted, like going from E minor back to E major—and with a slightly different rhythm. Whatever verse comes next after my bridge, it won't be what I once imagined. The story arc has changed. I don't know that any of us can ever fully defeat the midlife assassin. But for now, at least, I feel like we've reached a détente.

Taking a deep breath, I step forward off the cliff, close my eyes for a moment, and then leap into the clouds.

* * *

In a lifetime, if we are lucky, we may find a way to surmount walls we once believed impossible to overcome. And when we do so, certain fires of hurt, regret, and longing that smolder may go out forever. Rescuing that weak little-girl version of me through obstacle course racing did more than redeem my childhood; it made me a happier adult. Because while I know death is coming—it is the Insurmountable Obstacle—no longer do I move toward death feeling there is something untapped in my tank. It's true, what this quote so often attributed to Teddy Roosevelt says: "We must all wear out or rust out, every one of us." Roosevelt went on to say that to wear out was his choice. That is mine too. In choosing that path, I have become what I never expected to be. And with the gift of more time, I might yet be even more. Recently, I've been trying other types of races: a fast road race, a half-marathon trail run, and more obstacle races that aren't Spartans. Perhaps I'll eventually get strong enough to attempt a 50K Spartan Ultra event or a twenty-four-hour endurance challenge like the World's Toughest Mudder, or even—it somewhat terrifies me to type these next words—Joe De Sena's Death Race. Maybe I'll make it to Muddy Mildred's age and still be able to complete a 5K obstacle course race. Or I'll pivot altogether. There are some old fly-fishing rods gathering dust in our garage; we've been eyeing each other.

Still, some walls will inevitably be too tall to scale—Impossible with the capital *I*. And peace must be made with this truth. I am not talking about human performance or endurance when I say this. Because there are those rare individuals who do push the outer limits of what we believe is possible. I've met some of them through racing; they exist. Rather, it's the acceptance that not every idea we had as little girls or boys of what we would be when we grew up will pan out, and that we must find another path to avoid being consumed by the blaze of disappointment. That's perhaps the most enduring lesson obstacle course racing has taught me: How to pivot when things don't go as you've planned or dreamed. And to be content.

A few months after the Abu Dhabi race, I head back to the mountainous New Jersey Spartan racecourse on a cool morning. It's the same venue where I quit three years ago, when inexperience got the best of me, and then redeemed myself two years later with a bronze medal. Yesterday, I repeated that placement in the Beast. This morning, though, I walk past the adult registration and over to the Kids race.

"You ready?" I ask a lanky twelve-year-old blond boy. He is shaking his limbs like a nervous colt. It's his first Spartan Kids race, and he's eyeing the obstacles with awe and a little fear. Just as he should be, I think.

The boy's mother and father and his brother, Julian, stand out of earshot, giving Johnny and me our moment together. His mom, Dacia, has been my closest female friend since college, and while Johnny has her brilliant mathematical mind and competitive spirit, he is by eerie coincidence my physical and emotional doppelgänger—the child my body might have produced, had that been in the cards biologically. When we walk down the street, people will remark how much my son who is not my son looks like me. It makes us both laugh, but I'd be lying if I said my heart didn't break a little sometimes. This fire, I still can feel its heat.

Today, though, we are focused.

"Remember, make sure you're at the front of the pack to start," I tell him. "You are fast, so break hard. It's a short race. Use your speed so you don't get jammed up behind other racers at the obstacles."

He nods. Bounces on his toes. Steals a nervous glance at the other kids lining up. He's fast, lean, strong, super competitive, and, at twelve years old, the only seventh grader on the varsity cross-country team. These gifts make him a natural for this sport. Still, he doesn't know it yet, and I can feel his unspoken last-minute doubts bubbling up. *Why am I doing this? Why not just stick with cross-country running, where I'm already so good?*

I try to answer before he has to ask. "Johnny?" He meets my eyes.

"You'll know at the finish line."

Epilogue

A NEW VERSE

The T-shirts are gray, and emblazoned on the front is a round, cuddly blue-and-green creature wearing a fierce Spartan mask and leaping over a fire. Beneath the image is the word "SmartNews."

AJ is pulling the shirts out of a bag and handing them out to the ten of us who are milling about, adjusting our black Open race headbands, and stretching while rock music blares throughout this Salinas, California, field. Apart from AJ, all my new colleagues are about to run their first Spartan race. "Don't feel bad," I tell one of them as he fumbles with the latch on his timing-chip band. "I broke mine in my first race and had to run with it tied to my shoe."

The creature on our shirt is called Chikyu-kun. Chikyu-kun represents the earth and is the mascot of this late-stage tech start-up company called SmartNews, which uses artificial intelligence and human input to curate news and other information in an app. At fifty-one years old, I am one of the oldest employees at the company. And I am the senior racer today, with the rest of the group ranging from twenty-eight to forty-six years old. During the weekdays they teach me about engineering, generative AI, large language models, and product development. It's been nine months since I joined, and most days I've been drinking through a fire hose navigating new languages (both tech-speak and Japanese, as the company is based in Tokyo) and a work culture built around transparency, international hours, and a digital communication method called Slack. I felt far more at home on Slack after creating a custom emoji that said, AROO!

As is the case with most start-ups, the future is uncertain. The company might have a completely different business model by the time you read this. I might not still be there.

And yet it's the most fun I've had at work in a long time.

I'd certainly been happy enough at Consumer Reports. I held an executive position, was paid well for a journalism job, and was adding to a generous 401(k). I oversaw a well-oiled team who could mostly run the show without me, and I generally had the respect of my peers and superiors. It was the kind of job where in middle age you start thinking, "Hmmm, can I find a way to hold on to this until I retire?" And with that thinking comes inevitable temptation for compromise—step up and question a decision, or keep my head down and go with the flow? Fight to keep an innovative newsletter that needs investment to grow, or just let it go?

One Friday afternoon a year earlier, our CEO had asked me to join her for lunch, just the two of us, at her country home. Her husband cooked while we took a walk with her dog and sat by what appeared to be a small lake.

"You must be wondering why I asked you here," she said.

"Well, I figure I'm not getting fired, since you're serving lunch," I responded, smiling.

"No," she laughed. "I've been thinking about your future. And I want to talk with you about a possible new position."

What she described was a potential pathway to become a CEO one day—if not at Consumer Reports, then somewhere else. It was a role as chief of staff, reporting to her, that would be integral to the company's strategic decision-making, involved in every board meeting, and her counselor on big decisions. It was a genuinely good offer and a gracious one, because this woman was tough and discerning.

I nodded, digesting the information. And then, in what might go down as the biggest non sequitur in job offer history, I looked across the water and said: "Is that a turtle?"

The apropos-of-nothing response was my mind's way of quickly leaping over an obstacle. And the obstacle was that I was confused. Because by all the professional measures I'd valued through the years, I should have been thrilled. I should have been calculating all the ways this would give me security until retirement. I probably should have been a bit more politically deft in my response. "Turtle?" Lisa said later when I got home. "Really?"

However, a few months earlier, I'd received an email from a former *Wall Street Journal* colleague now working at SmartNews. This man, Rich Jaroslovsky, had been a digital pioneer, helping launch *WSJ*'s website, and he was attempting to lure me there as his eventual successor heading their content team. The job would be smaller in scope, the security of a comfortable 401(k) replaced with the insecurity of stock options, and with a less fancy title. I'd take meetings late into the evenings, given the time zone differences, and need to learn a new industry. But I would be working with cutting-edge technology and partnering with hungry young leaders who would push me out of my midlife comfort zone.

A few weeks after my lunch with the CEO, I said yes to SmartNews and resigned from Consumer Reports.

I made my resignation calls sitting in the hot courtyard of an Aloft Hotel in Columbia, South Carolina. The next morning, I awoke before dawn, laced up my racing shoes, and drove to Newberry. There, racing in humid, heavy air, I took second place in a 10K Spartan race after going neck and neck again with Tara (Running Skirt) and crossing the finish line a mere twenty-seven seconds before her. (She beat me by two seconds the next day in the 5K.) I also did not heed Muddy Mildred's advice to stay low on the barbed-wire crawl and consequently tore my shirt and shoulder in the first race. The scars are still visible, and they feel like the mark of a transition.

Let's address the elephant in the room. Would I have made such a professional leap without obstacle course racing in my life? If you've read this book and haven't skipped to the very end (it's OK if you have; Lisa does that), you'll know the answer. I would most likely still be at Consumer Reports. From a financial and employment-security standpoint, that would have been the less risky choice. And if I'd had children to put through college, staying put might well have been the right decision. Regardless, staying was certainly the safest path, the one tethered to my identity and what it meant to be successful. But as my former colleague Joanne Lipman, the author of *Next!*, put it to me, "Having an alternate identity is really protection for yourself." And she is right. My identity as a competitive obstacle racer acts like a shield against the barrage of what-ifs that come with hard decisions. Because now I know what it's like to leave the comfort zone, to crawl blindly until you reach a clearing and then to start running again, faster than you ever thought you could. I know what it's like to carry something heavy for a long time, not knowing when the end will come, and to keep going. And when everything goes to hell—well, I know how to pick myself up after that, reset my goals and expectations, and start moving again.

I thank this brutal, beautiful sport for those gifts.

We run as a team, my SmartNews colleagues and I, in the more relaxed Open wave, where we can help each other. I've already raced competitively that morning and the day prior, taking silver medals in both contests for my age group. We pause every so often to help one another over the walls and cheer one another through the obstacles. We laugh and take photos along the way. I give a tutorial at the rope climb and clap as AJ, our head of marketing, muscles his way to the top and smacks the bell. We sweat through our team T-shirts with Chikyu-kun emblazoned triumphantly on our chests and will ultimately cross the finish line together, holding hands.

As we jog down an open dirt road into the last mile together, I settle in next to a gutsy twenty-eight-year-old woman named Nhi, who has shown incredible dexterity climbing the walls today. Technically, I'm old enough to be her mother. We round a corner, and suddenly she looks up at me.

"Wendy, I bet you were always the first one picked for the team when you were growing up," she says, pivoting to avoid a pothole.

Her gracious assumption floats over to perch on my shoulder, an old demon whispering a false truth I no longer crave.

I laugh. And the demon tumbles onto the dusty road behind us.

"Nhi." I smile at her. "Let me tell you a story."

Acknowledgments

Four people supported me most when, approaching age fifty, I inex-
plicably began crawling under barbed wire and pushing my body up
and down ropes and mountains: my deeply patient spouse, Lisa
Bernhard; my mother and father (Norva and Mike); and my friend
Erle Norton. You were by my side before this journey began, and you
are still with me as I write this. My gratitude for that simple gift is
immeasurable.

Without my coaches, I would never have grown comfortable competing, nor would I have advanced in what will be a never-finished
mastery journey in this sport. Thank you to "Podium Pete" Jones for
the boundless belief you showed in all your students, and to the tal-
ented Faye Stenning and Jessica O'Connell of Grit Coaching, who
never let me use age as an excuse to not push harder.

There would be no book without my agent and friend, David
Black. My outstanding editor, Mary Reynics at Ballantine, from the
beginning envisioned what *Not Too Late* should be far more clearly
than I did. The entire team at Penguin Random House showed
incredible attention to detail and excellence throughout the publishing process.

Thank you to Cherie Bortnick and everyone at Spartan who
patiently answered my endless questions during the fact-checking
for this book. And a special nod of appreciation to all the Spartan
staff and volunteers who work in the heat and cold and make racing
possible on any given weekend.

Jonea Gurwitt was the tireless fact-checker for this manuscript
and sound editorial counsel for me on multiple fronts. Peter Sucheski

created the special illustrations introducing the chapters about obstacles. Both of you made this book better.

A pit crew of doctors and other specialists have kept my body intact during this journey. I probably wouldn't still be racing without you: Ellen Casey, Peter Duggan, Kirsten Healy, Jonathan Horey, James Hudson, Deborah Jones, Albert Knapp, Arlene Markowitz, Cristina Matera, Toni McGinley, Janet Prystowsky, and Richard Shapiro.

My Hudson Valley neighbor Suzanne Baker first suggested I write this book at a point when I was starting to struggle with the realities of mortality and middle age. My friend and fellow author Stefan Fatsis echoed her sentiment over dinner in D.C. (after he told me I was crazy for doing these races). I appreciate that you both saw a story in my journey. I am also grateful for the waves and thumbs-ups from my Hudson Valley neighbors as I ran, rucked, pulled tires, and carried buckets of gravel up and down our shared dirt roads.

Big shout-out to the SmartNews Spartans who teamed up to race with me in Salinas, California: Justin L. Abrotsky, Maya Bruhis, AJ Brustein, Taku Inaba, Mayu Kumaki, Nhi Nguyen, Kevin O'Kane, Adam Sandur, and Maria Shuckahosee. You crushed it, and that was the most fun I ever had at a race (despite nearly taking off my own leg on the Herc Hoist).

And finally, I want to thank every Spartan and other obstacle course racer out there pushing your own limits in this incredibly special sport. I draw inspiration from you—especially when you pass me.

Sources and Notes

At its heart, this book is a story—one person's story, mine—about the search for purpose, meaning, and inspiration in midlife, when the days in front of you are likely fewer than the ones behind you. While obstacle course racing anchors my journey, this is not an exhaustive book about the sport, or Spartan Race as a business. Also, this book captures a moment in time; rules and specifics mentioned about obstacle course racing continue to evolve, as do the science and data cited. If you have a fresh piece of noteworthy research applicable to the concepts in this book, or just want to say hello, please email me at gwendolynboundsauthor@gmail.com.

To learn more about obstacle course racing and how to train, a few places to start are the books *Down and Dirty: The Essential Training Guide for Obstacle Races and Mud Runs* by Matt B. Davis and *Spartan Fit!* by Joe De Sena, and the documentary film *Rise of the Sufferfests: A Film About Mud, Masochism & Modern Life,* written and directed by Scott Keneally.

Books

Aristotle. *Rhetoric.* Book 2, chapter 14. Translated by J. H. Freese. Cambridge and London: Harvard University Press; William Heinemann Ltd., 1926.

Attia, Peter, with Bill Gifford. *Outlive: The Science & Art of Longevity.* New York: Harmony Books, 2023.

Bercovici, Jeff. *Play On: The New Science of Elite Performance at Any Age.* Boston: Houghton Mifflin Harcourt, 2018.

Burkeman, Oliver. *Four Thousand Weeks: Time Management for Mortals.* New York: Farrar, Straus and Giroux, 2021.

292 Sources and Notes

Conley, Chip. *Learning to Love Midlife: 12 Reasons Why Life Gets Better with Age*. New York: Little, Brown Spark, 2024.

Conley, Chip. *Wisdom @ Work: The Making of a Modern Elder*. New York: Currency, 2018.

Conti, Paul. *Trauma, the Invisible Epidemic: How Trauma Works and How We Can Heal from It*. Boulder, Colo.: Sounds True, 2021.

Coyle, Daniel. *The Talent Code: Greatness Isn't Born. It's Grown. Here's How*. New York: Bantam Books, 2009.

Csikszentmihalyi, Mihaly. *Flow: The Psychology of Optimal Experience*. New York: Harper & Row, 1990.

Davis, Matt B. *Down and Dirty: The Essential Training Guide for Obstacle Races and Mud Runs*. Beverly, Mass.: Fair Winds Press, 2014.

De Sena, Joe, with John Durant. *Spartan Fit!: 30 Days. Transform Your Mind. Transform Your Body. Commit to Grit*. New York: Houghton Mifflin Harcourt, 2016.

Diviney, Rich. *The Attributes: 25 Hidden Drivers of Optimal Performance*. New York: Random House, 2021.

Dweck, Carol S. *Mindset: The New Psychology of Success*. New York: Ballantine Books, 2016.

Easter, Michael. *The Comfort Crisis: Embrace Discomfort to Reclaim Your Wild, Happy, Healthy Self*. New York: Rodale, 2021.

Epictetus. *The Enchiridion*.

Epstein, David. *Range: Why Generalists Triumph in a Specialized World*. New York: Riverhead, 2019.

Fields, R. Douglas. *Electric Brain: How the New Science of Brainwaves Reads Minds, Tells Us How We Learn, and Helps Us Change for the Better*. Dallas: BenBella, 2020.

Gladwell, Malcolm. *Outliers: The Story of Success*. New York: Little, Brown and Company, 2008.

Goggins, David. *Can't Hurt Me: Master Your Mind and Defy the Odds*. Austin, Tex.: Lioncrest Publishing, 2018.

Herbert, Frank. *Dune*. New York: Ace, 2005.

Holiday, Ryan. *Stillness Is the Key*. New York: Portfolio/Penguin, 2019.

Hutchinson, Alex. *Endure: Mind, Body, and the Curiously Elastic Limits of Human Performance*. New York: William Morrow, 2018.

James, William. *On Vital Reserves: The Energies of Men; The Gospel of Relaxation*. New York: Henry Holt and Company.

Kotler, Steven. *The Art of Impossible: A Peak Performance Primer*. New York: Harper Wave, 2021.

Leonard, George. *Mastery: The Keys to Success and Long-Term Fulfillment*. New York: Plume, 1992.

Levy, Becca. *Breaking the Age Code: How Your Beliefs About Aging Determine How Long & Well You Live*. New York: William Morrow, 2022.

Lipman, Joanne. *Next!: The Power of Reinvention in Life and Work*. New York: Mariner Books, 2023.

McKeown, Greg. *Essentialism: The Disciplined Pursuit of Less*. New York: Currency, 2020.

Nester, James. *Breath: The New Science of a Lost Art*. New York: Riverhead Books, 2020.

Roll, Rich. *Finding Ultra: Rejecting Middle Age, Becoming One of the World's Fittest Men, and Discovering Myself*. New York: Harmony Books, 2018.

Setiya, Kieran. *Midlife: A Philosophical Guide*. Princeton: Princeton University Press, 2017.

Sheehy, Gail. *Passages: Predictable Crises of Adult Life*. New York: Ballantine Books, 2006.

Vanderbilt, Tom. *Beginners: The Joy and Transformative Power of Lifelong Learning*. New York: Alfred A. Knopf, 2021.

Chapter Notes

Introduction: I Should Not Be Here

4   **It is the land of epic movie**   Lorraine Ali, "The Harsh Reality of Building a 'Star Wars' Fantasy in Abu Dhabi," *Los Angeles Times*, December 3, 2015.

Joshua St. Clair, "Here's Where Dune Filmed Its Amazing Desert Scenes," *Men's Health*, October 26, 2021, https://www.menshealth.com/entertainment/a38066111/dune-movie-filming-locations.

4   **Roughly six weeks from now**   Dion Nissenbaum, "Houthis Fired Drones and Missiles in Abu Dhabi Attack, Investigation Finds," *The Wall Street Journal*, January 18, 2022.

Alexander Cornwell, Alaa Swilam, and Phil Stewart, "Yemen's Houthis Fail in Second Missile Attack on UAE," Reuters, January 24, 2022.

"US to Send Destroyer, Fighter Jets to UAE Amid Houthi Attacks," Al Jazeera, February 2, 2022.

9   **The ancient Greek philosopher Aristotle**   Aristotle, *Rhetoric.*

Setiya, *Midlife.*

9   **It wasn't until the mid-1960s**   Setiya, *Midlife.*

9   **To start, tackling something new and challenging**   K. Warner Schaie, "Observations from the Seattle Longitudinal Study of Adult Intelligence," sls.psychiatry.uw.edu.

K. Warner Schaie and Sherry L. Willis, "The Seattle Longitudinal Study of Adult Cognitive Development," *International Society for the Study of Behavioural Development Bulletin* 57, no. 1 (2010): 24–29.

Marcel Schwantes, "A Yale Professor Shatters False Beliefs About Aging and Uncovers 4 Truths to a Longer and Happier Life," Inc.com, April 8, 2022.

10   **Over the past decade, OCR**   Christian Radnedge, "Obstacle-Course Racing Scaling Its Way to Olympic Inclusion," Reuters.com, May 11, 2019.

Luke de Costa, "Obstacle-Course Racing: Welcome to the World of a Growing Sport with Olympic Ambitions," BBC.com, June 13, 2023.

11   **And one way we can start**   Carol Dweck, "The Power of Believing You Can Improve," Ted.com, November 2014.

12   **With time not on my side**   Anne Trafton, "The Rise and Fall of Cognitive Skills," MIT News Office, March 6, 2015, https://news.mit.edu/2015/brain-peaks-at-different-ages-0306.

Kendra Cherry, "Fluid vs. Crystallized Intelligence," VerywellMind.com, November 11, 2022.

1: When You Grow Up

21   **Queued in the long list**   Scott Keneally, "DNF: The True Tale of Failure at a Spartan Race," *Outside,* February 6, 2014.

2: Sitting and Screens

24 **I was born the year before Title IX** U.S. Department of Education Office for Civil Rights, www2.ed.gov/about/offices/list/ocr/docs/tix_dis.html.

"The 14th Amendment and the Evolution of Title IX," United States Courts, www.uscourts.gov/educational-resources/educational-activities/14th-amendment-and-evolution-title-ix.

26 **Even the song blaring** Kenny Chesney, "Summertime," *The Road and the Radio,* BNA Records, 2005.

29 **The screen of my cellphone** Felix Richter, "How Facebook Grew from 0 to 2.3 Billion Users in 15 Years," World Economic Forum, February 5, 2019.

3: Stuck in the Chorus

35 **Maybe you'll get more** Burkeman, *Four Thousand Weeks.*

35 **In 2014, Setiya had penned** Kieran Setiya, "The Midlife Crisis," *Philosophers' Imprint* 14, no. 31 (November 2014).

36 **He discovered that while philosophers** Setiya, *Midlife.*

36 **In 1965 Jaques** Elliott Jaques, "Death and the Midlife Crisis," *International Journal of Psychoanalysis* 46 (1965): 502–14.

Carlo Strenger and Arie Ruttenberg, "The Existential Necessity of Midlife Change," *Harvard Business Review,* February 2008.

Setiya, *Midlife.*

37 **Take, for example, the U** David G. Blanchflower and Andrew J. Oswald, "Is Well-Being U-Shaped over the Life Cycle?" *Social Science & Medicine* 66, no. 8 (April 2008): 1733–49.

David G. Blanchflower and Andrew J. Oswald, "International Happiness: An Introduction and Review," *Academy of Management Perspectives* 25, no. 1 (February 2011): 6–22.

David G. Blanchflower and Andrew J. Oswald, "The Midlife Low in Human Beings," CEPR.org/voxeu, September 16, 2017.

40 **This is the difference between** Robert Groves, "(Telic vs. Atelic) or (Telic and Atelic)?" *The Provost's Blog,* Georgetown University website, September 28, 2022.

Massimo Pigliucci, "Telic vs Atelic Activities, and the Meaning of Life," Medium.com, September 27, 2019.

41   **Now we have ready access**   By one count, U.S. adults were spending nearly eight hours a day staring at screens with digital content (smartphones, desktops, other devices) in 2020 at the height of the Covid-19 pandemic. That's more hours than some of us sleep.

Brian Stelter, "8 Hours a Day Spent on Screens, Study Finds," *The New York Times,* March 26, 2009.

Centers for Disease Control and Prevention, "Sleep and Sleep Disorders," CDC.gov.

41   **Obesity in the United States**   Centers for Disease Control and Prevention, "Overweight & Obesity," CDC.gov.

Trust for America's Health, "The State of Obesity: Better Policies for a Healthier America 2023," September 2023, TFAH.org.

41   **We've also got a new**   Daniela David, Cosimo Giannini, Francesco Chiarelli, and Angelika Mohm, "Text Neck Syndrome in Children and Adolescents," *International Journal of Environmental Research and Public Health* 18, no. 4 (February 7, 2021): 1565.

41   **The noise accompanying this move**   Jancee Dunn, "What's Behind the 'Middle-Aged Groan'?" *The New York Times,* March 24, 2023.

42   **He has been studying the**   Recently, Austad's research has focused on why different species age at different rates. This interest in animal behavior came from work he did early in his career training large cats (like, *really* large—think: lions) for movies. He's since studied mice, opossums, quahog clams, and hydras, among others, through his research as a distinguished professor of biology at the University of Alabama at Birmingham and director of one of the Nathan Shock Centers of Excellence, which focus on aging biology.

Author interview with Steven Austad.

43   **If you hit**   Jane A Cauley, "Estrogen and Bone Health in Men and Women," *Steroids* 99, part A (July 2015): 11–15.

Brittany C. Collins, Eija K. Laakkonen, and Dawn A. Lowe, "Aging of the Musculoskeletal System: How the Loss of Estrogen Impacts Muscle Strength," *Bone* 123 (June 2019): 137–44.

Roger D. Stanworth and T. Hugh Jones, "Testosterone for the Aging Male; Current Evidence and Recommended Practice," *Clinical Interventions in Aging* 3, no. 1 (March 2008): 25–44.

43   **Against this bleak backdrop**   Frank J. Infurna, Denis Gerstorf, and Margie E. Lachman, "Midlife in the 2020s: Opportunities and Challenges," *American Psychologist* 75, no. 4 (May–June 2020): 270–85.

Ryan K. Masters, Andrea M. Tilstra, and Daniel H. Simon, "Explaining Recent Mortality Trends Among Younger and Middle-Aged White Americans," *International Journal of Epidemiology* 47, no. 1 (February 1, 2018): 81–88.

43   **Sure, muscle-and-respiratory fitness matters**   One doctor who sees the aftermath of our sit-and-stare-at-screens lifestyle up close is Ellen Casey, who is a sports medicine physiatrist at the renowned Hospital for Special Surgery in New York. Casey has worked with the USA Gymnastics Women's National Team and possesses a particularly keen understanding of the female physique. Increasingly, she is treating people of both sexes with a lot of weakness around the hips, often due to atrophied gluteal muscles. "Most people are sitting too much, which can lead to reduced strength, stability, and control. Many can't stand on one leg without losing their balance." One of the most challenging patients she sees fitting this description? "The sixty-year-old psychotherapist," Casey says. "Because they just sit all day with their clients."

44   **"Starting a new program"**   Kyle Mandsager et al., "Association of Cardiorespiratory Fitness with Long-Term Mortality Among Adults Undergoing Exercise Treadmill Testing," *JAMA Network Open* 1, no. 6 (October 19, 2018).

Karsten Keller and Martin Engelhardt, "Strength and Muscle Mass Loss with Aging Process," *Muscle, Ligaments, and Tendons Journal* 3, no. 4 (October–December 2013): 346–50.

45   **It involved a professor**   Alex Hutchinson, "4 Laws of Muscle," *Outside*, May 12, 2022.

45   **everything we could possibly measure**   Keller and Engelhardt, "Strength and Muscle Mass Loss."

Author interview with Alex Hutchinson.

46   **Perhaps what struck me most**   J. Eric Ahlskog et al., "Physical Exercise as a Preventive or Disease-Modifying Treatment of Dementia and Brain Aging," *Mayo Clinic Proceedings* 86, no. 9 (September 2011): 876–84.

Julian M. Gaitán et al., "Brain Glucose Metabolism, Cognition, and Cardiorespiratory Fitness Following Exercise Training in

Adults at Risk for Alzheimer's Disease," *Brain Plasticity* 5, no. 1 (December 26, 2019): 83–95.

Kristi L. Storoschuk et al., "Strength and Multiple Types of Physical Activity Predict Cognitive Function Independent of Low Muscle Mass in NHANES 1999–2002," *Lifestyle Medicine* 4, no. 4 (October 2023).

4: Path to a Bridge (and Superpower)

50   **Second, it requires strength**   Michael F. Leitzmann et al., "Physical Activity Recommendations and Decreased Risk of Mortality," *Archives of Internal Medicine* 167, no. 22 (December 10, 2007): 2453–60.

News release, "Moderate Physical Activity Linked with 50 Percent Reduction in Cardiovascular Death in Over-65s: The Cardiovascular Risks of Modern Life," *European Society of Cardiology* (August 27, 2016).

Xiuxiu Huang et al., "Comparative Efficacy of Various Exercise Interventions on Cognitive Function in Patients with Mild Cognitive Impairment or Dementia: A Systematic Review and Network Meta-analysis," *Journal of Sport and Health Science* 11, no. 2 (March 2022): 212–23.

51   **On the history of OCR**   Brett and Kate McKay, "The History of Obstacle Courses for Military Fitness, Sport, and All-Around Toughness," ArtofManliness.com, September 10, 2015.

"Methode Naturelle," Methodenaturelle.de/history.

51   **On the history of Tough Guy**   Scott Keneally, "Playing Dirty," *Outside*, November 2012.

52   **On the roots of Spartan Race**   Peter Vigneron, "Meet the Most Punishing Man in Fitness," *Outside*, June 10, 2014.

Michael Brick, "You Created It, Tough Guy. So Let's See You Finish It." *The New York Times*, July 6, 2009.

Mark Jenkins, "A Soul-Crushing Sufferfest I'll Never Do Again," *Outside*, October 19, 2010.

Melissa Malamut, "There's Something Called the 'Death Race' in Vermont," BostonMagazine.com, March 7, 2014.

Davis, *Down and Dirty*.

The Obstacle: Burpees

55   **As my former *Wall Street***   Jason Gay, "Please Stay Home. Please Stay Active. And Please Stay Yourself," *The Wall Street Journal,* April 13, 2020.

5: Fragile First Notes

59   **In his book *Beginners***   Vanderbilt, *Beginners.*

6: Be Content to Appear Foolish

71   **The ancient Greek Stoic philosopher**   Epictetus, *The Enchiridion.*

71   **If you fall in the latter "hard work"**   Dweck, *Mindset.*

Carol S. Dweck, "The Growth Mindset," Talks at Google, July 14, 2015, www.youtube.com/watch?v=-71zdXCMU6A.

Carol S. Dweck, "The Power of Yet," TEDx Norrkoping, November 2014, www.authentichappiness.sas.upenn.edu /videos/carol-s-dweck-tedxnorrk%C3%B6ping-power-yet-2014.

72   **Want to master diving**   Leonard, *Mastery.*

72   **each time we learn something new**   "Neural Plasticity," ScienceDirect, www.sciencedirect.com/topics/medicine-and -dentistry/neural-plasticity.

Donna J. Cech and Suzanne "Tink" Martin, "Nervous System Changes," in *Functional Movement Development Across the Life Span,* third edition, 2011.

David E. Vance et al., "Neuroplasticity and Successful Cognitive Aging: A Brief Overview for Nursing," *Journal of Neuroscience Nursing* 44, no. 4 (August 2012): 218–27.

72   **The Seattle Longitudinal Study**   Schaie, "Observations from the Seattle Longitudinal Study of Adult Intelligence."

Schaie and Willis, "The Seattle Longitudinal Study of Adult Cognitive Development."

73   ***On boredom***   Meeri Kim, "Boredom's Link to Mental Illnesses, Brain Injuries and Dysfunctional Behaviors," *The Washington Post,* July 17, 2021.

Ann Robinson, "Is Boredom Bad for Your Health?" *The Guardian,* October 14, 2012.

Nicole LePera, "Relationships Between Boredom Proneness, Mindfulness, Anxiety, Depression, and Substance Abuse," *The New School Psychology Bulletin* 8, no. 2 (2011): 15–25.

The Obstacle: Heavy Carries

80   **In Spartan races, some of these heavy**   Spartan Race, "Spartan 2023 Rules of Competition."

7: The Power of Firsts

87   **these emotional "flashbulb" memories**   William Hirst and Elizabeth A. Phelps, "Flashbulb Memories," *Current Directions in Psychological Science* 25, no. 1 (February 2016): 36–41.

R. Douglas Fields, "Making Memories Stick," *Scientific American,* February 1, 2005.

87   ***On the power of firsts and memory***   Fields has spent decades decoding the mysteries of our brain and nervous system and how they impact learning. His research has zeroed in on an explanation for why some events earn the distinction of sticking around more than others, which he delves into in his book *Electric Brain: How the New Science of Brainwaves Reads Minds, Tells Us How We Learn, and Helps Us Change for the Better.* When we spoke by phone, Fields was working at the National Institutes of Health as the head of the Section of Nervous System Development and Plasticity in the NIH's child health and human development division. The first thing he explained to me was completely counterintuitive. Memory, he noted, is not actually about the past. It's really about the future. "There is no value in having a recording of all our experiences," Fields said. "Most of them have no enduring value and there is no reason to retain them."

R. Douglas Fields, "The Brain Learns in Unexpected Ways," *Scientific American,* March 2020.

Author interview with R. Douglas Fields.

96   **That I am here in part**   Keneally, "DNF: The True Tale of Failure at a Spartan Race."

8: Coming from Behind

104   **I knew later-in-life success was possible**   Jake J. Smith, "How Old Are Successful Tech Entrepreneurs?" Kellogg

Insight, website for the Kellogg School of Management at Northwestern University, May 15, 2018.

"Martha Stewart," Academy of Achievement, achievement.org /achiever/martha-stewart/.

Frank Olito, "8 Famous Companies Started by People in Their 50s and Older," *Business Insider*, January 23, 2020.

Sujan Patel, "Success Can Come at Any Age. Just Look at These 6 Successful Entrepreneurs," *Entrepreneur*, January 25, 2015.

Know Your Value staff, "'Retired, Inspired, Qualified': How a Math Teacher Fought Age, Racial Barriers to Become the First Woman Elected as Mayor of Her Hometown," MSNBC, February 4, 2021.

Lisa Bernhard, "When Hockey Moms Lace Up," *The New York Times*, December 24, 2010.

Pierre Azoulay et al., "Age and High-Growth Entrepreneurship," *American Economic Review* 2, no. 1 (March 2020): 65–82.

Amy S. Fatzinger, "Learning from Laura Ingalls Wilder," *The Atlantic*, September 9, 2018.

Sareen Habeshian, "These Are the Five Oldest U.S. Presidents to Hold Office," *Axios*, November 19, 2022.

106   **One well-known framework for advancement**   Stuart E. Dreyfus, "The Five-Stage Model of Adult Skill Acquisition," *Bulletin of Science, Technology & Society* 24, no. 3 (June 2004): 177–81.

Adam Etzion, "In a Constantly Changing Environment, Can Anyone Ever Truly Be an Expert?" Gloat.com, October 5, 2020.

Adolfo Peña, "The Dreyfus Model of Clinical Problem-Solving Skills Acquisition: A Critical Perspective," *Medical Education Online* (June 14, 2010).

107   **In his book *Mastery***   Leonard, *Mastery*.

107   **A founding father of modern**   James, *On Vital Reserves*.

107   **This sentiment was echoed**   Hutchinson, *Endure*.

108   **You may have heard**   K. Anders Ericsson and Kyle W. Harwell, "Deliberate Practice and Proposed Limits on the Effects of Practice on the Acquisition of Expert Performance: Why the Original Definition Matters and Recommendations for Future Research," *Frontiers in Psychology* 10 (October 2019).

K. Anders Ericsson, Michael J. Prietula, and Edward T. Cokely, "The Making of an Expert," *Harvard Business Review,* July/ August 2007, 1114–21.

108   **On any journey**   Leonard, *Mastery.*

108   **Understanding the difference**   Kendra Cherry, "Extrinsic vs. Intrinsic Motivation: What's the Difference?" Verywellmind .com.

108   **That includes harnessing**   "Fluid and Crystallized Intelligence," ScienceDirect, www.sciencedirect.com/topics /neuroscience/fluid-and-crystallized-intelligence.

Dalia Khammash and Thad A. Polk, "The Neurobiology of Aging," in *Neurology of Brain Disorders* (second edition), 2023.

9: Don't Let Your Crop Die

111   **There's a well-traveled quote**   David Taylor, "Don't Ignore the Unimportance of Practically Everything," *Your Virtual Business Executive* (blog), Thinking Business, April 14, 2016, thinkingbusinessblog.com/2016/04/14/dont-ignore-the -unimportance-of-practically-everything.

113   **McKeown is polished**   Greg McKeown, "Essentialism: The Disciplined Pursuit of Less," Crucial Learning, YouTube video, March 14, 2018, youtube.com/watch?v=v7Nao8lpsIs&ab _channel=CrucialLearning.

McKeown, *Essentialism.*

The Obstacle: Rolling Mud and the Slip Wall

125   **He said this about fear**   *Finding Mastery* (podcast), episode 210, "The Relationship Between Fear and Motivation, with Mark Mathews," findingmastery.com/podcasts/mark-mathews/.

10: What's on the Other Side of Fear?

136   **In certain circumstances**   "5 Things You Never Knew About Fear," Northwestern Medicine, October 2020, nm.org/health- beat/healthy-tips/emotional-health/5-things-you-never-knew- about-fear.

136   **In this form, fear**   Herbert, *Dune.*

138 **It came, curiously enough**   Ed Knowles, "Runner Alexi Pappas Has a Great Idea to Make Marathon Races Even Better to Watch or Participate In," Olympics.com, January 20, 2021.

Mary Kate McCoy, "Olympic Athlete Alexi Pappas on Embracing Pain to Reach Your Dreams," audio, Wisconsin Public Radio, January 27, 2021, wpr.org/listen/1752926.

139 **On one page, there's a scrawled**   *Finding Mastery* (podcast), episode 208, "There Is No Bravery Without Fear, with Tony Blauer," January 22, 2020, findingmastery.com/podcasts/tony -blauer.

139 **I was out running while**   Tim Ferriss, *The Tim Ferriss Show* (blog), no. 533, "Paul Conti, MD—How Trauma Works and How to Heal from It," September 22, 2021, tim.blog /2021/09/22/paul-conti-trauma.

11: Learn, Unlearn, Relearn

149 **This benchmark of mastery**   Malcolm Gladwell, "Complexity and the Ten-Thousand-Hour Rule," *The New Yorker*, August 21, 2013.

Gladwell, *Outliers*.

149 **After years studying the nature**   Ericsson, Prietula, and Cokely, "The Making of an Expert."

150 **With this type of practice**   Mark Bonchek, "Why the Problem with Learning Is Unlearning," *Harvard Business Review*, November 3, 2016.

151 **When we learn a skill**   Coyle, *The Talent Code*.

Author interview with R. Douglas Fields.

12: Dips and Turning Points

154 **The Beast race at the Mountain Creek**   Kelsey Wynn, "These Are the 10 Hardest Spartan Races on the Schedule. Think You Can Handle One?" Spartan.com, December 26, 2021.

157 **But this steep rise**   Leonard, *Mastery*.

158 **Water, it turns out**   Occupational Safety and Health Administration, "Cold Water Immersion," OSHA.gov.

158 **On cold exposure**   Cleveland Clinic, "Hypothalamus," my.clevelandclinic.org/health/body/22566-hypothalamus.

MyHealth Alberta, "Cold Exposure: Ways the Body Loses Heat," myhealth.alberta.ca/health/pages/conditions .aspx?Hwid=tw9037.

Lauren Gelman, "9 Weird Things That Happen to Your Body When It's Cold—and 3 Things That Make It Worse," The Healthy, January 8, 2018, thehealthy.com/first-aid/avoid -hypothermia-and-frostbite.

Centers for Disease Control and Prevention, "Prevent Hypo- thermia & Frostbite," CDC.gov.

13: Edges and Equalizers

165 **Recently she'd been tapped**   Jordyn Taylor, "An Exclusive Look at the Defenders on *Million Dollar Mile,* the CBS Fitness Show Hosted by Tim Tebow," *Men's Health,* March 4, 2019.

169 **As it turns out, attributes**   Diviney, *The Attributes.*

170 **This is just one of many small**   Attia, *Outlive.*

170 **Journalist Jeff Bercovici spent three years**   Bercovici, *Play On.*

The Obstacle: Spear Throw

179 **It's the single most failed**   Rich Borgatti, "Follow These 4 Tips to Beat the Spartan Spear Throw," Spartan.com.

15: Do What You Can, When You Can, While You Can

197 **But for someone who**   Kotler, *The Art of Impossible.*

198 **My own coach Faye will nearly**   "2019 West Virginia North American Championship | Spartan Race," YouTube video, August 25, 2019, 54:14, www.youtube.com/watch?v=d2ov7lk SnIo&t=3123s.

202 **Fluid intelligence is often affected**   Patrick J. Skerrett, "Don't Overwork Your Brain," *Harvard Business Review,* October 27, 2009.

16: Age Is a Secret Weapon

213 **All of us generally**   Chad Stecher is a behavioral health econ- omist and assistant professor at Arizona State University and has served on the scientific advisory board of the sleep-and-mindfulness app Calm. His current research focuses on the habit-formation process.

One thorny question Stecher seeks to answer in his research is how you make a good habit and motivation stick for the long term. From his work in the United States and sub-Saharan Africa, he and his colleagues noted again and again that extrinsic incentive programs such as prizes work well in the short term, but that the efficacy wanes over time. "I can probably get someone up from the couch to run a 10K if I give them enough money," Stecher says. "But after that 10K, unless I provide additional incentives or support, their physical activity won't persist."

17: When There's No Bell to Ring

233   **Within weeks, that trickle**   Roni Caryn Rabin, "First Patient with Wuhan Coronavirus Is Identified in the U.S.," *The New York Times,* January 21, 2020.

Joseph Goldstein, "New York City Eyes First Suspected Case of Coronavirus," *The New York Times,* February 1, 2020.

234   **There was a book I'd begun reading**   Holiday, *Stillness Is the Key.*

237   **Lying in bed, I devour**   Nester, *Breath.*

Chapter 18: Finding Flow at Fifty

244   **The late Hungarian American**   Clay Risen, "Mihaly Csikszentmihalyi, the Father of 'Flow,' Dies at 87," *The New York Times,* October 27, 2021.

Csikszentmihalyi, *Flow.*

244   ***More on flow***   John Geirland, "Go with the Flow," *Wired,* September 1, 1996.

The Flow Channel, theflowchannel.com.

Steven Kolter, "Frequently Asked Questions on Flow," steven kotler.com/rabbit-hole/frequently-asked-questions-on-flow.

244   **In a sunny Mexico beachside**   Modern Elder Academy website: MEAwisdom.com.

Conley made his business mark as a boutique-hotel entrepreneur, and then by helping the young founders of Airbnb build their strategy when he was in his fifties. That journey is chronicled in his book *Wisdom @ Work: The Making of a Modern Elder.*

247   **Part of the secret to victory**   *The Gabby Reece Show* (podcast), episode 100, "Living the Adventure with Laird Hamilton: Navigating Life, Love, and the Waves of Change with the Innovative Surfer," November 9, 2021, gabriellereece.com/laird-hamilton-big-wave-surfer-innovator/.

19: The Final Stretch

250   **This woman, "Muddy Mildred"**   "83-Year-Old Woman Becomes Oldest Tough Mudder Competitor," Scripps News, May 19, 2022, scrippsnews.com/stories/83-year-old-woman-becomes-oldest-tough-mudder-competitor.

Andy Corbley, "After Husband Dies 83-Year-Old 'Muddy Mildred' Runs Her Third Tough Mudder Race to Provide Clean Water," Good News Network, May 5, 2022, goodnewsnetwork.org/mildren-wilson-83-years-old-completes-third-tough-mudder-to-raise-money-for-africa.

251   **A few months earlier, I'd seen a similarly**   Pinstripes Media, "Paul Lachance Is a Spartan Warrior Who Continues to Inspire; He Turns 82 Years Old This Year," EIN Presswire, January 17, 2023.

Kelsey Wynn, "80-Year-Old Navy Veteran Paul Lachance Completes 100th Spartan Race," Spartan.com.

252   **The VO₂ Max test is considered one**   UC Davis Health, "VO2max and Aerobic Fitness," Sports Medicine, health.ucdavis.edu/sports-medicine/resources/vo2description.

Peter Attia, "AMA #27: The Importance of Muscle Mass, Strength, and Cardiorespiratory Fitness for Longevity," September 20, 2021, peterattiamd.com/ama27.

Kyle Mandsager et al., "Association of Cardiorespiratory Fitness with Long-Term Mortality Among Adults Undergoing Exercise Treadmill Testing," *JAMA Network Open* 1, no. 6 (October 19, 2018), https://jamanetwork.com/searchresults?author=Kyle+Mandsager&q=Kyle+Mandsager.

252   **Every four minutes**   UC Davis Health, "Lactate Profile," *Sports Medicine,* health.ucdavis.edu/sports-medicine/resources/lactate.

253   **From prior research**   Mandsager et al., "Association of Cardiorespiratory Fitness."

Attia, *Outlive.*

254   **One note: you don't need access**   Stephen W. Farrell, "50 Years of the Cooper 12-Minute Run," The Cooper Institute, June 18, 2018, cooperinstitute.org/blog/50-years-of-the -cooper-12-minute-run.

254   **And that's bad, because falling**   Centers for Disease Control and Prevention, "Keep on Your Feet—Preventing Older Adult Falls," cdc.gov/injury/features/older-adult-falls.

Richard W. Bohannon, "Grip Strength: An Indispensable Biomarker for Older Adults," *Clinical Interventions in Aging* 14 (2019): 1681–91.

255   **Then there is grip strength**   Dawn E. Alley, Michelle D. Shardell, and Katherine W. Peters, "Grip Strength Cutpoints for the Identification of Clinically Relevant Weakness," *The Journals of Gerontology* 69, no. 5 (May 2014): 559–66.

255   **And holding our screens**   Connie Chang, "Why Your Grip Strength Matters and How to Improve It," *The New York Times,* October 19, 2023.

255   **There are plenty of others**   One good place to start if you want to dig in more is a podcast called *Huberman Lab,* hosted by the neuroscientist Andrew Huberman, who is a professor at the Stanford School of Medicine. In the first episode of a six-part series with Andy Galpin, a professor of kinesiology at California State University, the two health experts outline a myriad of well-accepted assessments to measure fitness and protocols for improvement. hubermanlab.com/episode/dr-andy -galpin-how-to-assess-improve-all-aspects-of-your-fitness.

256   **And I know that if left**   Cleveland Clinic, "Blood Glucose (Sugar) Test," my.clevelandclinic.org/health/diagnostics /12363-blood-glucose-test.

Centers for Disease Control and Prevention, "All About Your A1C," cdc.gov/diabetes/managing/managing-blood-sugar/a1c .html.

Johns Hopkins Medicine, "Alternative Markers of Glycemia: Fructosamine, Glycated Albumin, 1,5-AG," hopkinsguides. com/hopkins/view/Johns_Hopkins_Diabetes_Guide/547055 /all/Alternative_markers_of_glycemia:_fructosamine_glycated _albumin_15_AG.

Michael J. LaMonte, Steven N. Blair, and Timothy S. Church, "Physical activity and diabetes prevention," *Journal of Applied Physiology* 99, no. 3 (September 1, 2005): 1205–13.

Mayo Clinic, "Diabetes," mayoclinic.org/diseases-conditions/diabetes.

258   **In his book *Outlive***   Attia, *Outlive*.

259   ***On "will to live"***   Marcel Schwantes, "A Yale Professor Shatters False Beliefs About Aging and Uncovers 4 Truths to a Longer and Happier Life," *Inc.*, April 8, 2022, inc.com/marcel-schwantes/a-yale-professor-shatters-false-beliefs-about-aging-uncovers-4-truths-to-a-longer-happier-life.html.

Becca R. Levy et al., "Longevity Increased by Positive Self-Perceptions of Aging," *Journal of Personality and Social Psychology* 83, no. 2 (August 2002): 261–70.

Robert C. Atchley, "Ohio Longitudinal Study on Aging and Retirement, 1975–1995," Harvard Dataverse, 1996, dataverse.harvard.edu/dataset.xhtml?persistentId=doi:10.7910/DVN/XL2ZTO.

Levy, *Breaking the Age Code*.

20: You'll Know at the Finish Line

267   **"I don't even know if Godzilla"**   T. J. Murphy, "The Complete Guide to the 2021 Spartan World Championship in Abu Dhabi," Spartan.com.

270   **All this has left**   Dreyfus, "The Five-Stage Model of Adult Skill Acquisition."

272   **He holds it up and shows**   David McKenzie et al., "Omicron, a New Covid-19 Variant with High Number of Mutations, Sparks Travel Bans and Worries Scientists," CNN, November 25, 2021, cnn.com/2021/11/26/africa/new-covid-variant-discovered-south-africa-b11529-intl/index.html.

277   ***On David Goggins***   Peter Economy, "Use the 40 Percent Rule to Break Through Every Obstacle and Achieve the Impossible," *Inc.*, April 23, 2019, inc.com/peter-economy/use-40-percent-rule-to-achieve-impossible.html.

"Fittest Real Athletes: David Goggins" (video), *Outside*, February 24, 2022, outsideonline.com/video/fittest-real-athletes-david-goggins.

Goggins, *Can't Hurt Me*.

About the Author

GWENDOLYN BOUNDS is an award-winning journalist and author whose career spans influential media brands including *The Wall Street Journal*, ABC News, Consumer Reports, CNBC, Smart-News, and more. Her first book, *Little Chapel on the River*, earned wide acclaim for its poignant portrayal of life inside a small-town pub after the terrorist attacks of September 11, 2001. Raised in North Carolina, Bounds now lives in New York's Hudson River Valley.

gwendolynbounds.com
Facebook.com/gwendolynbounds
Instagram: @gbounds
LinkedIn: linkedin.com/in/gwendolynbounds
X: @gwendolynbounds